Images of Modern America

THE RICHMOND CRUSADE FOR VOTERS

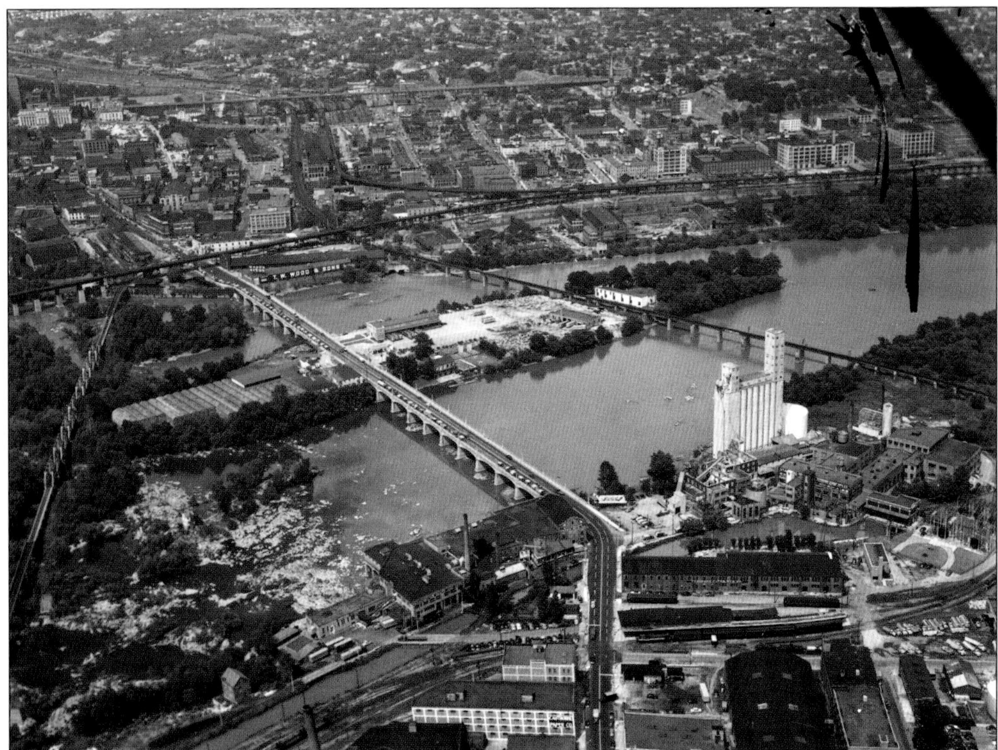

This is a scenic aerial view of Lower Richmond and the James River by Adolph B. Rice from 1952. The James River is 340 miles long and is the 12th-longest river in the United States that remains entirely within a single state. (Courtesy of the Library of Virginia.)

Front Cover: Pictured in 1947, Calvin Hopkins (left), Lester Banks (center), and A. Washington "Puss" Owens of Richmond are encouraging people to pay their poll tax and to vote through "Getting out the Vote" campaigns. These campaigns took place throughout the year in predominantly African American neighborhoods. (Courtesy of the Scott Henderson Collection, L. Douglas Wilder Library, Virginia Union University.)

Upper Back Cover: Pictured is a poll tax bill from 1940 for Mary E. Harrison of Lawrenceville, Virginia, for $4.01, the equivalent of approximately $68 today. Poll taxes had to be paid in full before one could register to vote in the commonwealth of Virginia. In addition to poll taxes, literacy tests were also employed to prevent African Americans from registering to vote. Requirement loopholes allowed local election officials to exempt poor and illiterate white voters while disqualifying African Americans. (Courtesy of the Harrison family.)

Lower Back Cover (from left to right): At left, Lt. Gov. Tim Kaine visited the Richmond Crusade for Voters in September 2005 to speak with the membership about his run for governor. Kaine won the Richmond Crusade for Voters endorsement and the election to become Virginia's 70th governor. The Richmond Crusade for Voters endorsed Kaine throughout his political career. Pictured at center are campaign signs outside the Military Retirees Club at the October 2006 endorsement meeting. The Military Retirees Club has been a frequent meeting place for the Richmond Crusade for Voters. At the August 2006 general body meeting, pictured on the right, members of the Richmond Crusade for Voters and the community were provided a tutorial on how to use the new electronic voting machines from a board of elections official. (All, courtesy of Ralph Cramer).

Images of Modern America

THE RICHMOND CRUSADE FOR VOTERS

DR. KIMBERLY A. MATTHEWS

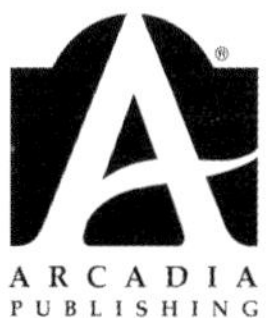

ISBN 978-1-4671-2492-8

Published by Arcadia Publishing
Charleston, South Carolina

Printed in the United States of America

Library of Congress Control Number: 2016958649

For all general information, please contact Arcadia Publishing:
Telephone 843-853-2070
Fax 843-853-0044
E-mail sales@arcadiapublishing.com
For customer service and orders:
Toll-Free 1-888-313-2665

Visit us on the Internet at www.arcadiapublishing.com

I dedicate this book to my parents, Albert and Lindell Matthews.

Contents

Acknowledgments

I would like to give a heartfelt thank-you to those who shared their stories and photographs with me to preserve a small portion of African American history.

For the encouragement and assistance with the creation of this book, I would like to thank the following: Selicia Gregory Allen, Londo Andrews, Francine Archer, Ray Bonis, Malcolm O. Carpenter, Elliott Eddie, Reginald D. Ford, Dr. Carmen Foster, Dr. Katrice A. Hawthorne, Dr. Raymond Hylton, Nicole Kappatos, Kelly Kerney, Dr. John Moeser, Dr. William Ferguson Reid, Benjamin Ross, Shiela Scott, Faye Smith, Meghan Townes, and Willie Williams III.

INTRODUCTION

The Richmond Crusade for Voters emerged from a racially charged environment at a critical moment in history. In 1954, the US Supreme Court unanimously ruled school segregation unconstitutional. The white leadership structure in Virginia was outraged by the decision; some even suggested secession. Well-known segregationist Sen. Harry F. Byrd Sr. acted quickly and ordered his political organization, known as the Byrd Machine, to create and develop alternatives to maintain racial segregation in Virginia. In 1956, the Virginia General Assembly passed an Act of Interposition, which declared Virginia's right to reject the federal mandate. Also, a new set of Jim Crow laws that provided the legal authority for massive resistance were introduced in the general assembly, giving the governor the ability to close schools forced to integrate, to establish whites-only private schools, and to provide financial assistance to whites who could not afford private school tuition. Byrd put forward a referendum to amend Section 141 of the Virginia Constitution, which would allow public funds to be provided statewide to white students to attend private schools through a tuition grants program promoting segregation.

Some Virginia residents supported Byrd's endeavors, but there were pockets of opposition that believed that equal public education for all was a right—not a privilege. The Committee to Save Public Schools, an interracial group of Richmond residents, opposed the statewide referendum intended to circumvent the *Brown v. Board of Education of Topeka* decision. Despite the Committee to Save Public Schools' opposition, the referendum passed by a four to one margin on January 9, 1956. African American voter turnout was disappointing. Of the 8,500 registered African American voters, fewer than 4,000 voted. This committee, which was formed specifically to defeat the referendum, disbanded shortly after the election. However, some members foresaw a new route to continue the fight for equality.

Thus, the Richmond Crusade for Voters was created in 1956 to increase the strength of the minority electorate in the city. This endeavor took time to gain momentum, but once it did, it was a dominant force in the city of Richmond. Dr. William S. Thornton, a podiatrist was the first president of the Richmond Crusade for Voters and is often referred to as its founding father. Dr. Thornton devised a plan for an independent nonpartisan organization focused on increasing voter registration and voter education. Dr. Thornton called for a meeting to address these concerns at Greater Mt. Moriah Baptist Church on North First Street in Jackson Ward. Dr. William Ferguson Reid, a physician and John Mitchell Brooks, a businessman attended the founding meeting. During the organization's development, Christopher French Foster Sr., a well-known elder in Richmond, proposed the name Crusade for Voters.

The organization quickly established its purpose, objectives and preamble. The Richmond Crusade for Voters' purpose is "to increase the voting strength of the population of the city of Richmond and to improve the moral, social, economic, educational, and general welfare. To establish voter registration and voter education in the city of Richmond and issue such policy statements or institute such programs that will improve the economic, educational, general welfare and solidarity of the people." The preamble states that "in order to maintain a democratic form of government and lay a firm foundation upon which the freedom of all people can be protected and under which a government of the people shall remain, we dedicate ourselves to this organization." In 1956, the four objectives of the organization were 1) To increase the Negro vote in Richmond, Virginia, through year-round voter registration activities, 2) To increase Negroes' political awareness, 3) To study the records of candidates and give recommendations, and 4) To push for equal job opportunities in city hall.

The Richmond Crusade for Voters created a precinct system in Richmond's African American neighborhoods that were highly effective in educating, organizing, galvanizing, and motivating voters. The precinct system included a structured leadership, which included precinct captains, block leaders, officers and volunteers within each precinct. Since each precinct was unique, this system made it easy for information to be disseminated throughout the neighborhoods through block meetings. To those outside of the movement, block meetings seemed like evening social gatherings with beverages and food; however, serious business was discussed.

Few are aware of the Richmond Crusade for Voters' connection to the National Association for the Advancement of Colored People (NAACP). During the 1950s, the Virginia General Assembly worked diligently to eliminate the NAACP and to obtain its membership list. The NAACP filed more lawsuits related to school segregation than any organization in the state and vehemently opposed the Act of Interposition. The NAACP had to remain apolitical; thus, members of the NAACP voter registration committee joined the Richmond Crusade for Voters and helped the voter registration and research committees to vet and endorse a slate of candidates. The two organizations worked collaboratively and most African American Richmond residents were members of both organizations. The NAACP fought through the courts and the Richmond Crusade for Voters fought through the ballot box.

Over the years, the Richmond Crusade for Voters experienced great victories, including Dr. William Ferguson Reid's election to the Virginia House of Delegates in 1968, the election of L. Douglas Wilder to the Senate of Virginia in 1969, the election of the first African American–majority Richmond City Council in 1977, and the election of Richmond's first African American mayor, Henry L. Marsh III, also in 1977. In 2016, the Richmond Crusade for Voters celebrated its 60th anniversary. This historical organization continues to advocate for voter empowerment through the political process by remaining visible, vocal, and educational.

One

The Struggle Begins

In 1877, the US government withdrew its troops from the southern states, ending Reconstruction. The structure that was created to make sure African Americans had a voice in their future was dismantled. The achievements of African Americans that took place during this era, including winning elections to southern state legislatures and to the US Congress, ended. From the end of Reconstruction through the 1960s, Jim Crow laws, which separated the races and stripped African American of their political and civil rights, were enacted. African Americans lacked opportunities to obtain a proper education, adequate and affordable housing, reasonable medical care, and gainful employment. White southerners often resorted to campaigns of violence and intimidation, which included lynching and riots. Groups such as the Ku Klux Klan killed over 3,000 African Americans, and burned homes, businesses, churches, and schools in the quest to destroy stable African American communities. New developments and projects, such as new highways, were constructed through thriving African American neighborhoods. For example, in 1955, the Richmond-Petersburg Turnpike, now part of Interstate 95, went through Jackson Ward, a thriving African American neighborhood considered the Harlem of the South.

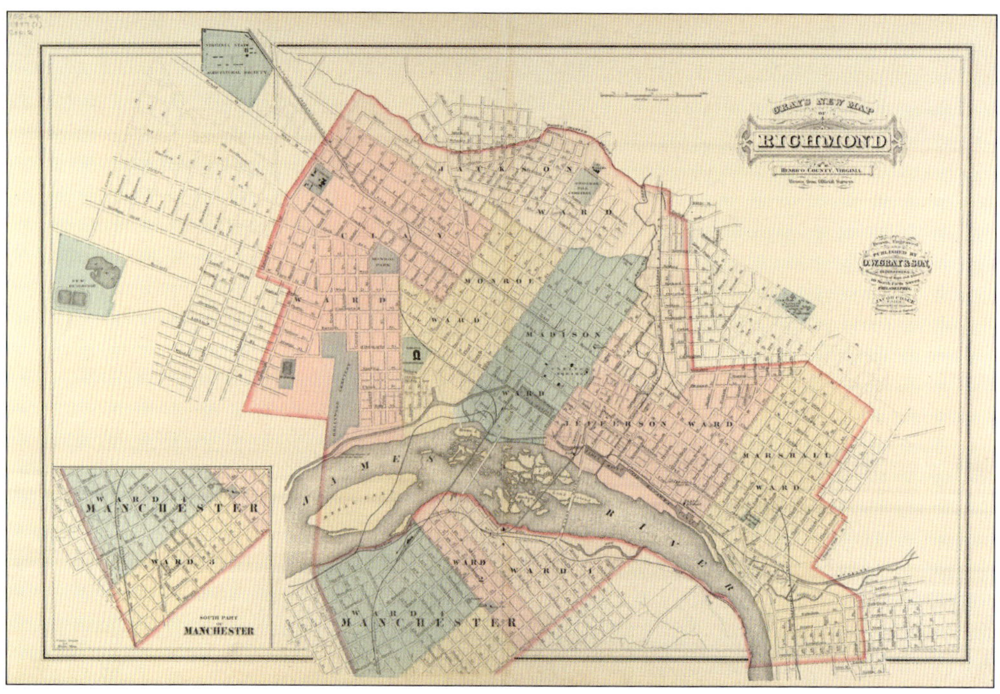

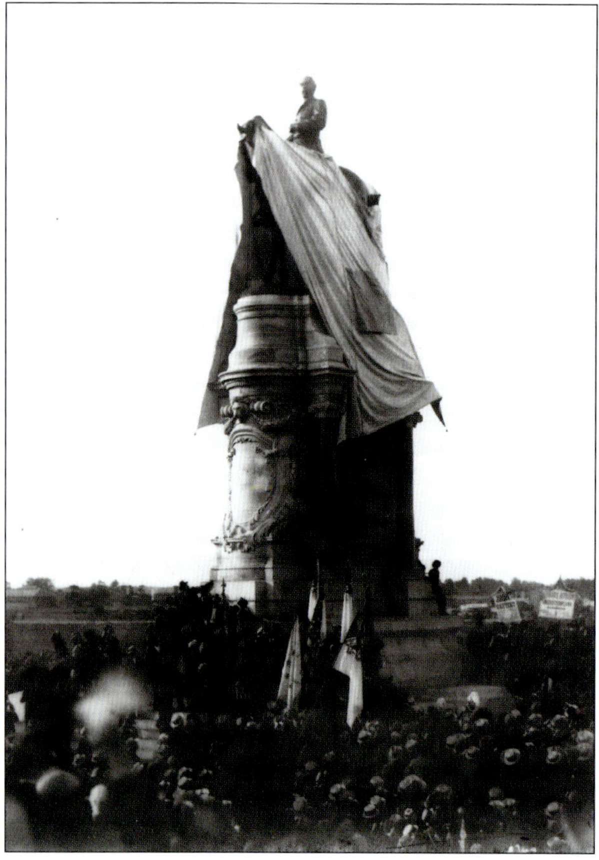

This 1882 map of the city of Richmond shows the division of land into seven wards: Clay, Jackson, Monroe, Madison, Jefferson, Marshall, and Manchester. The creation of Jackson Ward as an all–African American ward was intended to limit African American voting influence to one ward, but it also assured representation on the Richmond City Council for African Americans long after Reconstruction. (Courtesy of the Library of Virginia.)

Thousands of veterans and their families gather for the dedication and unveiling of the statue of Robert E. Lee on Monument Avenue in 1890. Lee was an American general known for commanding the Confederate army in the American Civil War from 1862 until his surrender in 1865. African Americans believed the monument was a symbol of white supremacy. (Courtesy of the Cook Collection, the Valentine.)

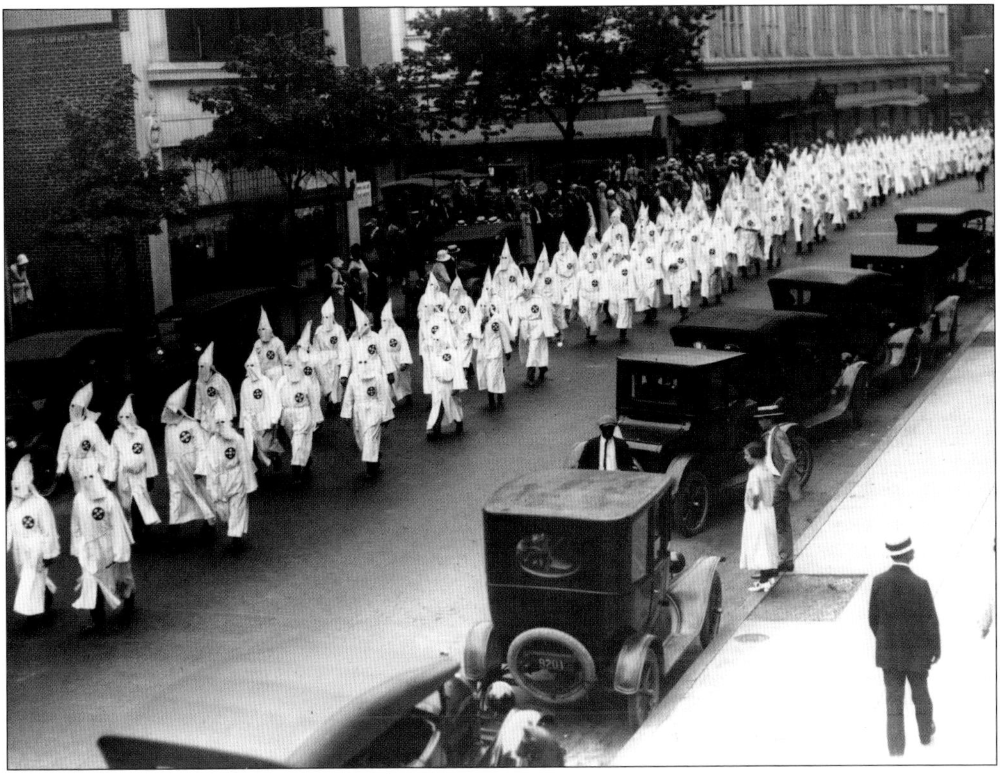

This is a photograph of a Ku Klux Klan parade in downtown Richmond in 1920. In Richmond, the white supremacy movement centered in Anglo-Saxon clubs begun by local musician John Powell, who contributed to the drafting and passage of the Racial Integrity Act of 1924. This act established the one-drop rule by classifying as black anyone with African ancestry. (Courtesy of the Valentine.)

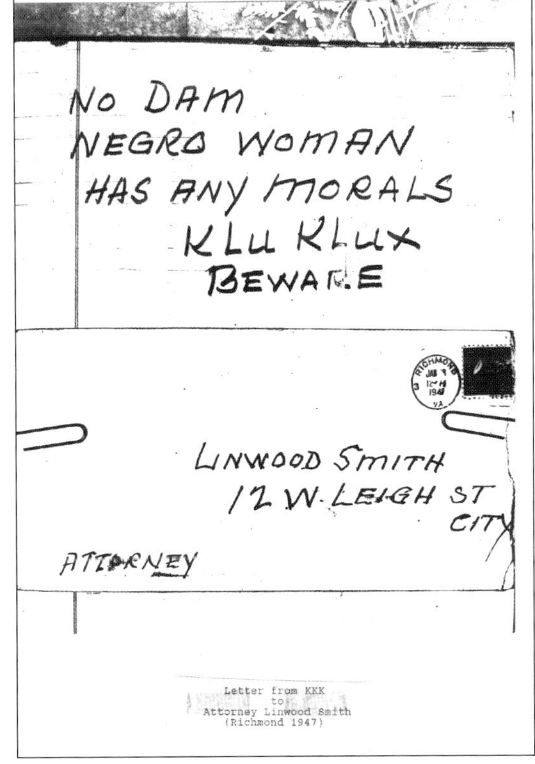

NO DAM
NEGRO WOMAN
HAS ANY MORALS
KLU KLUX
BEWARE

LINWOOD SMITH
12 W. LEIGH ST
CITY

ATTORNEY

Letter from KKK
to
Attorney Linwood Smith
(Richmond 1947)

Shown is a letter written to local attorney Linwood Smith from the Ku Klux Klan in 1947. The Ku Klux Klan used these types of tactics to frighten those in the African American community. (Courtesy of the Scott Henderson Collection, L. Douglas Wilder Library, Virginia Union University.)

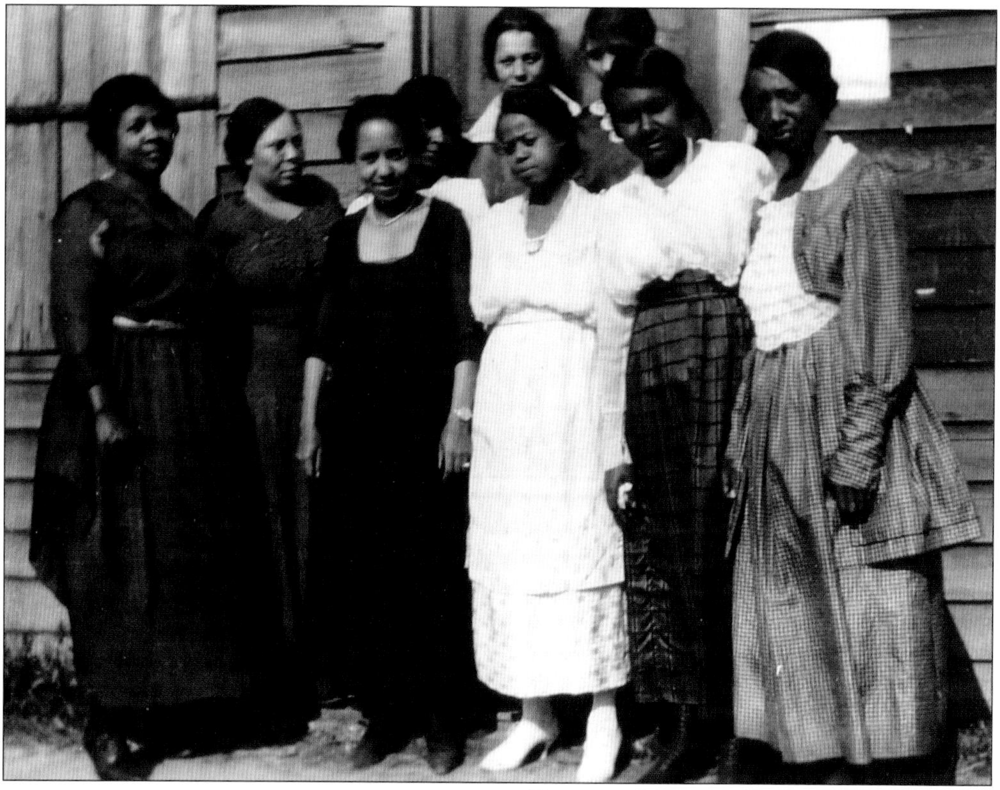

Shown is the First Colored Women Voters Club of Ettrick in 1920. These eight founders were faculty members at Virginia Normal and Industrial Institute (now Virginia State University). Standing in front of the Ettrick Courthouse from left to right are (first row) Mary Branch, Anna Lindsay, Edna Colson, Edwina Wright, Johnella (Frazer) Jackson, and Nannie Nichols; (second row) Eva Conner, Evie Lee (Carpenter) Spencer, and Odelle Green. (Courtesy of Special Collections and University Archives, Johnston Memorial Library, Virginia State University.)

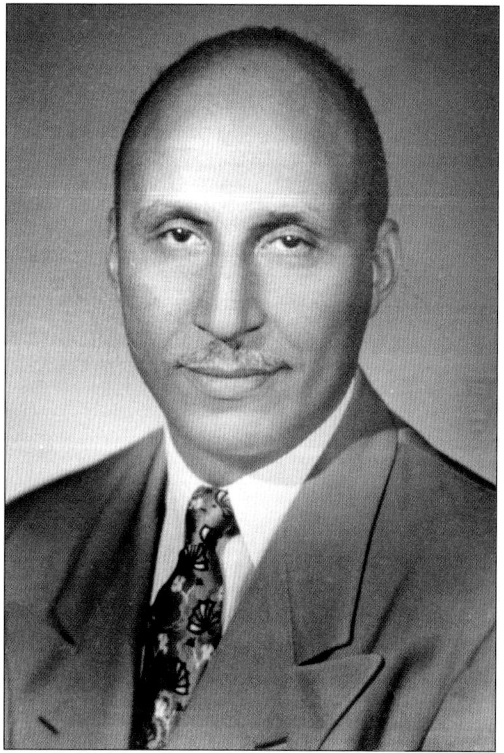

In 1948, at age 41, Richmond native and civil rights attorney, Oliver W. Hill Sr. (1907–2007) made history when he became the first African American to win election to the Richmond City Council since 1896. During his political and law careers, Hill worked tirelessly against racial discrimination. He is most famous for successfully litigating court cases that ended the "separate but equal" doctrine. (Courtesy of Oliver W. Hill Jr.)

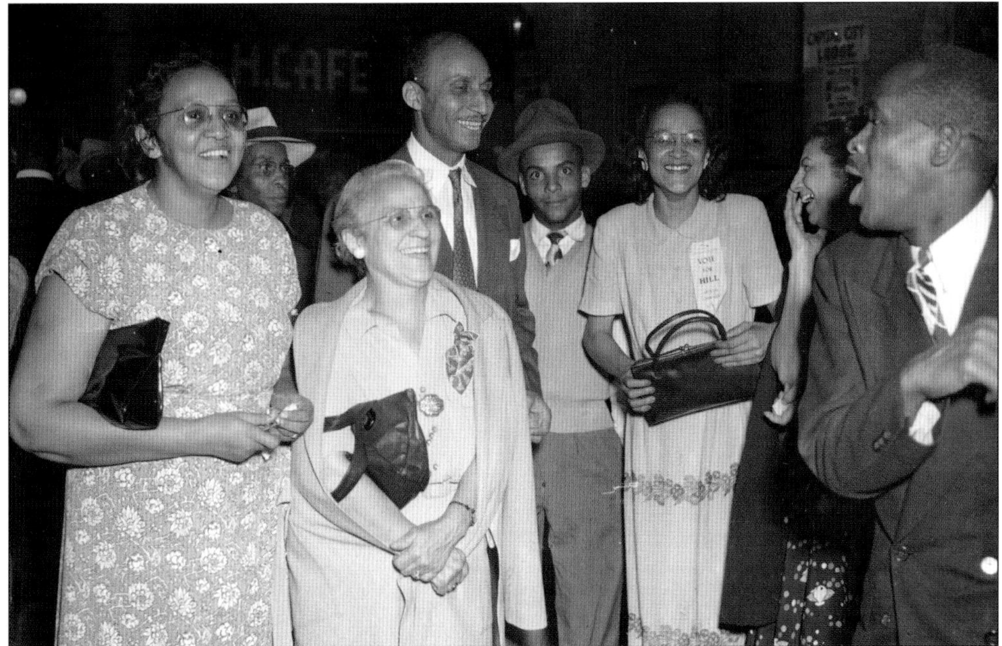

This photograph was taken during the victory celebration of Oliver W. Hill Sr. to Richmond City Council in 1948. Pictured from left to right are Beresenia Hill, Olivia Hill, Oliver W. Hill Sr., unidentified, Evalyn Shaed, Lillian Brown, and Dr. Felix Brown. (Courtesy of Oliver W. Hill Jr.)

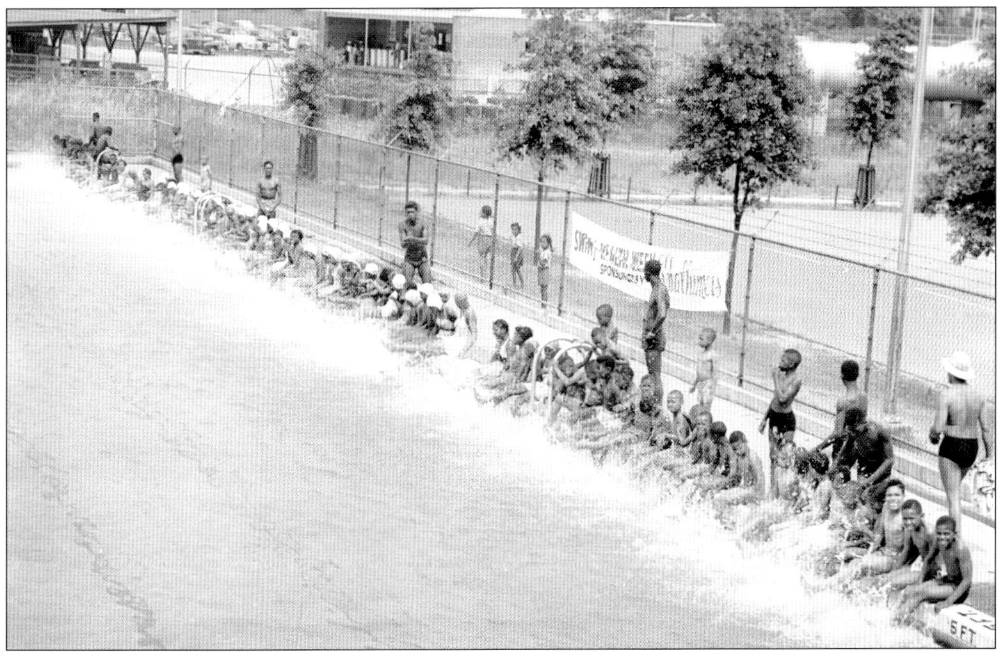

In June 1950, children prepare for lessons at Brook Pool in Richmond. This was the only pool that served the city's African American population. Across the country, officials usually shut down their community pools rather than integrate. Whites typically used private pools in their neighborhoods, where segregation was permitted. (Courtesy of the *Richmond Times-Dispatch*.)

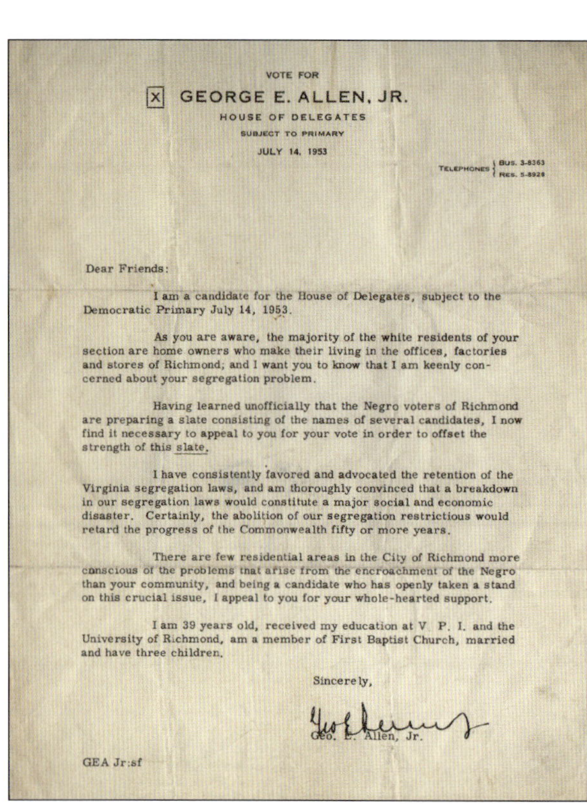

VOTE FOR

☒ GEORGE E. ALLEN, JR.

HOUSE OF DELEGATES

SUBJECT TO PRIMARY

JULY 14, 1953

TELEPHONES { BUS. 3-8363
RES. 5-8928

Dear Friends:

I am a candidate for the House of Delegates, subject to the Democratic Primary July 14, 1953.

As you are aware, the majority of the white residents of your section are home owners who make their living in the offices, factories and stores of Richmond; and I want you to know that I am keenly concerned about your segregation problem.

Having learned unofficially that the Negro voters of Richmond are preparing a slate consisting of the names of several candidates, I now find it necessary to appeal to you for your vote in order to offset the strength of this slate.

I have consistently favored and advocated the retention of the Virginia segregation laws, and am thoroughly convinced that a breakdown in our segregation laws would constitute a major social and economic disaster. Certainly, the abolition of our segregation restrictious would retard the progress of the Commonwealth fifty or more years.

There are few residential areas in the City of Richmond more conscious of the problems that arise from the encroachment of the Negro than your community, and being a candidate who has openly taken a stand on this crucial issue, I appeal to you for your whole-hearted support.

I am 39 years old, received my education at V. P. I. and the University of Richmond, am a member of First Baptist Church, married and have three children.

Sincerely,

Geo. E. Allen, Jr.

GEA Jr:sf

This letter was written to White Richmonders by George E. Allen Jr. (1914–1990), a pro-segregation candidate for the Virginia House of Delegates in 1953. Allen served in the house of delegates from 1954 to 1982. (Courtesy of Special Collections and Archives, James Branch Cabell Library, Virginia Commonwealth University [VCU] Libraries.)

This photograph from November 1957 shows Sixth Mount Zion Baptist Church in Richmond's Jackson Ward district amid the construction of the Richmond-Petersburg Turnpike, now part of Interstate 95. Renowned reverend John Jasper founded the church in 1867. (Courtesy of the *Richmond Times-Dispatch*.)

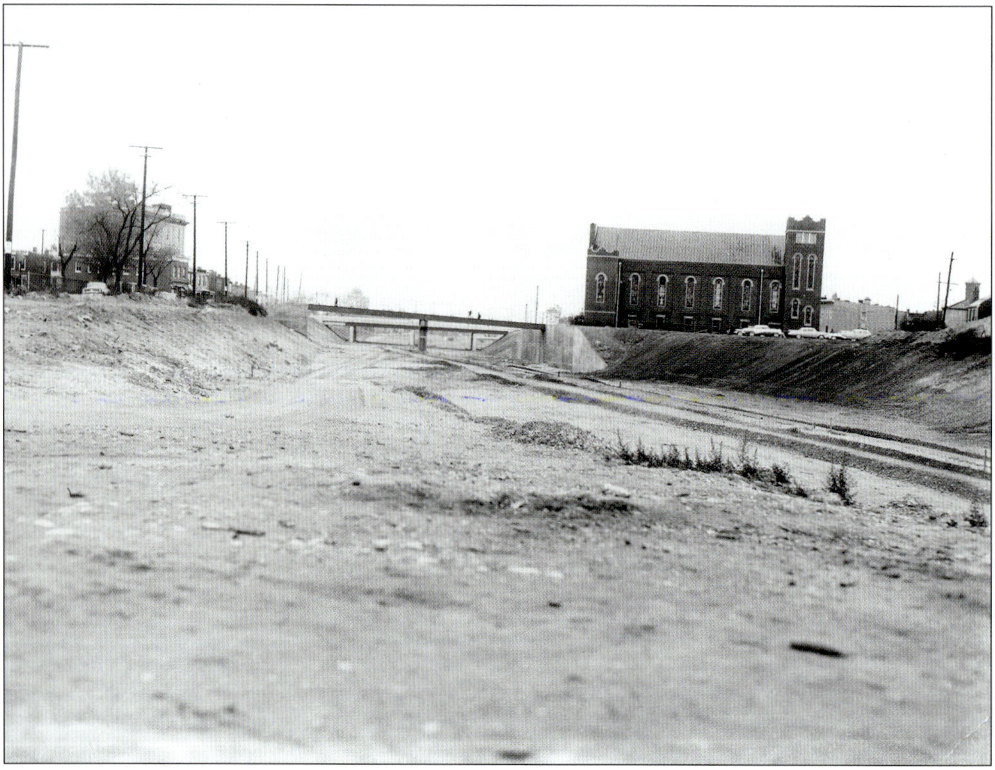

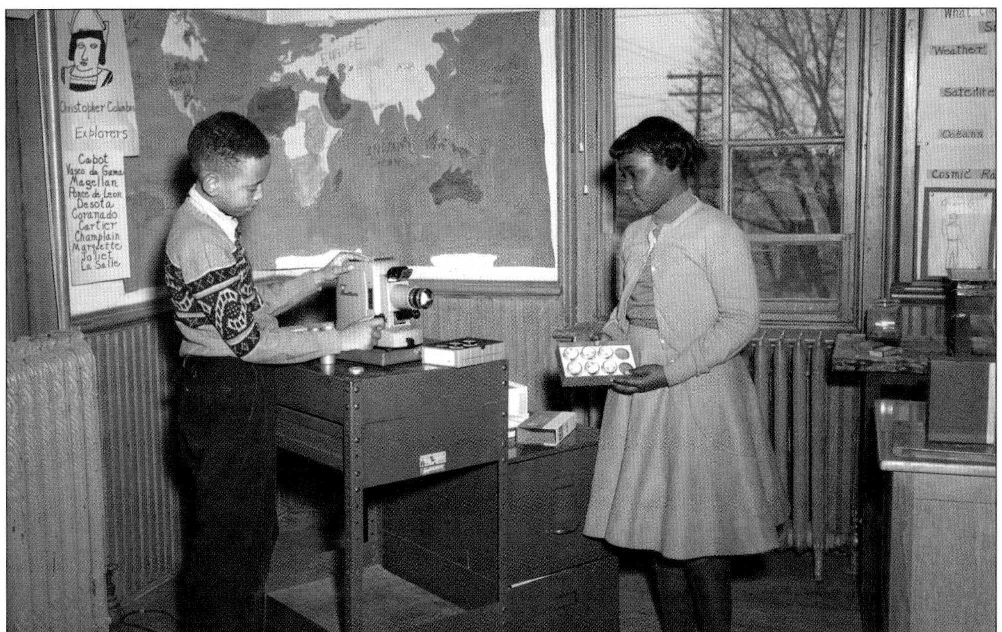

The Navy Hill School earned its name from the Navy Hill suburb in which it was located. The school, which housed grades one through seven, closed September 17, 1965, and its pupils transferred to local public schools. The building was demolished to accommodate the interchange between Interstate 64 and the Richmond-Petersburg Turnpike. (Courtesy of the Library of Virginia.)

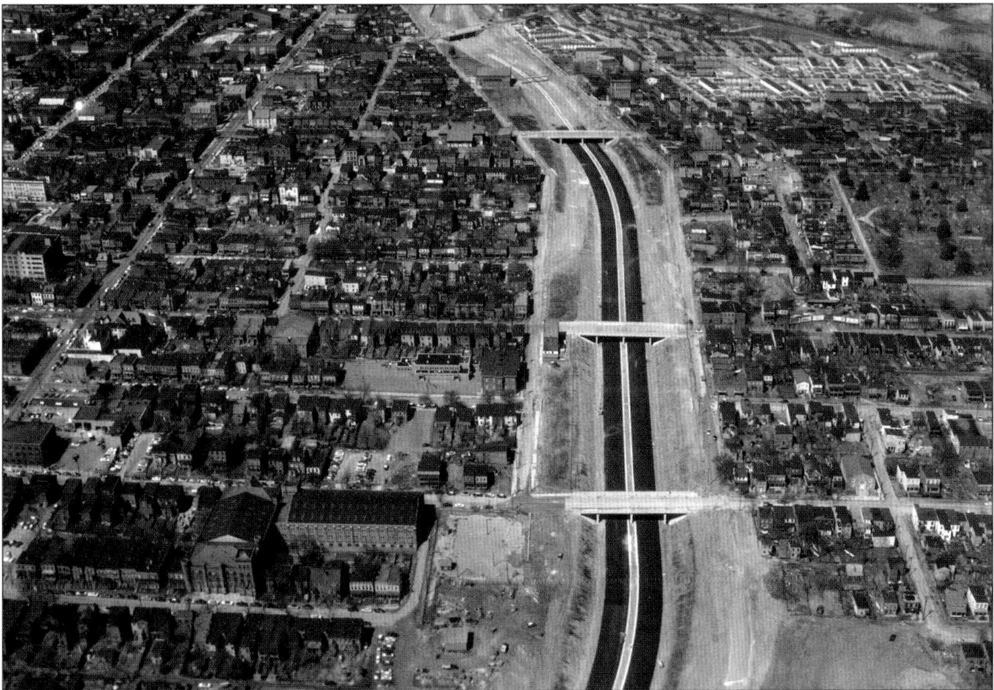

This 1958 aerial view of Richmond by Adolph B. Rice shows the construction of the six-lane Richmond-Petersburg Turnpike (Interstate 95) that cut directly through the heart of Jackson Ward, dividing the community in half. (Courtesy of the Library of Virginia.)

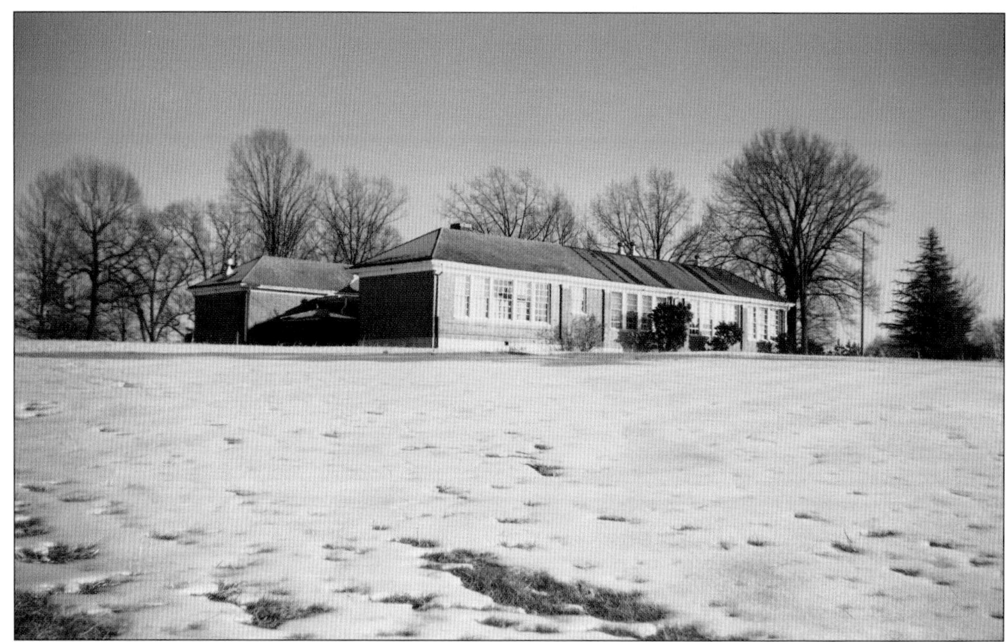

Seventy miles outside of Richmond in Prince Edward County, officials decided to close the entire public school system rather than integrate. Pictured is Darlington Heights Elementary School (for whites) on secondary road 660 in Prince Edward County in 1962. The school was equipped with steam or hot water heat and indoor plumbing. (Courtesy of Special Collections and Archives, James Branch Cabell Library, VCU Libraries.)

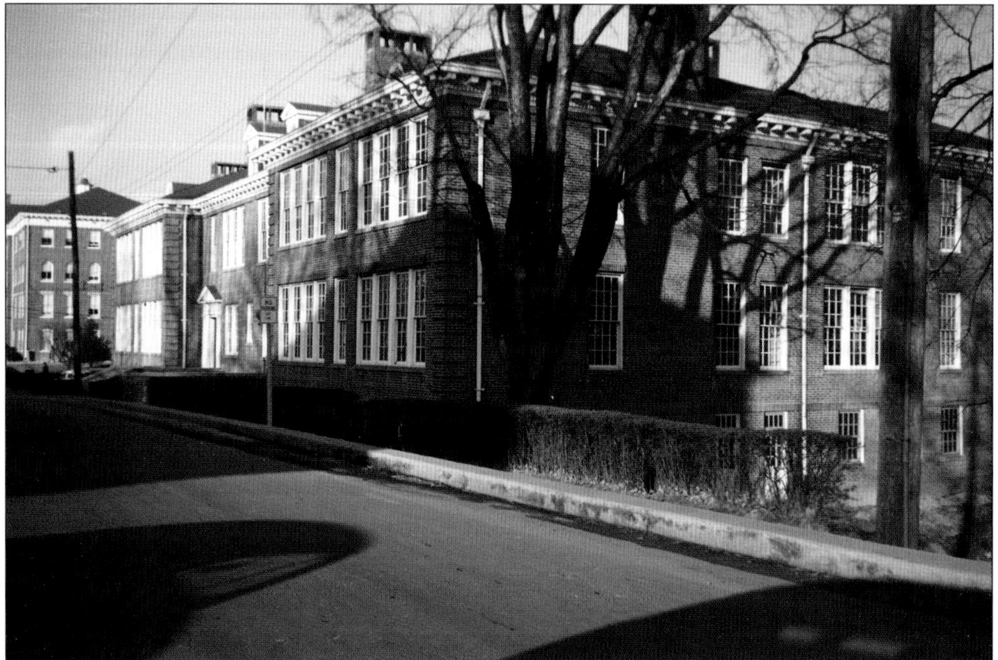

This photograph shows Farmville Elementary School (for whites) on Pine Street in Farmville in 1962. The school, which closed in 1959, was located at what is now Longwood University. (Courtesy of Special Collections and Archives, James Branch Cabell Library, VCU Libraries.)

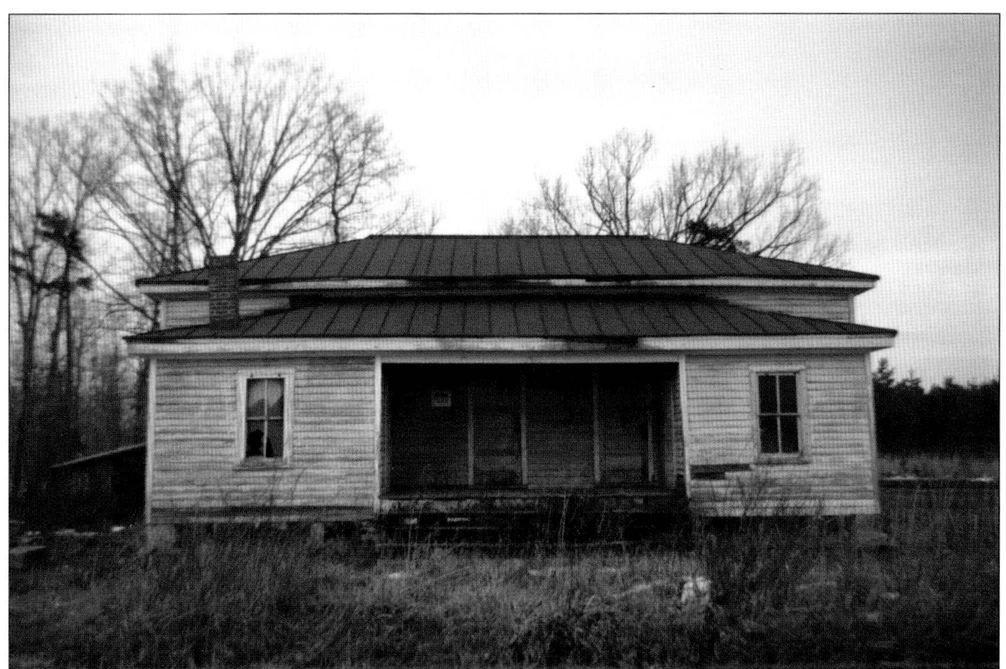

This is an image of Epps Elementary School (for African Americans) on secondary road 620 in Prince Edward County in 1962. The school had neither indoor plumbing nor heat. (Courtesy of Special Collections and Archives, James Branch Cabell Library, VCU Libraries.)

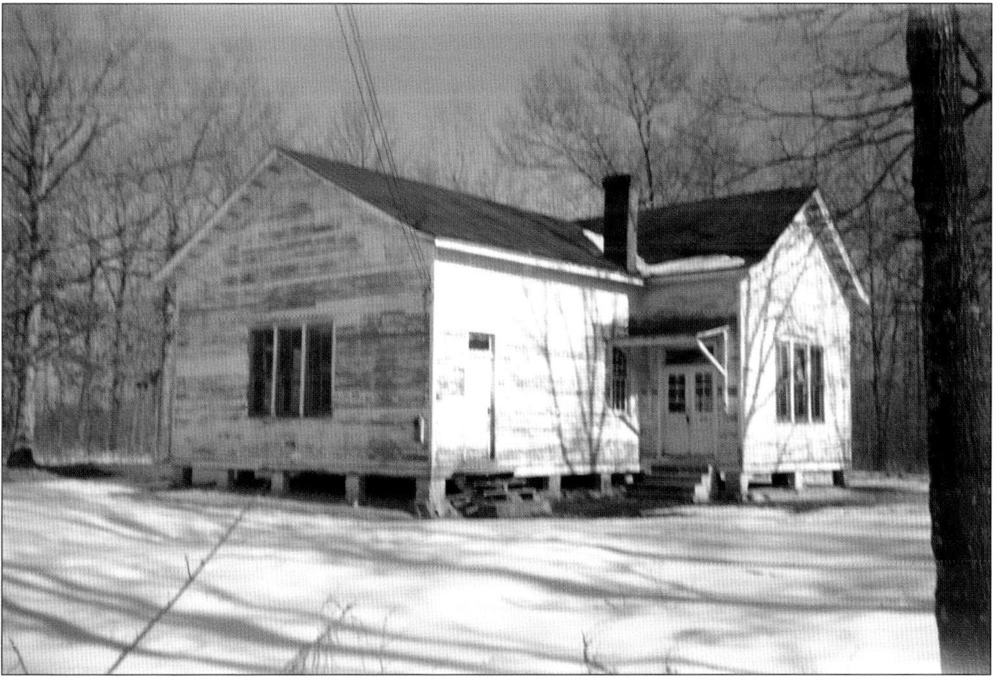

Felden Elementary School (for African Americans) was on secondary road 647 (formerly 677) in Prince Edward County. The school housed 90 students and lacked indoor plumbing and heat. (Courtesy of Special Collections and Archives, James Branch Cabell Library, VCU Libraries.)

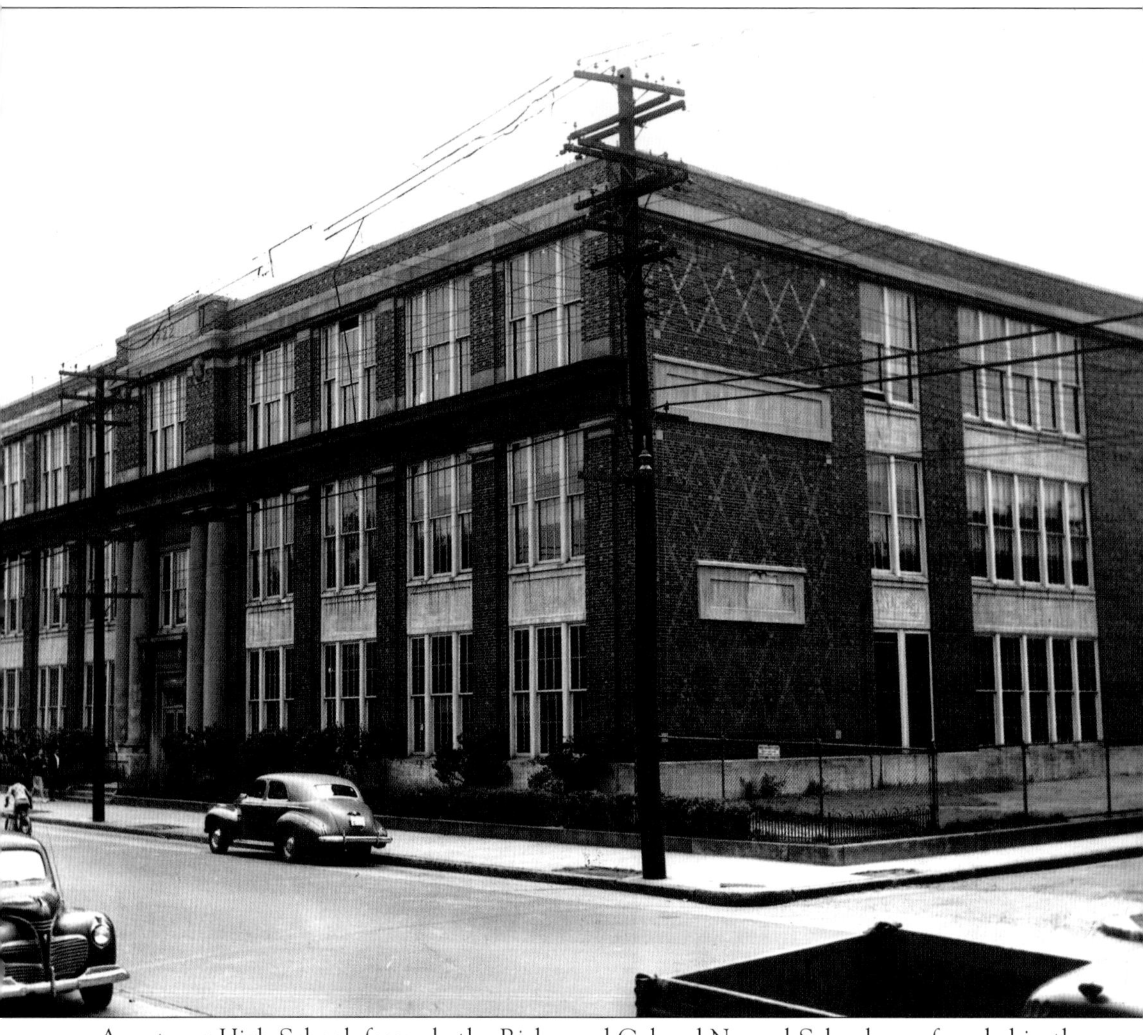

Armstrong High School, formerly the Richmond Colored Normal School, was founded in the 1870s and joined the Richmond Public School system in 1909. The school was renamed in honor of Civil War commander Samuel Chapman Armstrong, who led the US Colored Troops. In 1923, Armstrong High School moved to a three-story building at the corner of Prentis and Leigh Streets. All three founders of the Richmond Crusade for Voters—Dr. William Ferguson Reid, Dr. William S. Thornton, and John Mitchell Brooks—are Armstrong High School alumni. (Courtesy of the Scott Henderson Collection, L. Douglas Wilder Library, Virginia Union University.)

Two

A Brighter Future

In 1946, the US Supreme Court started ruling against segregation and the previous "separate but equal" dictums. Segregated interstate busing was ruled unconstitutional and some graduate schools were ordered to integrate. As a result of the historic *Brown v. Board of Education* Supreme Court decision in 1954, African Americans began to fight for better education for their children in their local school districts. However, segregationists like Harry F. Byrd Sr., the principal architect of massive resistance in Virginia, wanted to block desegregation. In 1956, despite the efforts of the Richmond Committee to Save Public Schools, a local interracial group committed to integration, Virginia passed the Stanley Plan, which allowed localities to close public schools rather than integrate. After the disbandment of the committee, the Richmond Crusade for Voters emerged in 1956 to register and educate African Americans in Richmond. The three cofounders of the organization—Dr. William S. Thornton, Dr. William Ferguson Reid, and John Mitchell Brooks—helped the Richmond Crusade for Voters become an instrumental force effecting political and social change in Richmond. History was made when Dr. William Ferguson Reid was elected to the Virginia House of Delegates in 1968, thus becoming the first African American member of the Virginia General Assembly since Reconstruction. The 1960s brought about the beginning of the activist movement in Richmond, specifically the Campaign for Human Dignity, which included sit-ins and boycotts.

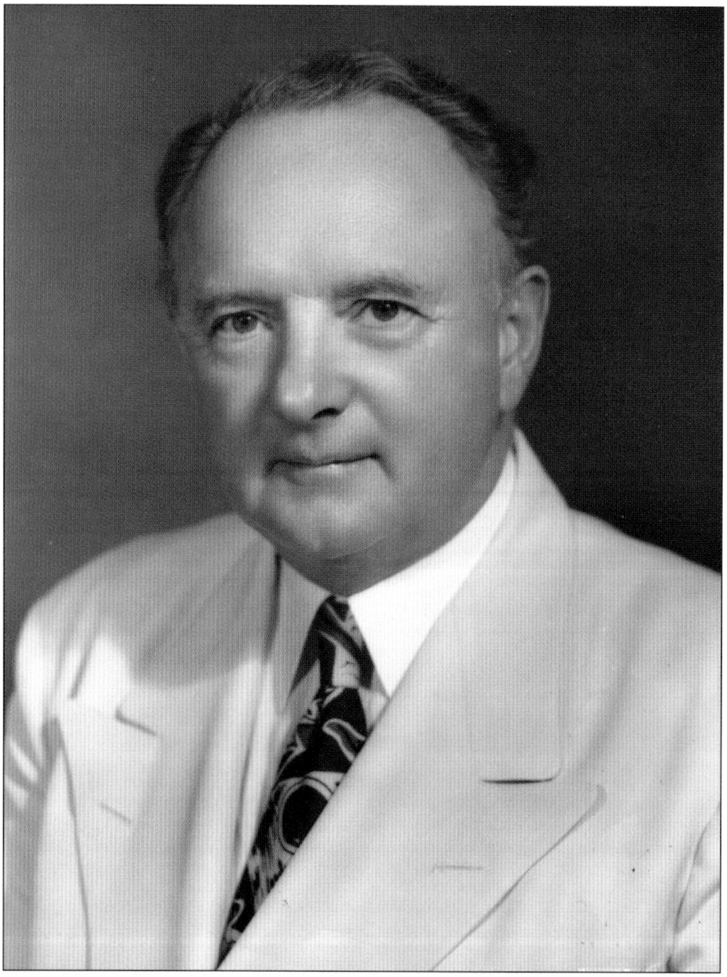

Former Virginia Governor and US senator Harry F. Byrd Sr., (1887–1966) was the architect of massive resistance, a series of laws passed in 1956 to prevent school integration, in the commonwealth. He created the Byrd Machine, a political organization that controlled Virginia politics from the mid-1920s to 1969. (Courtesy of the Valentine.)

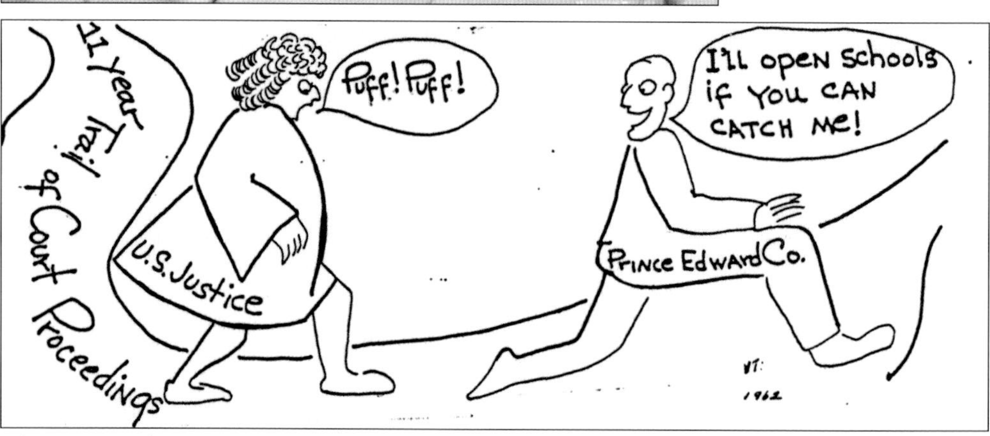

This cartoon by Virginia Tyack appeared in the *Powelton Post*, a neighborhood newsletter in Philadelphia, in 1962. It shows US Justice chasing Prince Edward County. On May 1, 1959, Prince Edward County was ordered to integrate its schools. Instead of heeding the call to integrate, the county closed its entire public school system for five years. (Courtesy of Special Collections and Archives, James Branch Cabell Library, VCU Libraries.)

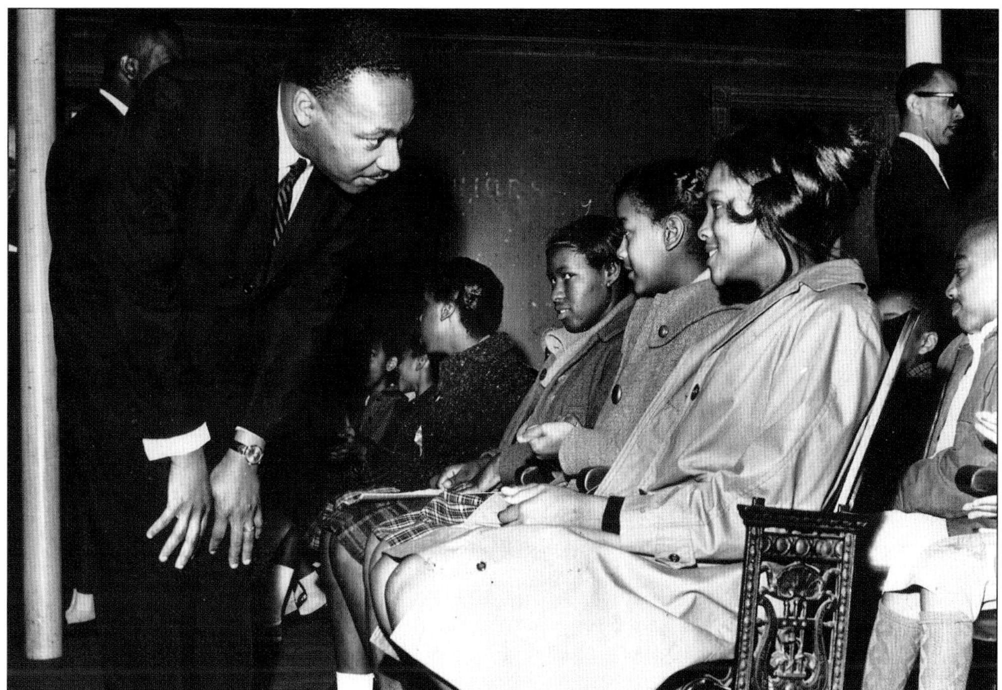

Martin Luther King Jr. visited students from Prince Edward County, Virginia, who were not able to attend school because of massive resistance. The Prince Edward Foundation created private schools to teach the county's white students, while no accommodations were made for teaching the county's African American students. (Courtesy of the Scott Henderson Collection, L. Douglas Wilder Library, Virginia Union University.)

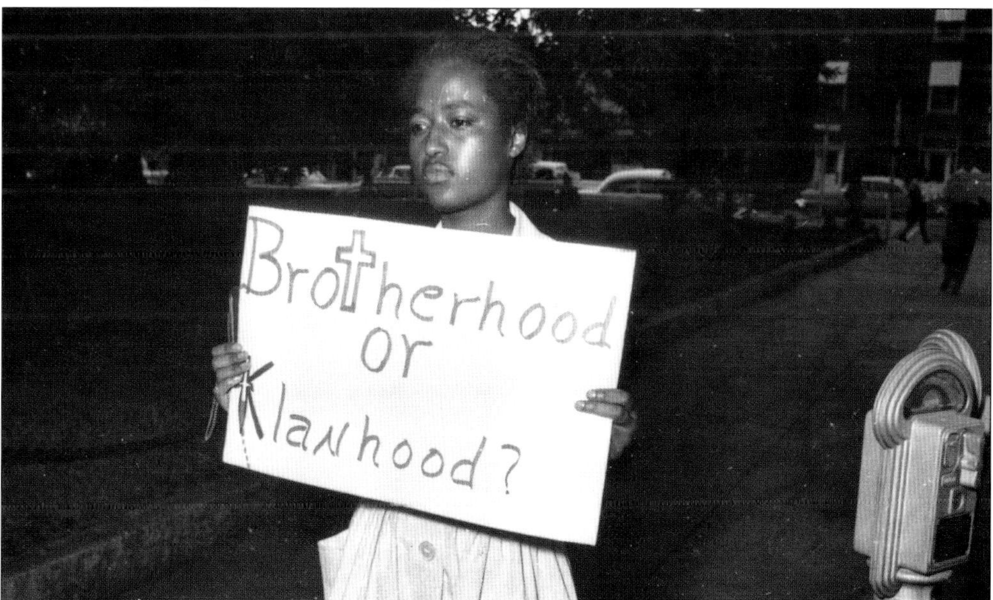

Shown is a civil rights protester in Prince Edward County, Virginia, in 1963. The demonstration was held to protest the school closure in Farmville. The public schools remained closed for five years. (Courtesy of Special Collections and Archives, James Branch Cabell Library, VCU Libraries.)

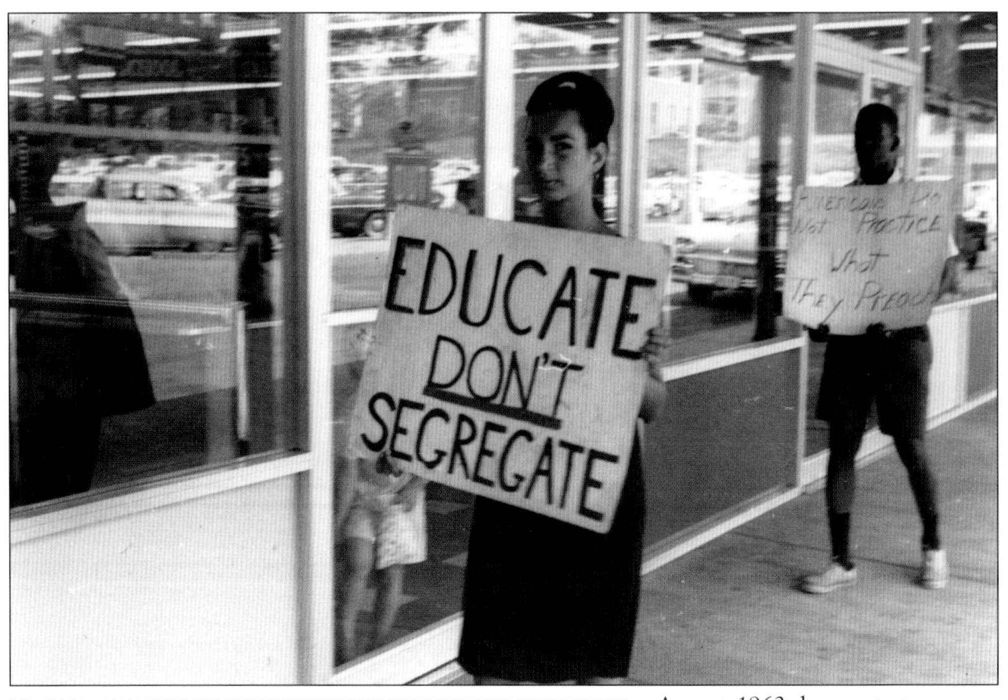

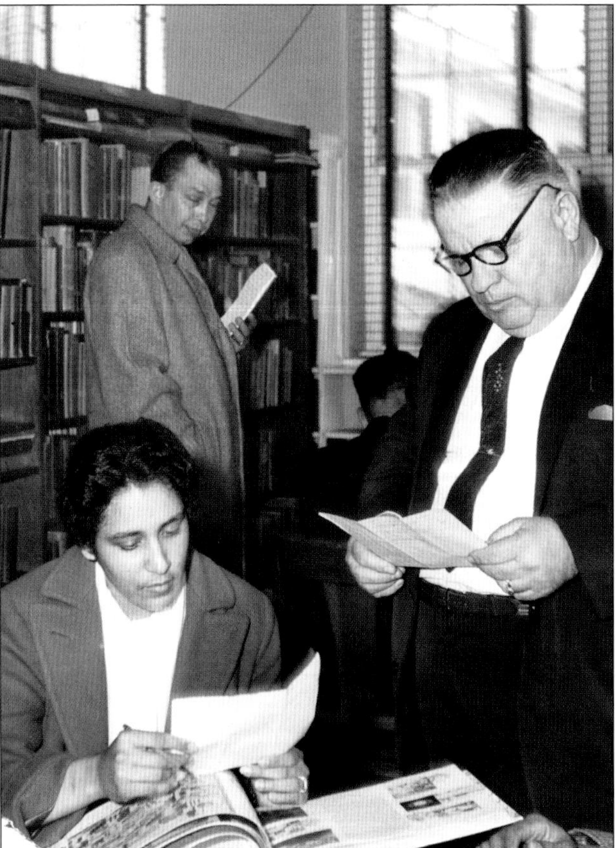

August 1963 demonstrators outside Safeway grocery store in Farmville, Virginia, protest massive resistance. Racial tensions ran very high in Farmville. (Courtesy of Special Collections and Archives, James Branch Cabell Library, VCU Libraries.)

On March 8, 1960, Lillian Pride, a Virginia State College (now Virginia State University) student, was served a warrant by Chief W.E. Traylor for sitting in a section reserved for whites in the Petersburg Public Library. Students at Virginia State College were very active in the civil rights movement. (Courtesy of the *Richmond Times-Dispatch*.)

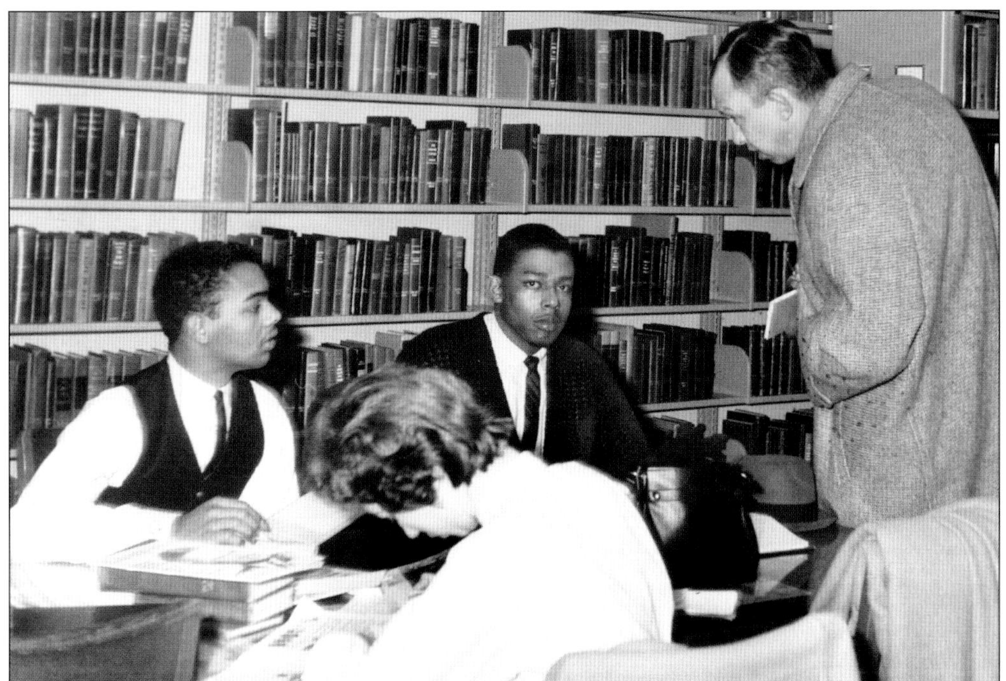

High school students Leonard Walker (seated left) and Horace Brooks (seated right) were arrested along with nine others on March 8, 1960, for trespassing at the Petersburg Public Library for sitting in portions of the library reserved for whites. (Courtesy of the *Richmond Times-Dispatch*.)

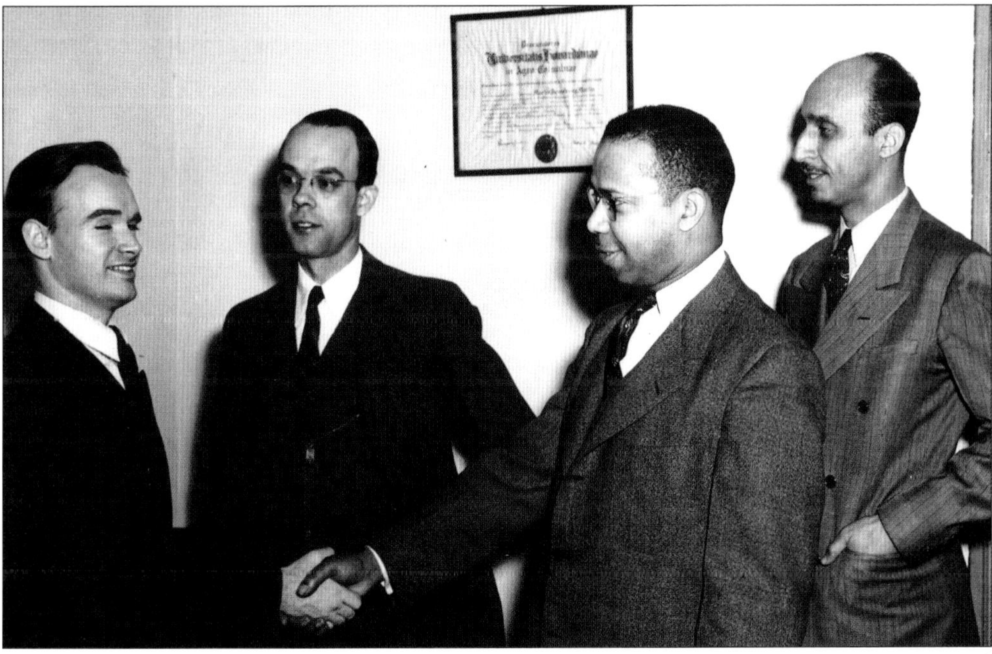

Pictured here, from left to right, are an unidentified man and Civil Rights attorneys Spottswood William Robinson III, Martin A. Martin, and Oliver W. Hill Sr. Robinson, Martin, and Hill worked tirelessly and successfully to challenge segregation in education. (Courtesy of the Scott Henderson Collection, L. Douglas Wilder Library, Virginia Union University.)

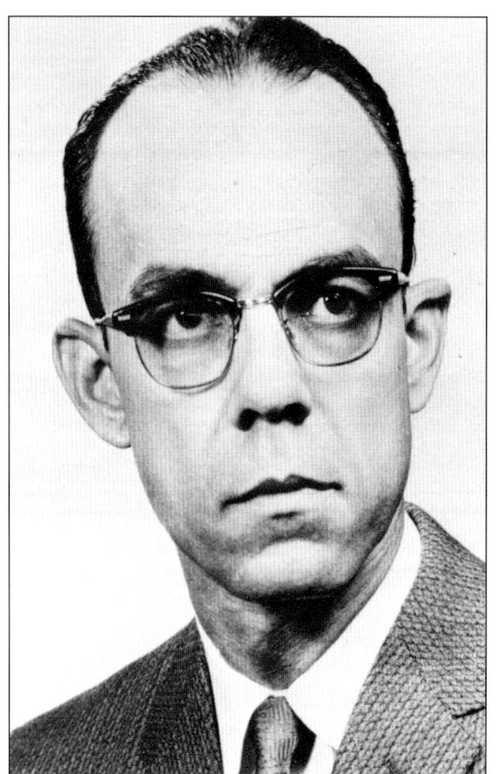

Civil rights attorney Spottswood William Robinson III (1916–1998) was born in Richmond, Virginia, and graduated from Howard University Law School, where he later became the dean. He was the law partner of Oliver W. Hill Sr., and the two successfully argued one of the five cases that led to the Supreme Court's 1954 desegregation ruling in *Brown v. Board of Education.* Robinson would later become chief judge of the US Circuit Court of Appeals for the District of Columbia. (Courtesy of the L. Douglas Wilder Library, Virginia Union University.)

The three cofounders of the Richmond Crusade for Voters are pictured here with concerned citizens who wanted to learn more about the interworkings and success of the organization. Second row, second from the left, is Dr. Ferguson Reid and second from the right is Dr. William S. Thornton. On the first row, third from the right, is John Mitchell Brooks. (Courtesy of Special Collections and Archives, James Branch Cabell Library, VCU Libraries.)

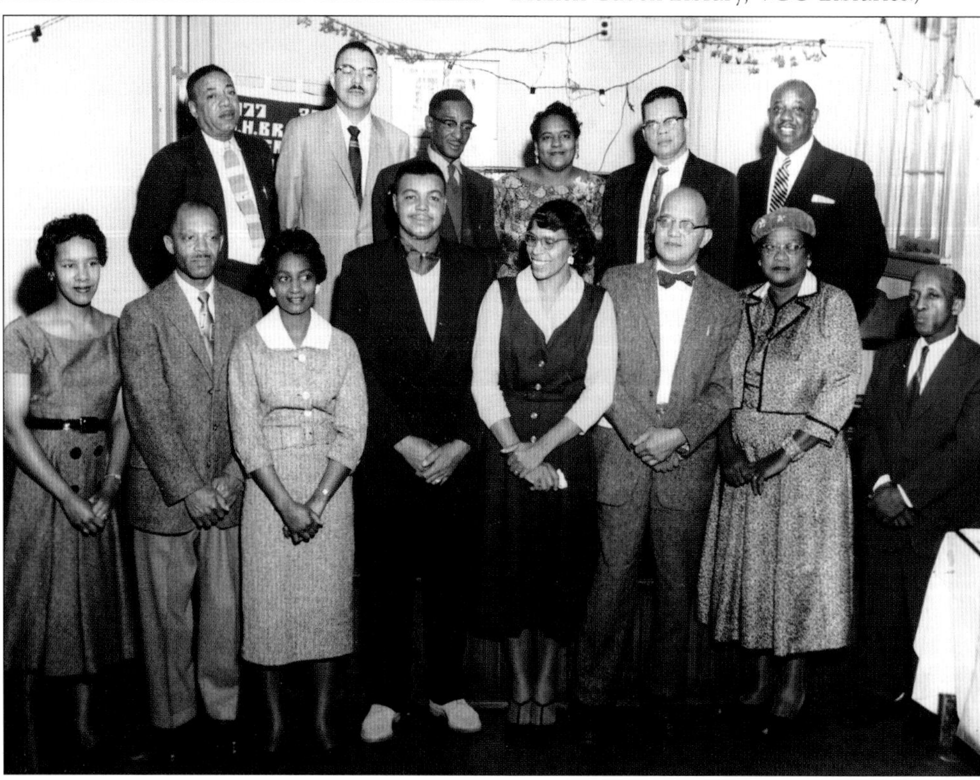

Native Richmonder Dr. William S. Thornton (1920–1999) graduated from Armstrong High School, Virginia Union University, and Ohio College of Podiatric Medicine. Dr. Thornton was a prominent African American podiatrist and cofounder of the Richmond Crusade for Voters. Dr. Thornton served as the first president of the Richmond Crusade for Voters from 1956 to 1961. He was heavily involved in spreading the Richmond Crusade for Voters model and message across the commonwealth. Dr. Thornton is affectionately referred to as the "godfather" of the African American political movement in Richmond. (Courtesy of the Thornton family.)

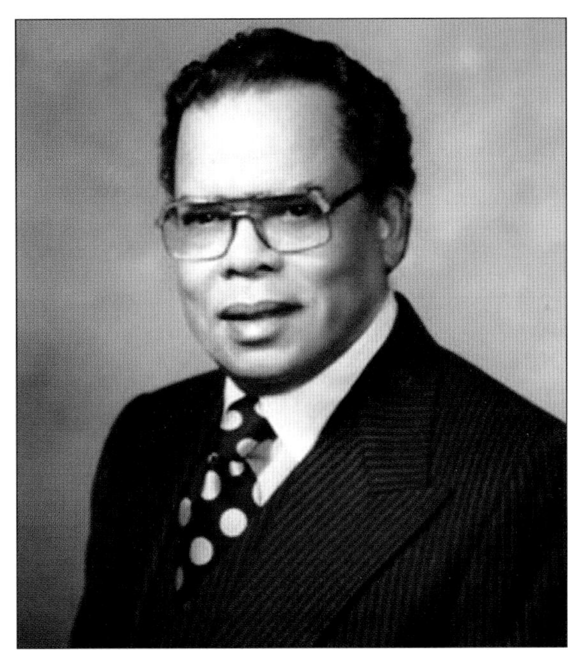

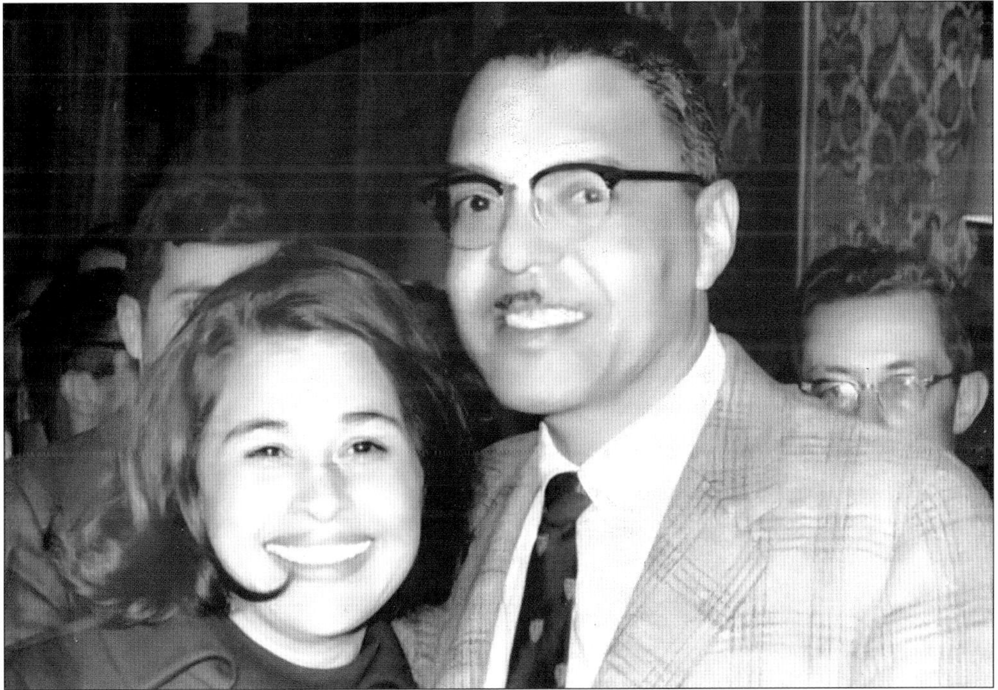

Native Richmonder Dr. William Ferguson Reid was born on March 18, 1925. He graduated from Armstrong High school, Virginia Union University, and Howard University. Dr. Reid was a prominent African American physician. He cofounded the Richmond Crusade for Voters in 1956 with the mission to register and educate African American voters during massive resistance. In 1968, Dr. Reid became the first African American elected to the Virginia General Assembly since Reconstruction, where he served from 1968 to 1973. Pictured are Dr. Reid and his wife, Jacqueline, at his election victory party in 1967. (Courtesy of Brenda Hill.)

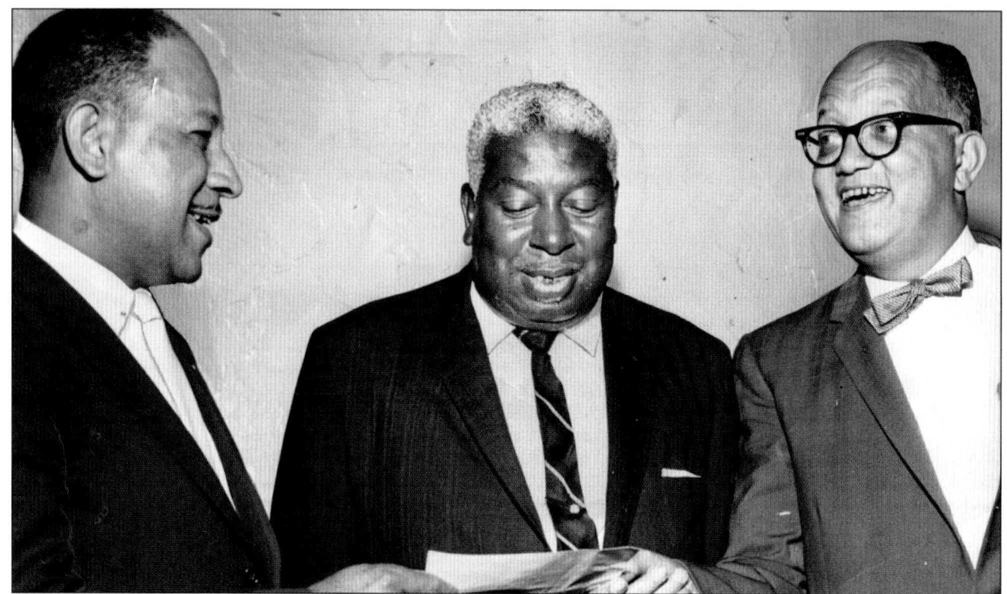

Civil rights activist and keen political strategist John Mitchell Brooks (1917–1980) of Pennsylvania moved to Richmond in 1931. He became one of the first African American Eagle Scouts in the state and graduated from Virginia Union University and West Virginia State College. Brooks was a cofounder of the Richmond Crusade for Voters and, from 1958 to 1975, served as the director of the NAACP national voter registration and education program. Brooks had a unique ability to organize and motivate people to take action in a cause for justice and fair play. Pictured from left to right are R. William M. Banian, J.A. Riddick, and Brooks. (Courtesy of Afro-American Newspapers.)

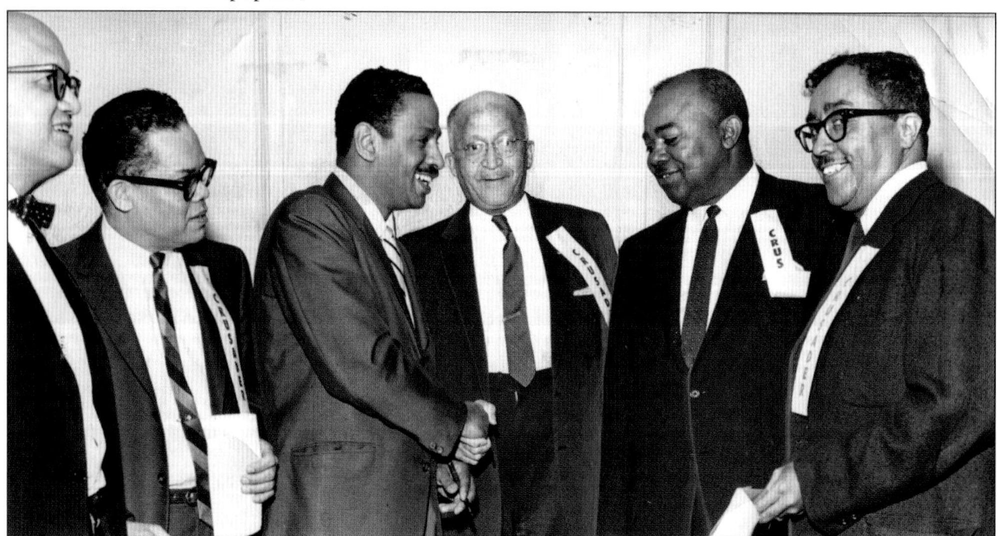

This Richmond Crusade for Voters meeting held on March 27, 1965, emphasized the payment of the state poll tax by May 1 and voter registration for this year's Virginia elections. Pictured from left to right are John Mitchell Brooks, national NAACP voter registration director; Dr. William S. Thornton, Richmond Crusade for Voters board chairman; John Conyers Jr., a Michigan congressman who was the guest speaker; C.B. Case, attorney and Virginia House of Delegates candidate; Colston A. Lewis; and Wilbert Foster. (Courtesy of Afro-American Newspapers.)

This photograph taken in 1958 in celebration of the 50th wedding anniversary of Christopher French Foster and Lucy Ann Jackson Foster. Christopher provided the name for the Crusade for Voters. He was a postal worker with the Richmond Post Office for almost 50 years. He also served as treasurer of the Richmond Branch of the NAACP for 40 years. His sons Christopher, Wendell, Richard, Wilbert ("Skip"), and Francis followed in their father's footsteps and participated in Richmond's African American civic scene. His daughter Ada Foster Fisher returned to Richmond in the early 1960s. Thanks to her encyclopedic knowledge of the history of Jackson Ward, her contributions enabled Jackson Ward to receive a designation in the National Register of Historic Places. (Courtesy of the Foster family collection.)

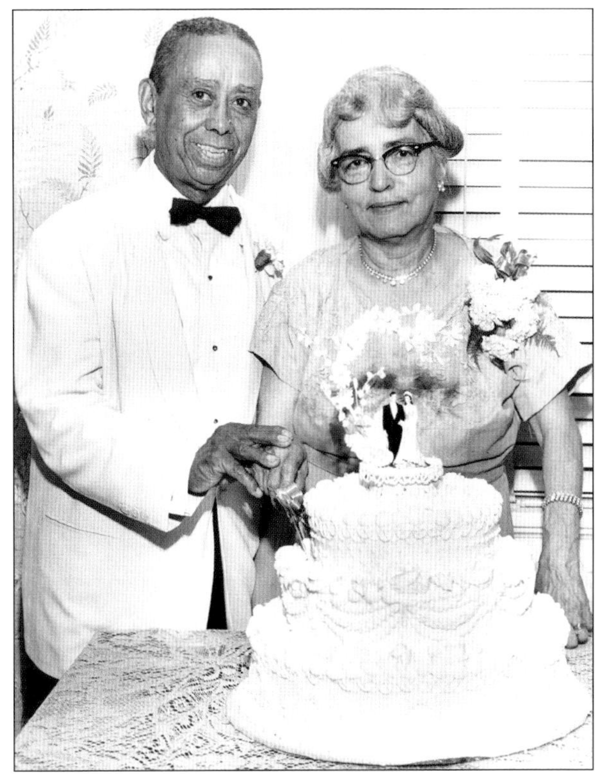

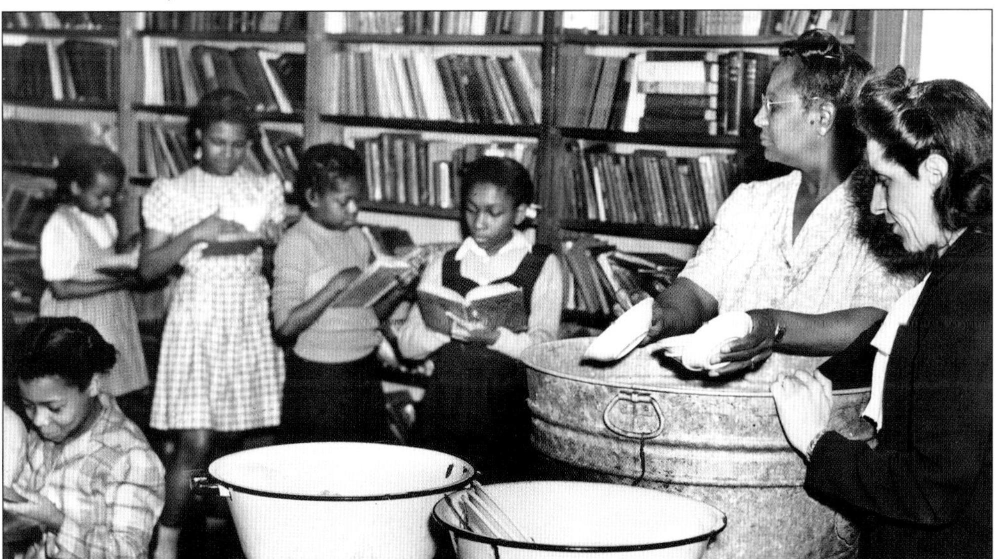

Ethel T. Overby (1892–1997), the first African American woman to serve as principal in the Richmond Public Schools, chaired the Richmond Crusade for Voters Finance Committee. Ethel and her husband, Floyd Overby, worked tirelessly to raise funds. Most notably, proceeds from their sale of donated newspapers helped finance the organization. Overby-Sheppard Elementary School, located at 2300 First Avenue in Richmond was named in her honor. Pictured second from the right, Ethel is washing lunch dishes at Elba School while the children visit the library. She was installed as principal of Elba School in 1933. (Courtesy of the *Richmond Times-Dispatch*.)

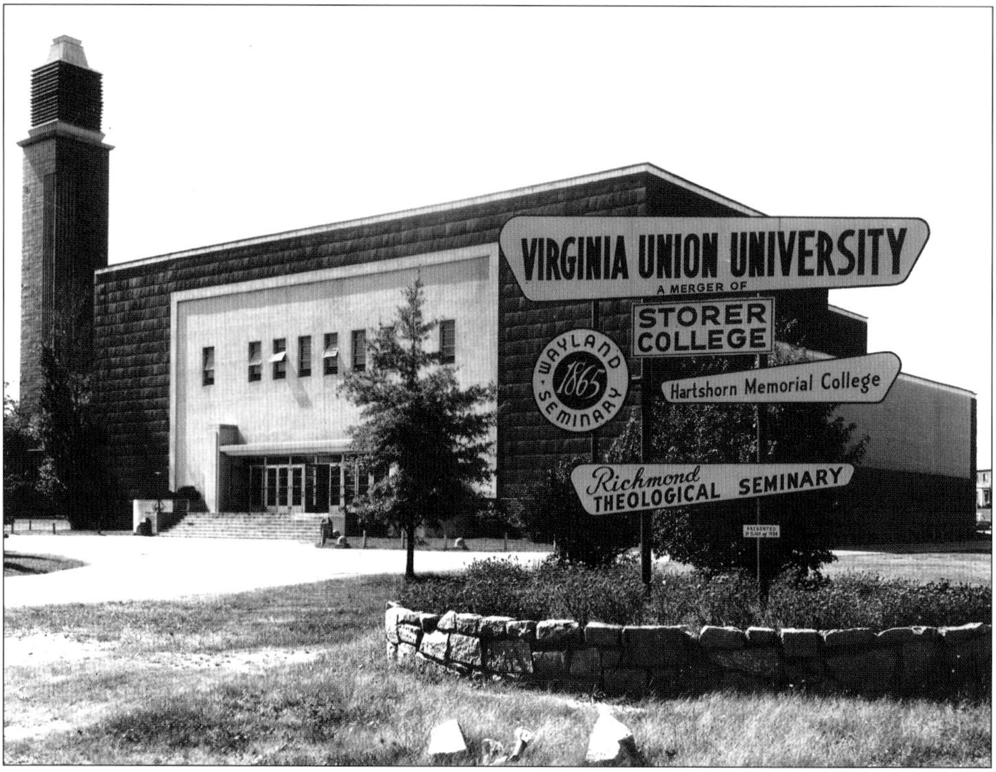

Virginia Union University played a pivotal role in the Richmond Crusade for Voters. All three founders—Dr. William S. Thornton, Dr. William Ferguson Reid and John Mitchell Brooks—graduated from the university, where the seeds of activism were planted. Virginia Union University, a historically black university, was founded in 1865 to educate newly emancipated freedmen. (Courtesy of the L. Douglas Wilder Library, Virginia Union University.)

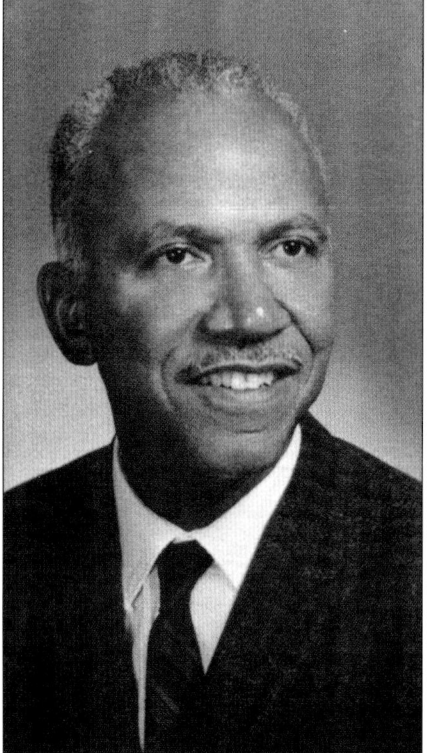

Dr. Franklin Johnson Gayles was born in 1920 in Marshallville, Georgia. Dr. Gayles was a member of Virginia Union University's faculty for 33 years. He served as a professor of social and political science, department chair, and as an academic dean. Gayles was instrumental in the formation and success of the Richmond Crusade for Voters, where he served for many years as the research committee chairman. (Courtesy of the L. Douglas Wilder Library, Virginia Union University.)

Virginia Union University professor Dr. Tinsley Spraggins (1910–2000) taught history and political science. He was very active in the civil rights movement and counseled student protesters in Richmond. (Courtesy of the L. Douglas Wilder Library, Virginia Union University.)

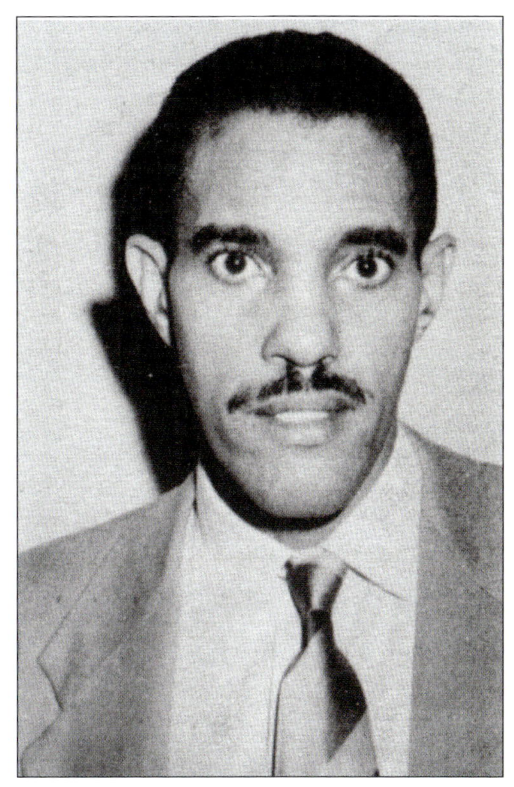

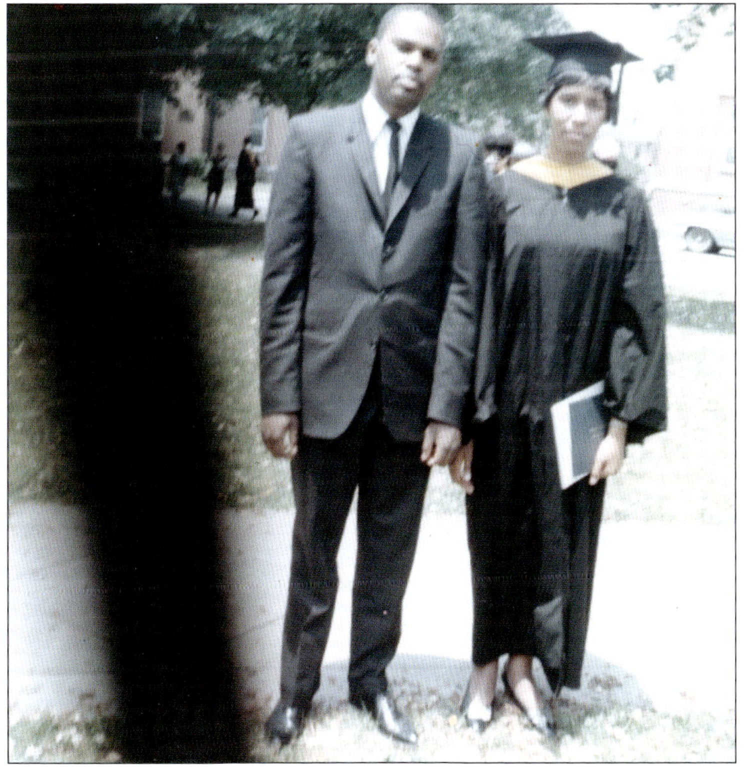

After meeting with Dr. Reid, one of the cofounders of the Richmond Crusade for Voters at Virginia Union University, Thomas Francis volunteered to drive voters to the polls for the 1963 election. He is pictured with his wife, Edna Francis, in June 1967. (Courtesy of the Francis family.)

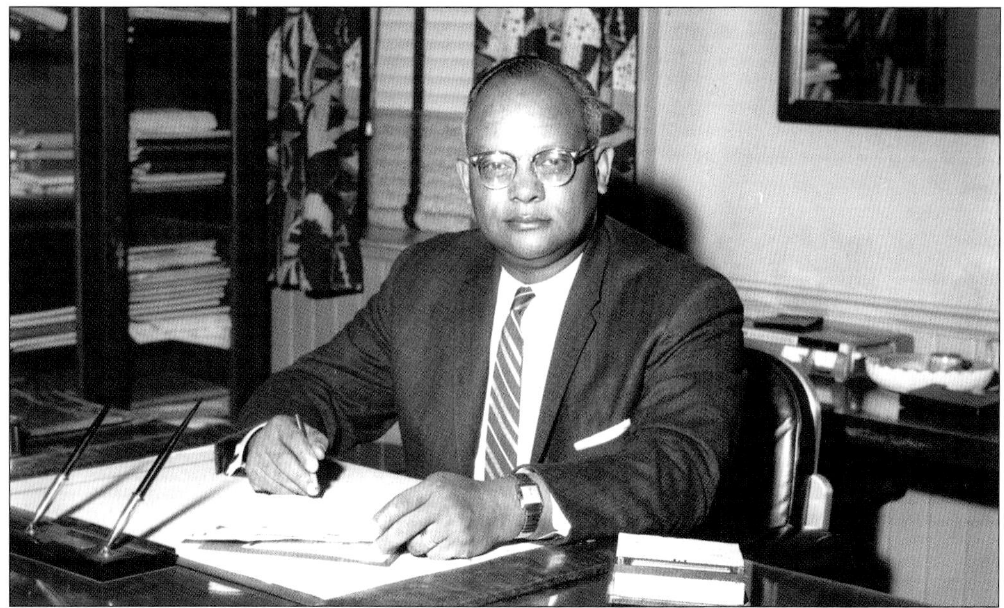

Dr. Thomas Howard Henderson (1910–1970), a 1929 Virginia Union University graduate, assumed the presidency of the university in 1960. Dr. Henderson's tenure as president coincided with the civil rights movement. He met with students Wendell T. Foster, Charles Sherrod, and Frank Pinkston the evening of February 21, 1960, the night before the Thalhimers sit-in protests. (Courtesy of the L. Douglas Wilder Library, Virginia Union University.)

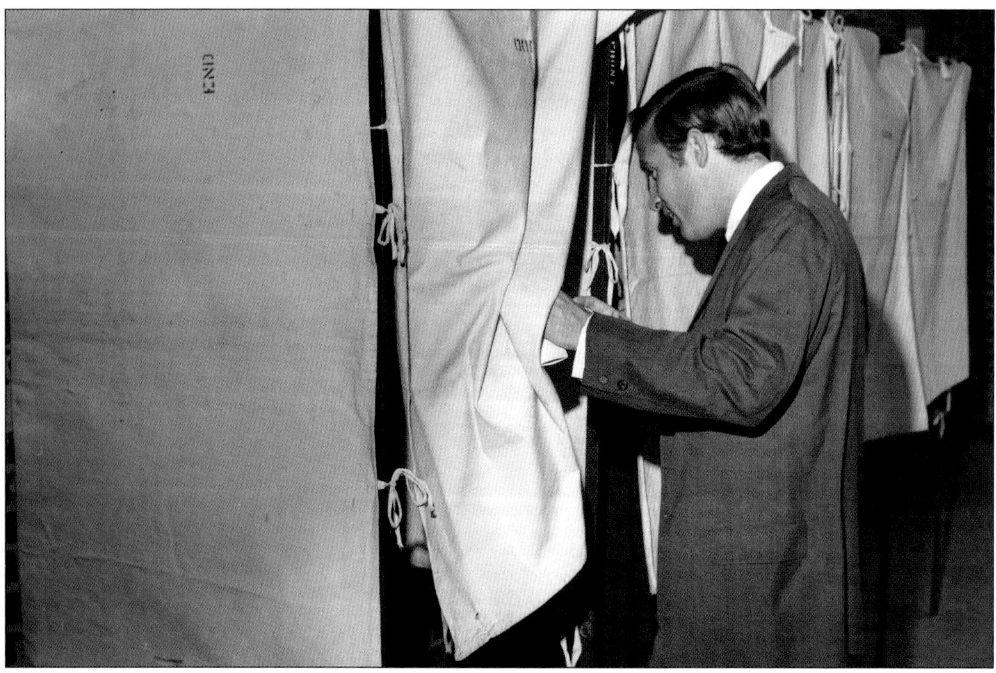

J. Sargeant Reynolds (1936–1971) served in the Virginia House of Delegates from 1966 to 1967, the Senate of Virginia from 1968 to 1969, and as the 30th lieutenant governor of Virginia (1970–1971). Reynolds was an ally to the Richmond Crusade for Voters and used his privilege to advocate for the less fortunate. (Courtesy of the *Richmond Times-Dispatch* Collection, the Valentine.)

Delegate Dr. William Ferguson Reid (right) walks the halls of the Virginia General Assembly with Sen. L. Douglas Wilder in 1970. The two men had a close relationship during their tenures at the general assembly. (Courtesy of the L. Douglas Wilder Library, Virginia Union University.)

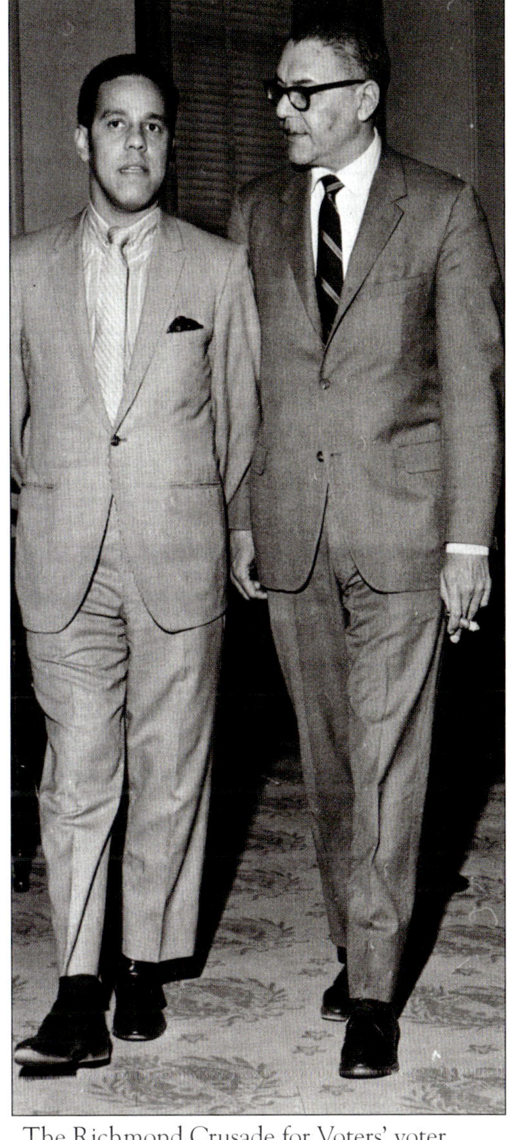

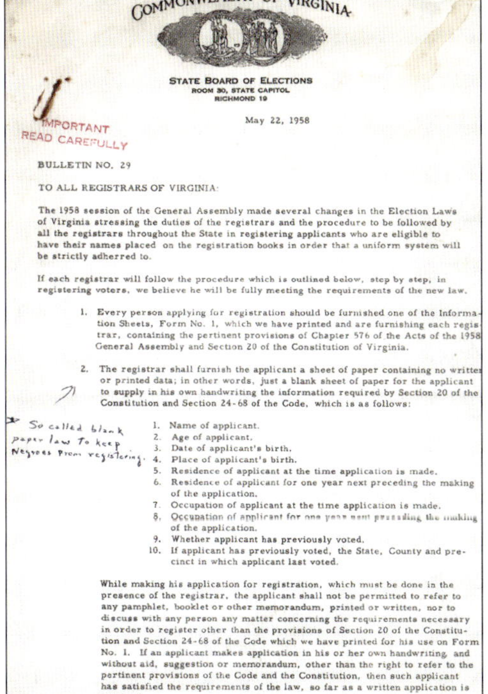

COMMONWEALTH OF VIRGINIA

STATE BOARD OF ELECTIONS
ROOM 30, STATE CAPITOL
RICHMOND 19

IMPORTANT
READ CAREFULLY

May 22, 1958

BULLETIN NO. 29

TO ALL REGISTRARS OF VIRGINIA:

The 1958 session of the General Assembly made several changes in the Election Laws of Virginia stressing the duties of the registrars and the procedure to be followed by all the registrars throughout the State in registering applicants who are eligible to have their names placed on the registration books in order that a uniform system will be strictly adherred to.

If each registrar will follow the procedure which is outlined below, step by step, in registering voters, we believe he will be fully meeting the requirements of the new law.

1. Every person applying for registration should be furnished one of the Information Sheets, Form No. 1, which we have printed and are furnishing each registrar, containing the pertinent provisions of Chapter 576 of the Acts of the 1958 General Assembly and Section 20 of the Constitution of Virginia.

2. The registrar shall furnish the applicant a sheet of paper containing no written or printed data; in other words, just a blank sheet of paper for the applicant to supply in his own handwriting the information required by Section 20 of the Constitution and Section 24-68 of the Code, which is as follows:

So called blank paper law to keep Negroes from registering.

1. Name of applicant.
2. Age of applicant.
3. Date of applicant's birth.
4. Place of applicant's birth.
5. Residence of applicant at the time application is made.
6. Residence of applicant for one year next preceding the making of the application.
7. Occupation of applicant at the time application is made.
8. Occupation of applicant for one year next preceding the making of the application.
9. Whether applicant has previously voted.
10. If applicant has previously voted, the State, County and precinct in which applicant last voted.

While making his application for registration, which must be done in the presence of the registrar, the applicant shall not be permitted to refer to any pamphlet, booklet or other memorandum, printed or written, nor to discuss with any person any matter concerning the requirements necessary in order to register other than the provisions of Section 20 of the Constitution and Section 24-68 of the Code which we have printed for his use on Form No. 1. If an applicant makes application in his or her own handwriting and without aid, suggestion or memorandum, other than the right to refer to the pertinent provisions of the Code and the Constitution, then such applicant has satisfied the requirements of the law, so far as a written application is required.

The Richmond Crusade for Voters' voter registration drive "Miracle of Richmond" registered 3,500 new African American voters. As a result, new campaigns were created by white politicians to suppress the African American vote. This 1958 letter from the state board of elections was sent to Virginia registrars and mandated new procedures for registering applicants, most notably through "blank sheet" registration forms, which served as a literacy test for African Americans. (Courtesy of Special Collections and Archives, James Branch Cabell Library, VCU Libraries.)

20,000 voters is goal set by Crusade for voters in 1959

RICHMOND

The Crusade for Voters will sponsor a meeting at Slaughter's Hotel February 2 to kick-off its 1959 effort to get 20,000 qualified voters in the city.

Each person attending the meeting is asked to get five other "crusaders" to help in the compaign for more voters.

Bill Thornton, president of the Crusade for Voters, speaking on the current drive for 20,000 voters, said:

"This is a year of decision for colored citizens of Richmond. We have reached a point where with a little more effort we can become an important part of Richmond's political picture.

"When I say we, I mean the group as a whole, not our Crusade for Voters which is a non partisan coordinating organization. This is a year of decision because:

1. Petty politicians may set in motion, through a referendum, the machinery for the abolition of our public schools.

2. Petty politicians may also call for referendums to annex bordering counties in order to bring into the city a vast number of white voters to offset the gains made by the colored population.

"We cannot meet these referendums with only emotional cries of indignation; we must have the ballot waiting and ready in the hands of at least 20,000 colored citizens.

"Many of our southern politicians believe that we are not capable of looking ahead and analyzing political events. They believe we react only when the crisis is upon us and it's too late to do anything other than make emotional speeches.

"That is why our election laws allow so long a period between elections and the deadline for becoming a qualified voter. The deadline this year is May 2, 1959. We are of age and with y[illegible] help the politicians will get a rude surprise this year."

The Crusade of Voters has headquarters at 420 N. First St. Johnny Brooks is executive secretary and Fergie Reid, suffrage chairman.

This February 7, 1959, headline from the *Richmond Afro-American* emphasizes the Richmond Crusade for Voters' goal to register 20,000 new African American voters. The organization set annual registration targets. (Courtesy of Afro-American Newspapers.)

MARTIN LUTHER KING

JOINS YOUR

Religious and Civic Leaders

IN

Urging All Virginians

TO

Come To Richmond

IN

A Pilgrimage Of Prayer For Public Schools

ON

EMANCIPATION DAY January 1, 1959

YOU WILL ASSEMBLE AT **THE MOSQUE** LAUREL and MAIN STREETS

PROMPTLY AT 2:30 P. M.

"Let us not deceive ourselves! We have among us politicians who will not hesitate to CLOSE ALL PUBLIC SCHOOLS IN VIRGINIA. We must demonstrate to Virginia and the nation by our presence and action that we will not tolerate this crime against Virginia's children."

— DR. PHILIP Y. WYATT

WHICH WILL IT BE?

Free Education? or Closed Schools?

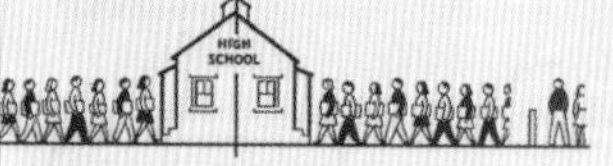

"Only through the preservation of a free, desegregated public school system can a people be fully emancipated from the shackles of prejudice and inequality. American democracy itself is at stake. This is your pilgrimage."

—THE REV. WYATT TEE WALKER

A flyer publicizes the arrival of Martin Luther King Jr. to the Mosque (now the Altria Theater) for a rally to save Richmond's public schools. The purpose of this event was to educate and galvanize the African American community. (Courtesy of Special Collections and Archives, James Branch Cabell Library, VCU Libraries.)

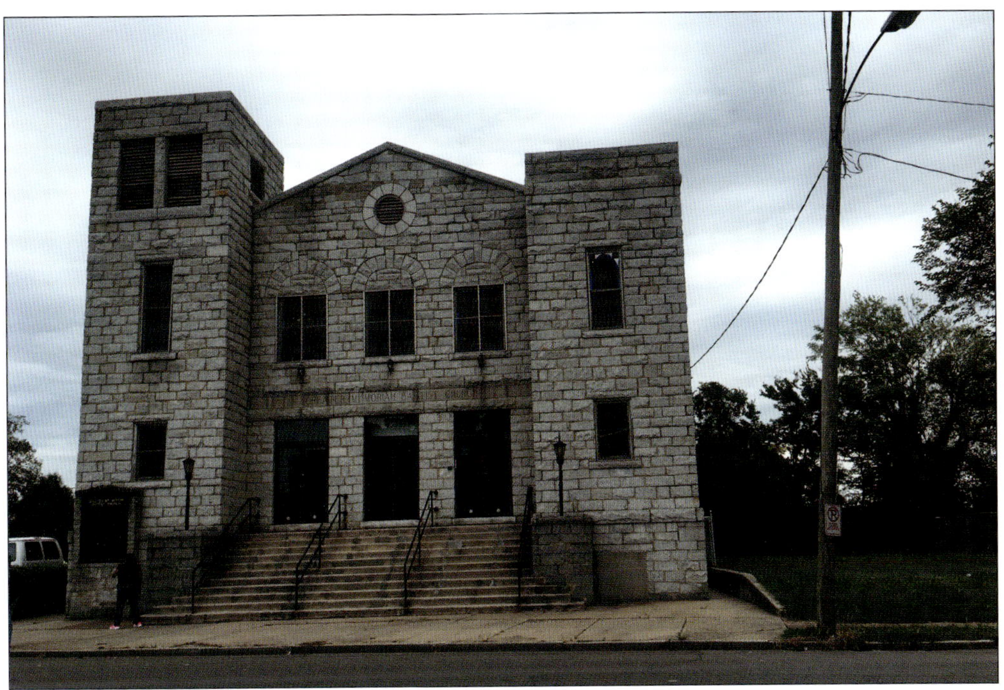

Greater Mt. Moriah Baptist Church, located on 913 North First Street in Jackson Ward, was the first meeting location of the three cofounders of the Richmond Crusade for Voters. (Author.)

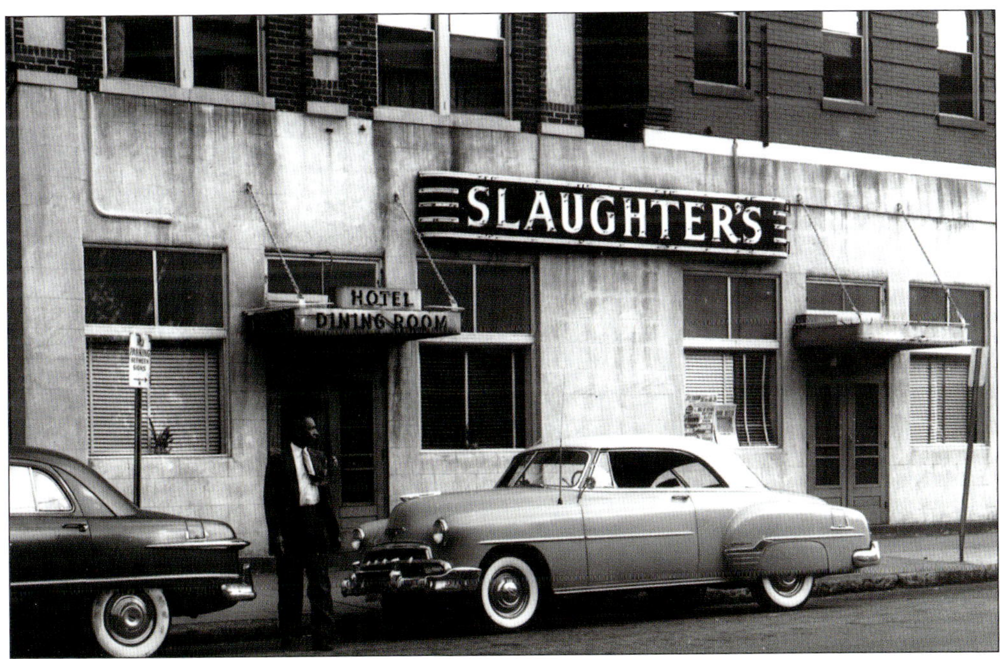

Slaughter's Hotel located on Second Street in Jackson Ward was a popular gathering place for African Americans. The founders of the Richmond Crusade for Voters met there almost daily during the early days of the organization to discuss strategy. (Courtesy of the Scott Henderson Collection, L. Douglas Wilder Library, Virginia Union University.)

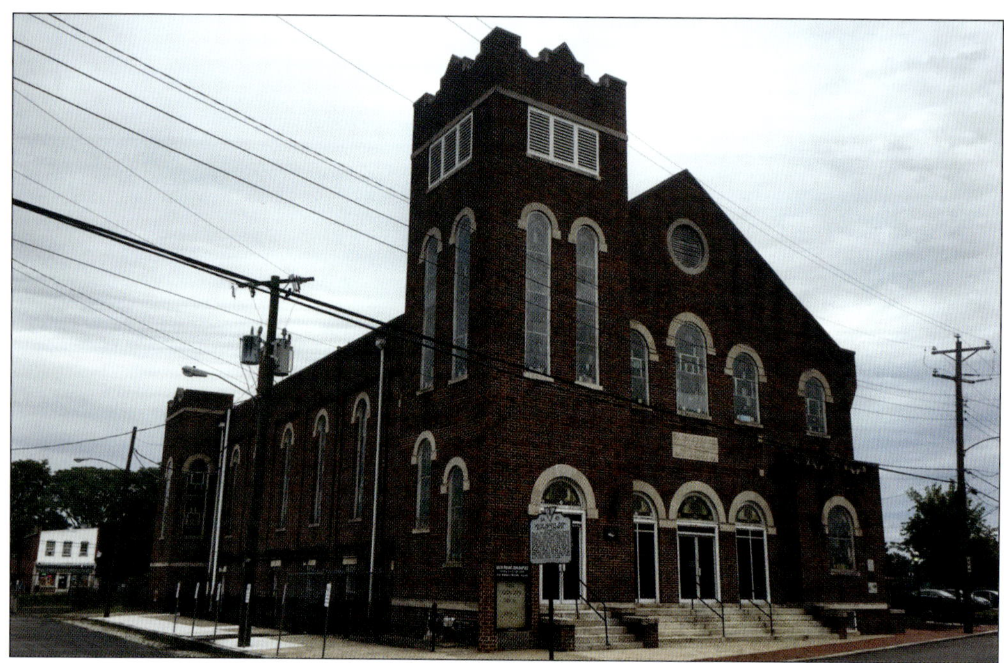

Sixth Mount Zion Baptist Church, located at 14 West Duval Street in Jackson Ward, was one of the meeting locations of the Richmond Crusade for Voters. This church was almost demolished by the construction of Interstate 95 in the 1950s. (Photograph by the author, courtesy of Sixth Mount Zion Baptist Church and Benjamin C. Ross.)

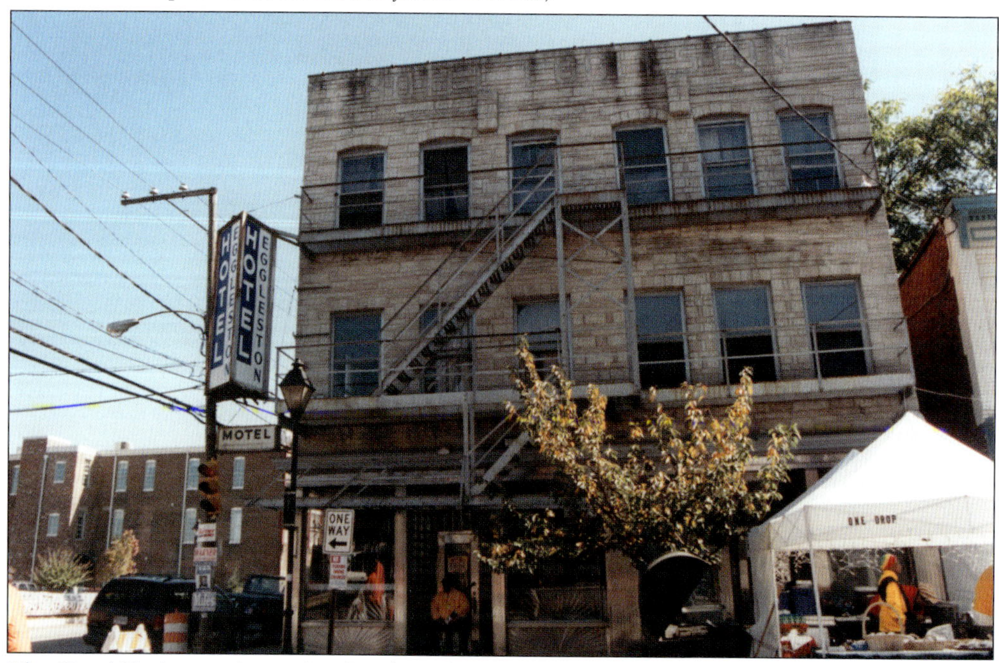

The Hotel Eggleston, located at Leigh and Second Streets in Jackson Ward, was a three-story building with brick side and rear elevations and a rusticated limestone block facade. This famous hotel was a frequent meeting location for the organization and hosted big names such as Louis Armstrong, Jackie Robinson, and James Brown. (Courtesy of the Valentine.)

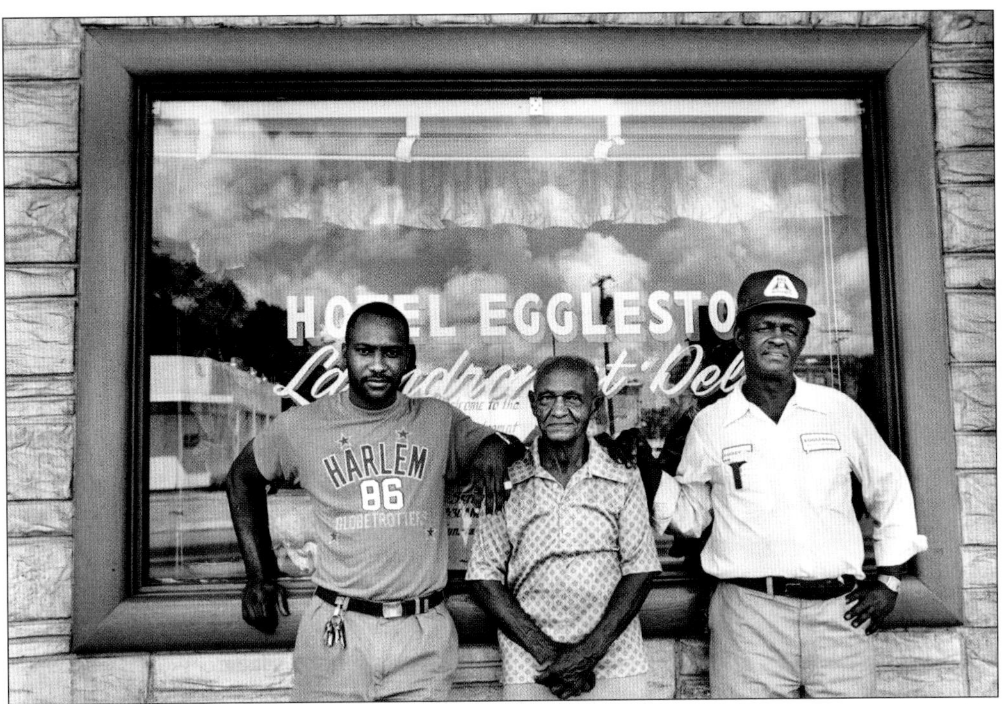

The Eggleston Hotel was owned and operated by the Eggleston family beginning in the 1930s. It was one of only three hotels in Richmond that permitted African American guests. From left to right are Neverett A. Eggleston III, Neverett A. Eggleston Sr., and Neverett A. Eggleston Jr. (Courtesy of the *Richmond Times-Dispatch.*)

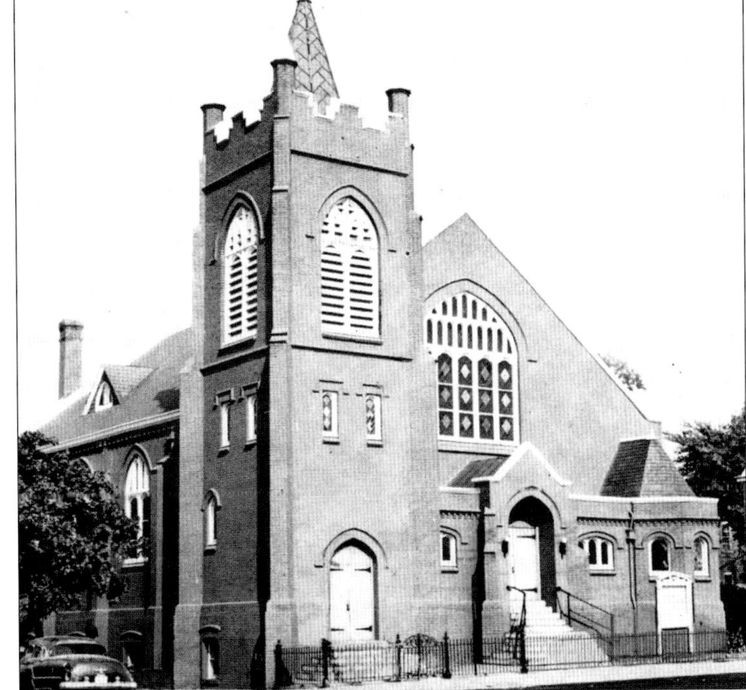

St. Paul's Baptist Church on Twenty-Fifth and Marshall Streets in Richmond's Church Hill was a location for Richmond Crusade for Voters meetings. The church was founded in 1909. (Courtesy of Dr. Lance D. Watson and St. Paul's Baptist Church.)

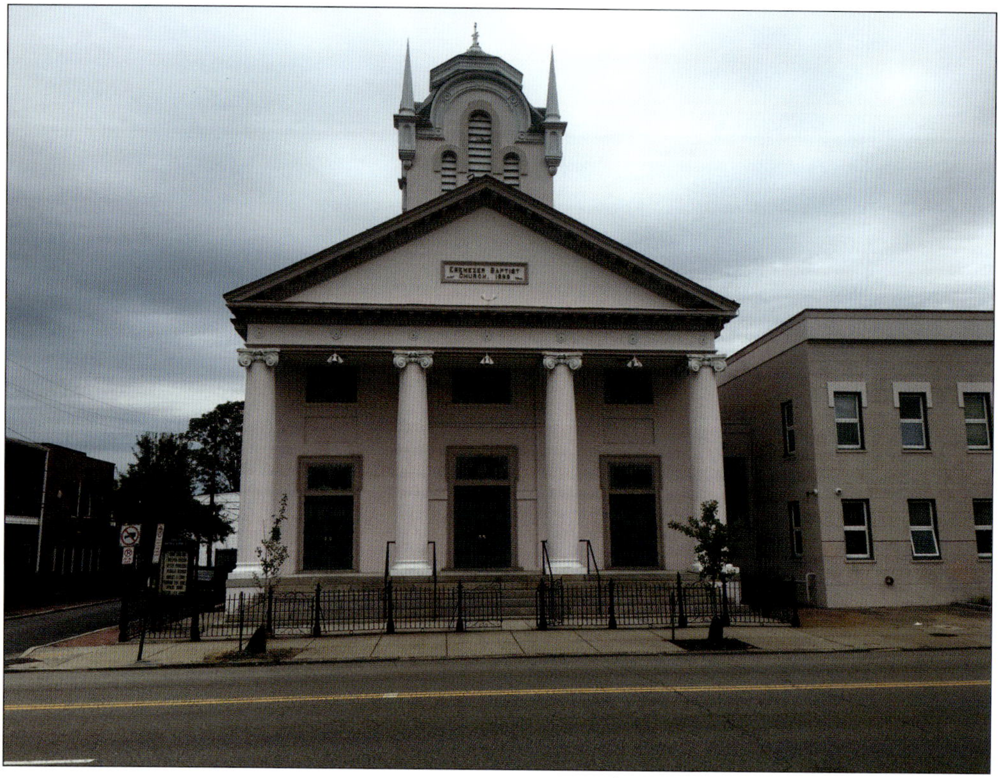

Early Richmond Crusade for Voters meetings took place at Ebenezer Baptist Church located at 216 West Leigh Street. The church was organized in 1857, and in 1866, Ebenezer established Richmond's first free school for African Americans. (Author.)

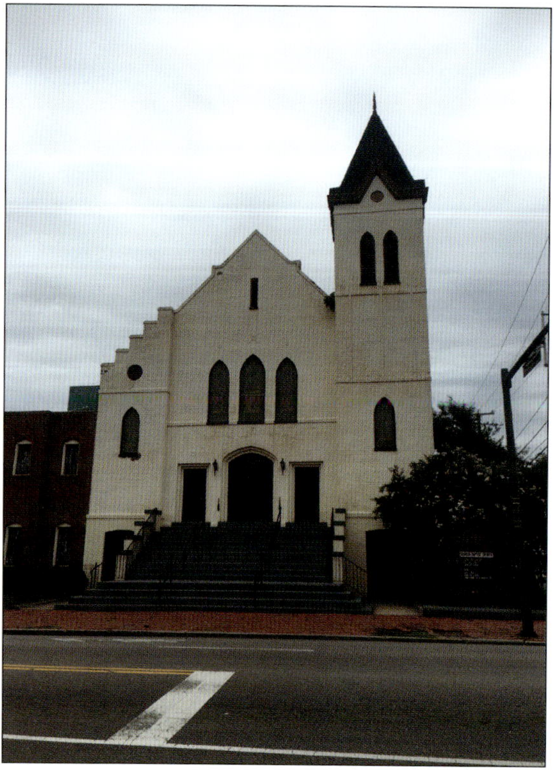

Sharon Baptist Church, built in 1887 at 22 East Leigh Street, was a meeting venue for the organization. (Author.)

St. Philip's Church, erected in 1870 and located at 1 West Leigh Street (at the intersection with St. James Street), was an early meeting place for the Richmond Crusade for Voters. (Author.)

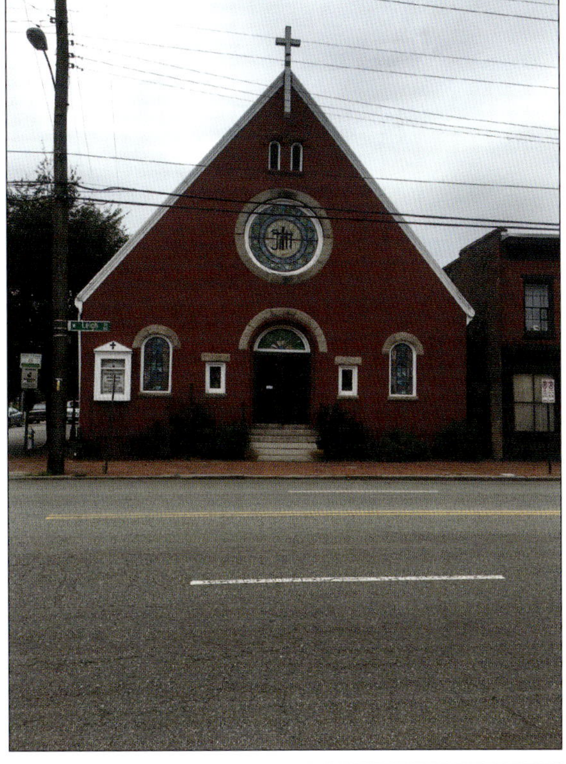

Jackson Ward was home to Maggie Lena Walker (1864–1934), the first woman bank president in the United States. Walker was also a community leader and educator. Walker's residence, located at 110½ East Leigh Street, was built in 1883. (Author.)

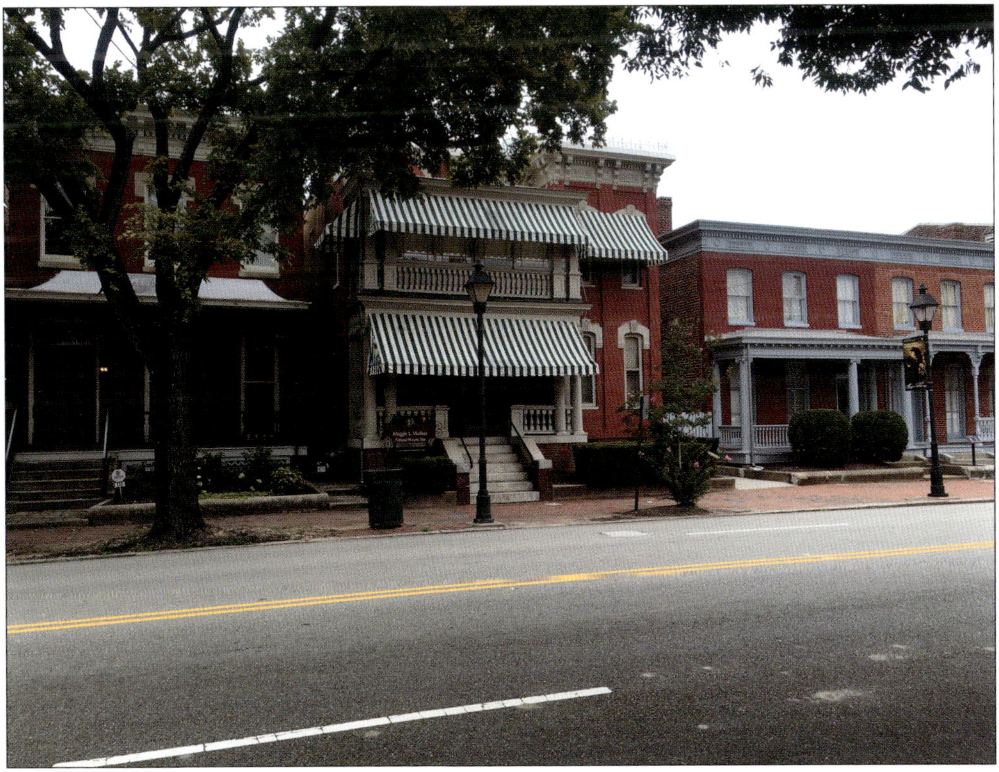

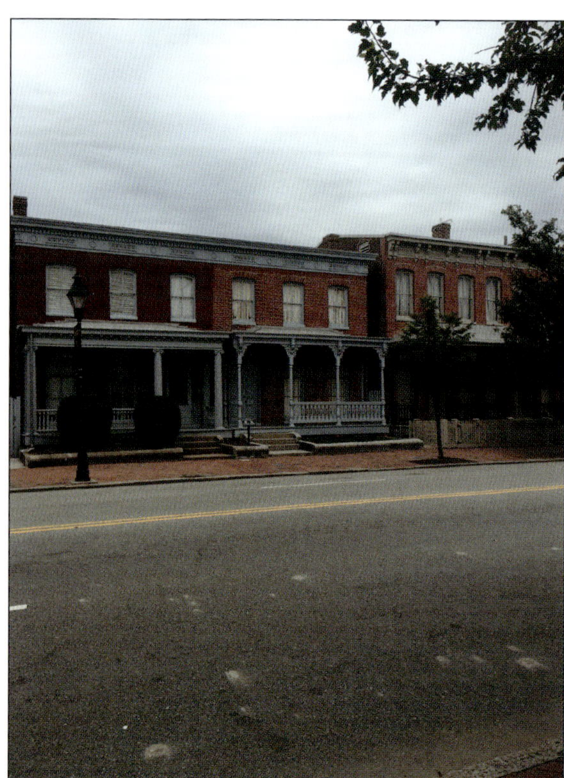

Many influential African Americans called Historic Jackson Ward home. Pictured are homes located on Leigh Street. (Author.)

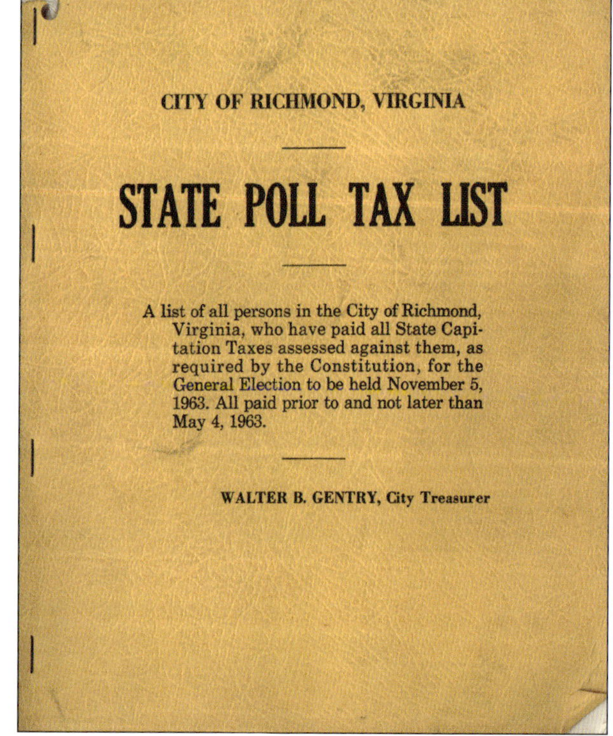

CITY OF RICHMOND, VIRGINIA

STATE POLL TAX LIST

A list of all persons in the City of Richmond, Virginia, who have paid all State Capitation Taxes assessed against them, as required by the Constitution, for the General Election to be held November 5, 1963. All paid prior to and not later than May 4, 1963.

WALTER B. GENTRY, City Treasurer

Shown is the cover of a 1963 state poll tax list distributed by the Richmond Crusade for Voters. The poll tax was a prerequisite to voter registration, and those listed were paid in full. (Courtesy of Special Collections and Archives, James Branch Cabell Library, VCU Libraries.)

Thornton William
Thornton William A
Thornton Willis S
Thorpe Archie L
Thorpe Bertie A
Thorpe Herman
Thorpe Lucille
Threatt Inez
Threatts Frank Jr
Threatts Joyce

Inside the 1963 state poll tax list were notable names connected to the Richmond Crusade for Voters. The name of William A. Thornton, longtime historian of the Richmond Crusade for Voters, is shown. (Courtesy of Special Collections and Archives, James Branch Cabell Library, VCU Libraries.)

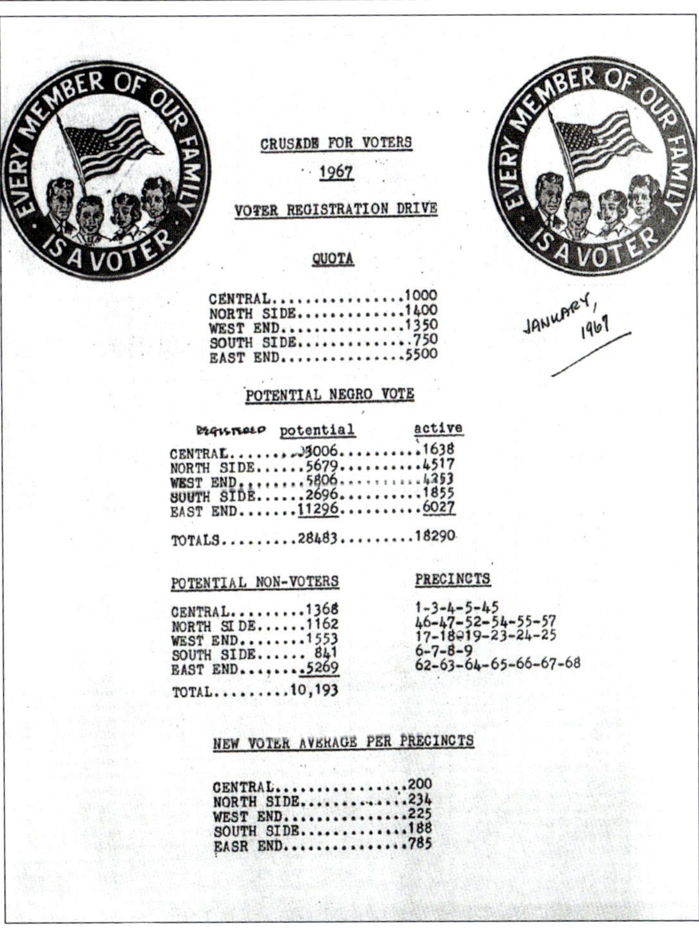

CRUSADE FOR VOTERS

1967

VOTER REGISTRATION DRIVE

QUOTA

CENTRAL	1000
NORTH SIDE	1400
WEST END	1350
SOUTH SIDE	750
EAST END	5500

POTENTIAL NEGRO VOTE

	REGISTERED potential	active
CENTRAL	3006	1638
NORTH SIDE	5679	4517
WEST END	5806	4253
SOUTH SIDE	2696	1855
EAST END	11296	6027
TOTALS	28483	18290

POTENTIAL NON-VOTERS		PRECINCTS
CENTRAL	1368	1-3-4-5-45
NORTH SIDE	1162	46-47-52-54-55-57
WEST END	1553	17-18-19-23-24-25
SOUTH SIDE	841	6-7-8-9
EAST END	5269	62-63-64-65-66-67-68
TOTAL	10,193	

NEW VOTER AVERAGE PER PRECINCTS

CENTRAL	200
NORTH SIDE	234
WEST END	225
SOUTH SIDE	188
EASR END	785

This January 1967 document shows voter registration drive quotas. There were quotas created for each voter registration event. (Courtesy of Special Collections and Archives, James Branch Cabell Library, VCU Libraries.)

Year	African American Registered Voters
1956	8,500
1960	15,759
1963	17,269
1966	32,500

Due to the efforts of the Richmond Crusade for Voters, the number of registered voters in the city of Richmond quadrupled in less than a decade. African Americans went from 15 percent of the total electorate in 1956 to over 35 percent of the electorate in 1966. This data was compiled by the author from a report by Ethel T. Overby, chairperson of finance. (Author.)

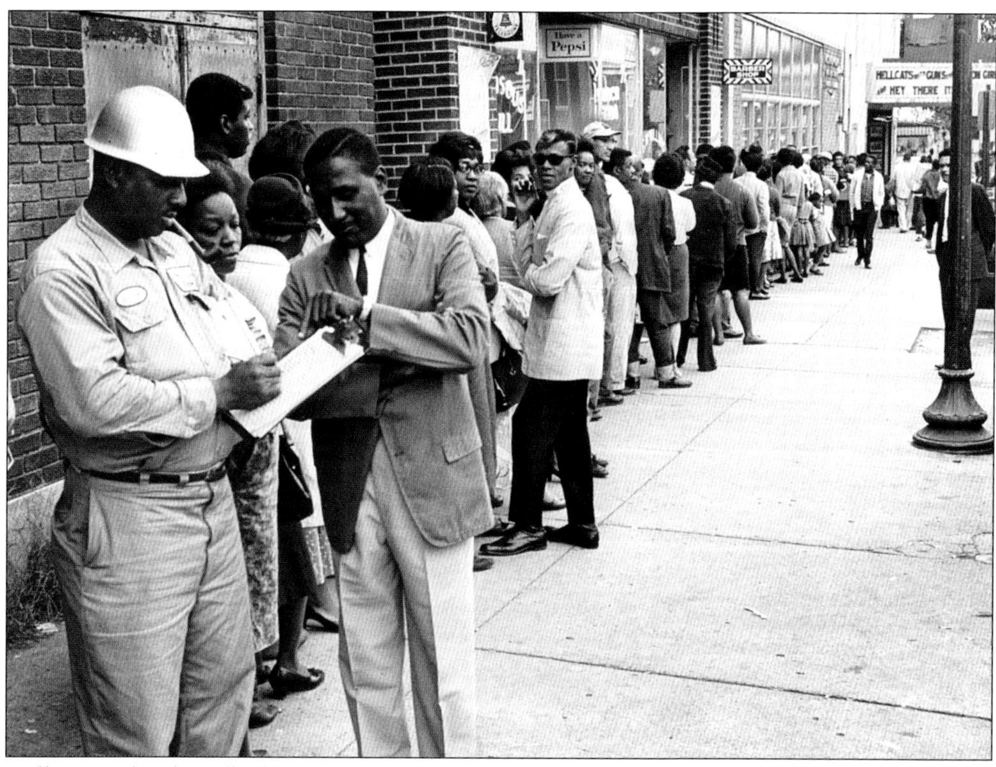

William Richardson (left) provides his name to Earl Carter during a voter registration drive in 1964. (Courtesy of the *Richmond Times-Dispatch*.)

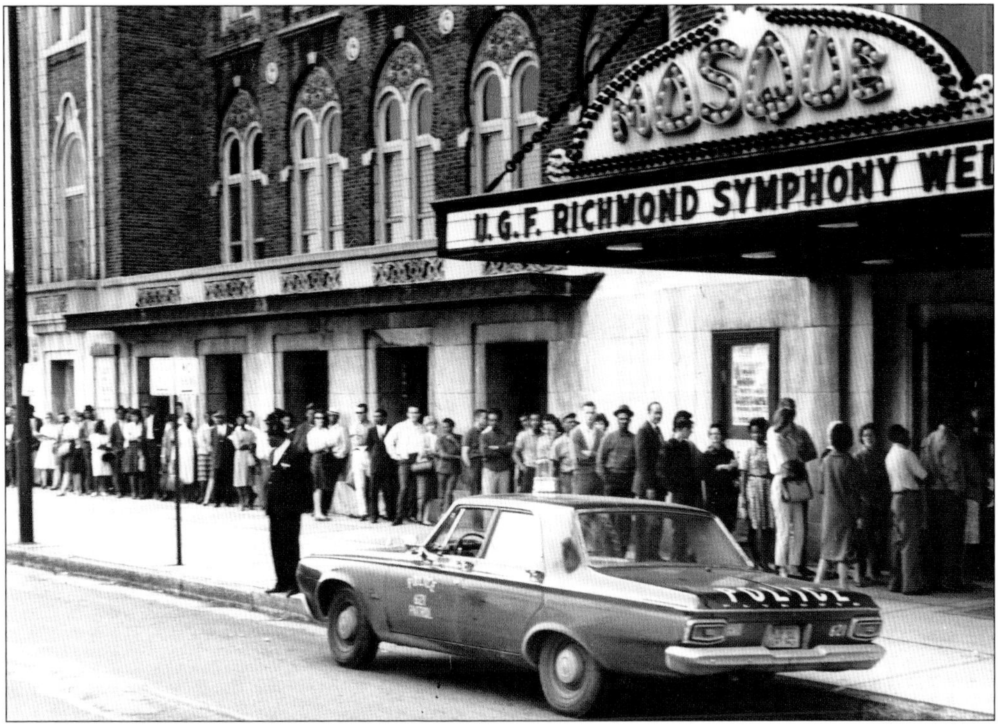

A Richmond Crusade for Voters voter registration campaign at the Mosque (now the Altria Theater) on Main and Laurel Streets is pictured here in the 1960s. Voter registration drives were held year-round. (Photograph by Scott Henderson, courtesy of John M. Brooks Jr.)

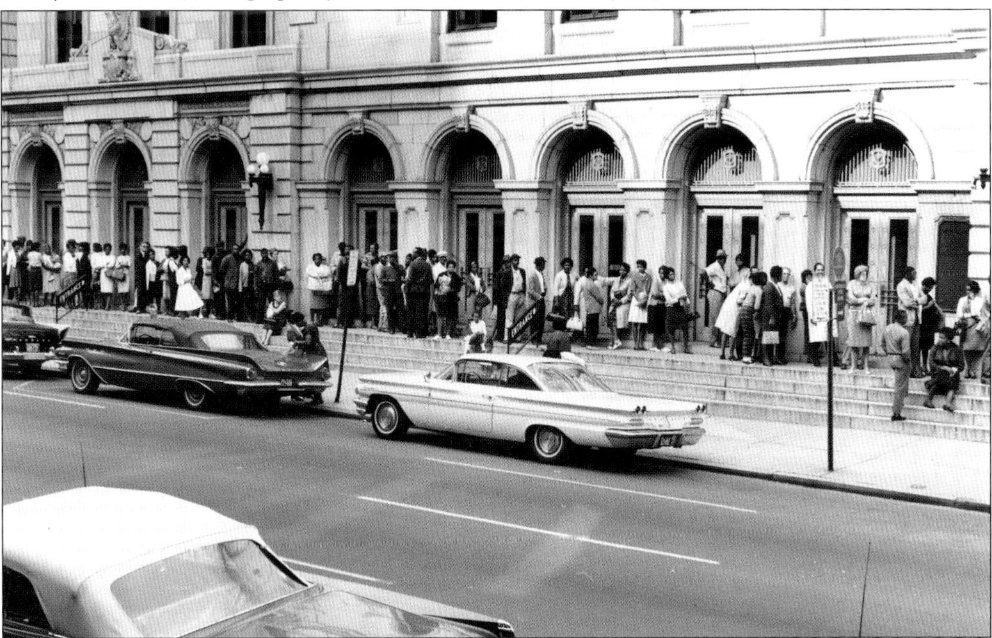

A 1960s voter registration drive at the post office on Main Street. Registration drives were held in popular locations that were accessible by public transportation. (Photograph by Scott Henderson, courtesy of John M. Brooks Jr.)

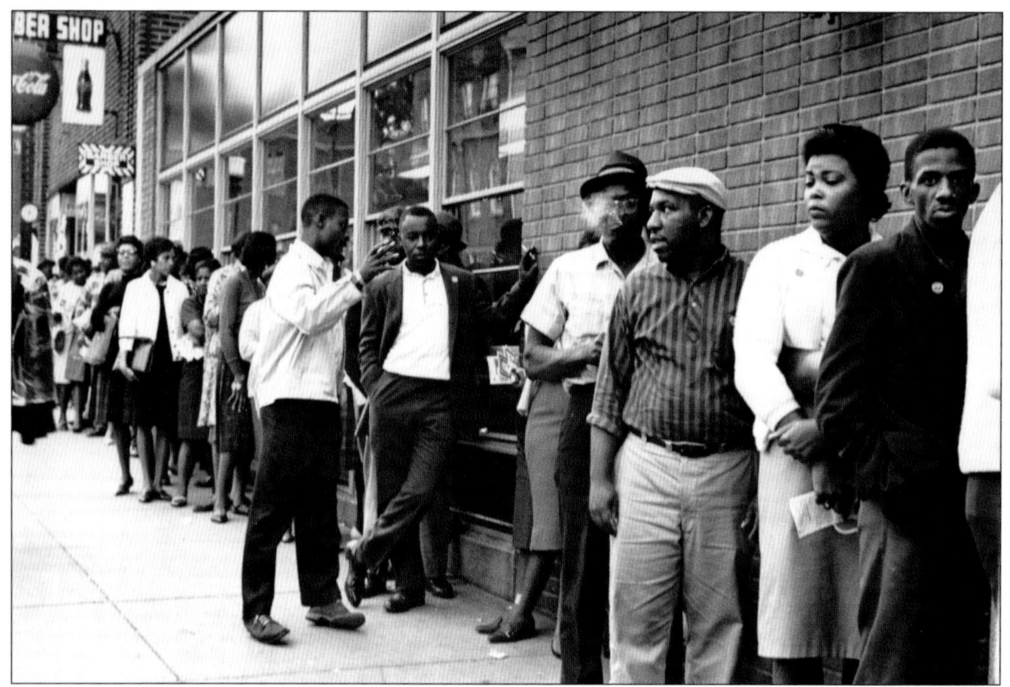

This image was captured during a voter registration drive held by the Richmond Crusade for Voters on Twenty-Fifth Street in Richmond. (Photograph by Scott Henderson, courtesy of John M. Brooks Jr.)

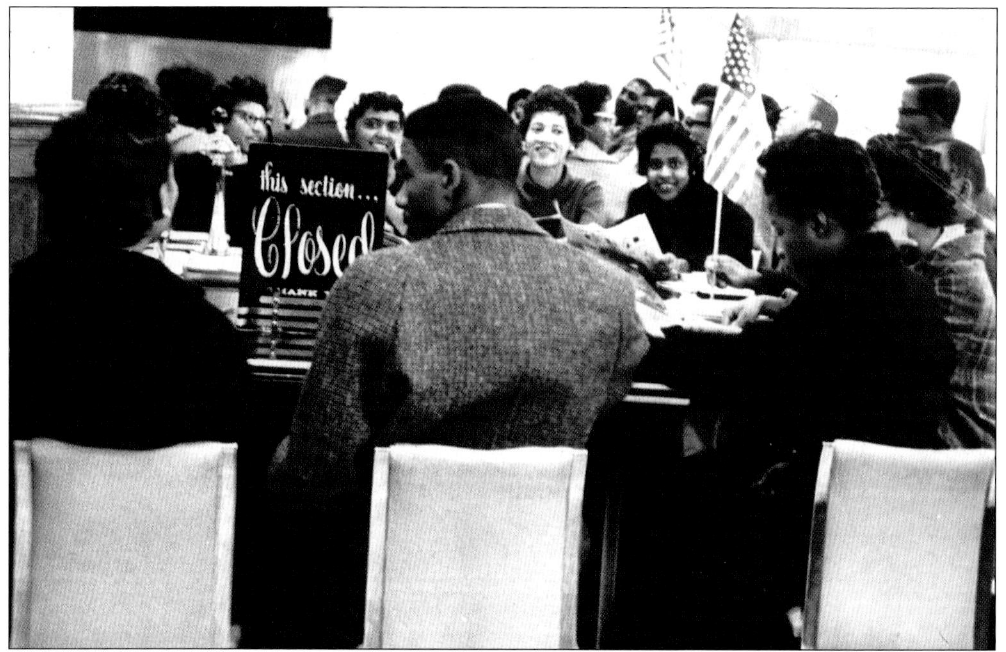

Sit-in demonstrations started in Greensboro, North Carolina, and quickly spread to Norfolk, Newport News, and then Richmond. Pictured is a sit-in at Murphy's Department Store by Virginia Union University students. (Courtesy of the Thomas H. Henderson Papers, L. Douglas Wilder Library, Virginia Union University.)

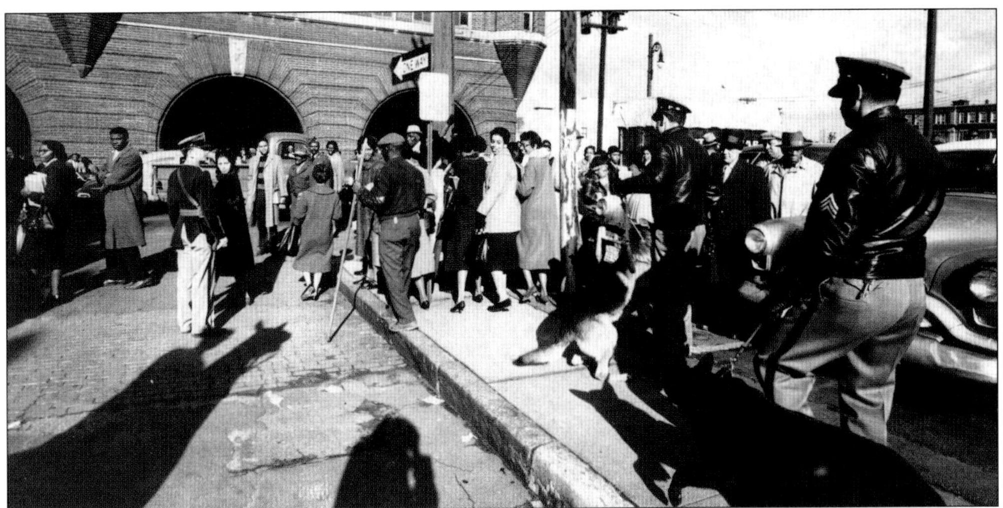

Police officers with K-9 units break up a crowd outside Richmond's lockup after the February 22, 1960, arrests of 34 African Americans who were charged with trespassing when they refused to vacate Thalhimers Department Store after being denied service at a tearoom and a lunch counter. The Richmond 34 are Elizabeth Patricia Johnson, Joanna Hinton, Gloria C. Collins, Patricia A. Washington, Barbara A. Thornton, Lois B. White, Thalma Y. Hickman, Celia E. Jones, Carolyn Ann Horne, Marise L. Ellison, Virginia G. Simms, Frank, George Pinkston, Charles Melvin Sherrod, Albert Van Graves Jr., Ford Tucker Johnson Jr., Leroy M. Bray Jr., Wendell T. Foster Jr., Anderson J. Franklin, Ronald B. Smith, Larry Pridgen, Woodrow B. Grant, Joseph E. Ellison, Gordon Coleman, Milton Johnson, Donald Vincent Goode, Robert B. Dalton, Samuel F. Shaw, Randolph A. Tobias, Clarence A. Jones, Richard C. Jackson, George Wendall Harris Jr., John J. McCall, Leotis L. Pryor, and Raymond B. Randolph Jr. (Courtesy of the *Richmond Times-Dispatch*.)

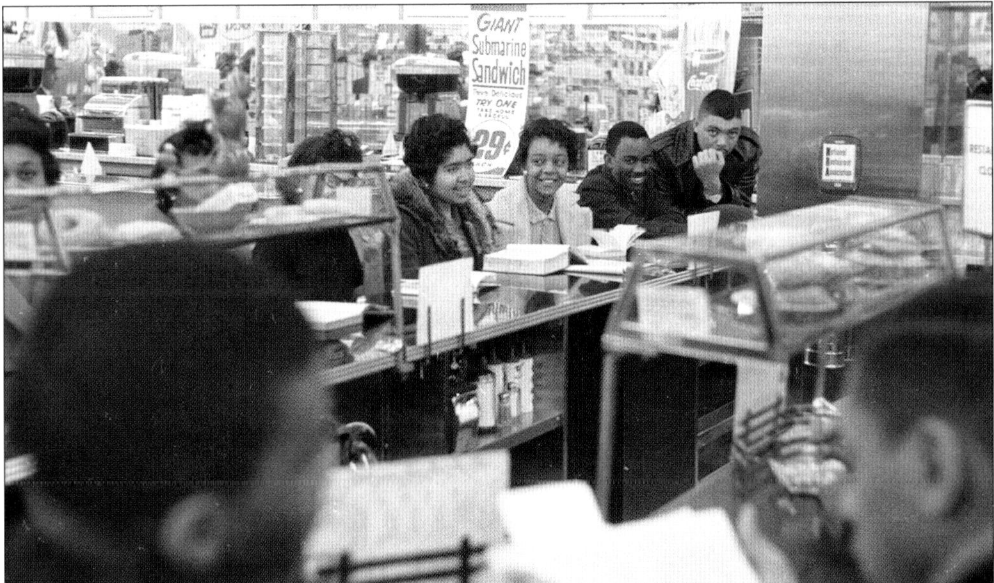

Pictured are students from Virginia Union University at a sit-in at a Woolworth's counter. Many of them brought homework and reading materials to the sit-in. (Malcolm O. Carpenter photograph, Prints & Photographs Division, Library of Congress.)

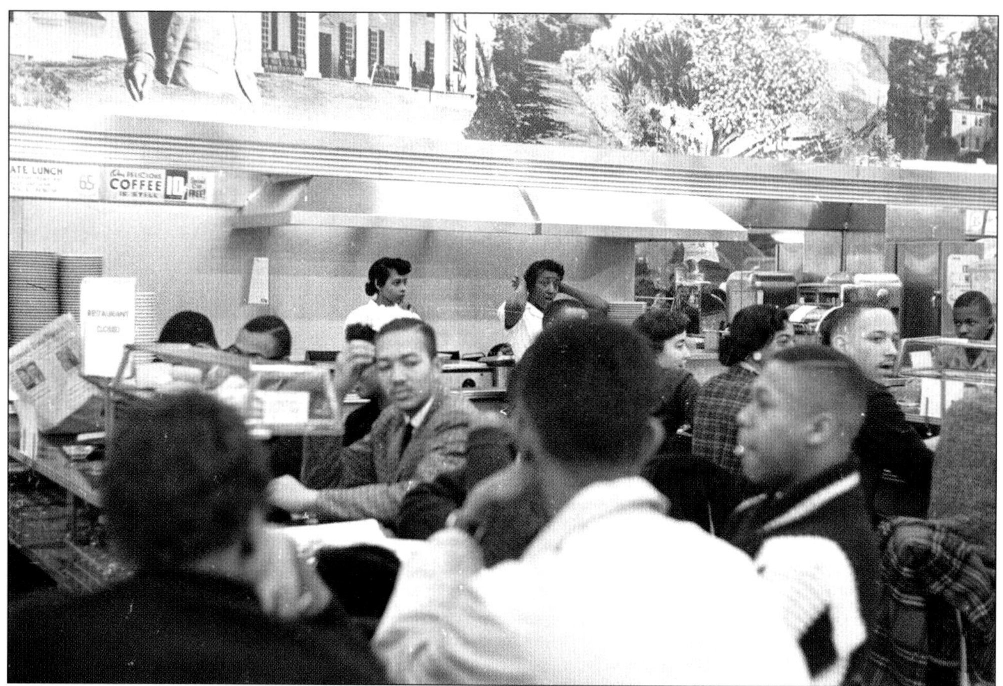

The serving personnel, who were mostly African American, were told by their supervisors not to serve the sit-in students. (Malcolm O. Carpenter photograph, Prints & Photographs Division, Library of Congress.)

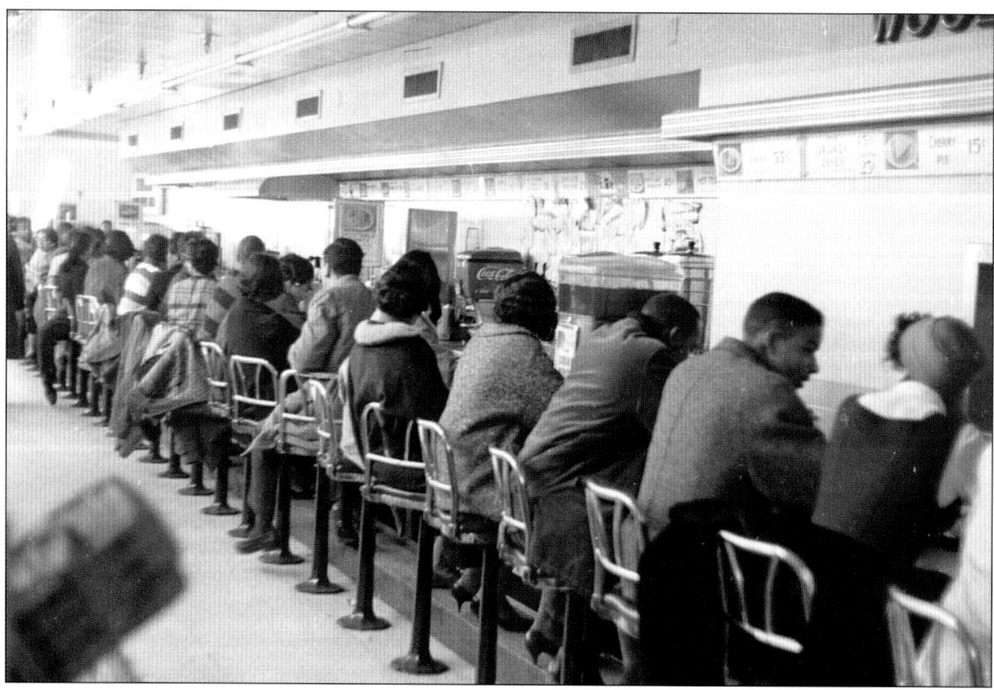

Sit-in demonstrators from Virginia Union University occupy Woolworth's segregated lunch counter. (Malcolm O. Carpenter photograph, Prints & Photographs Division, Library of Congress.)

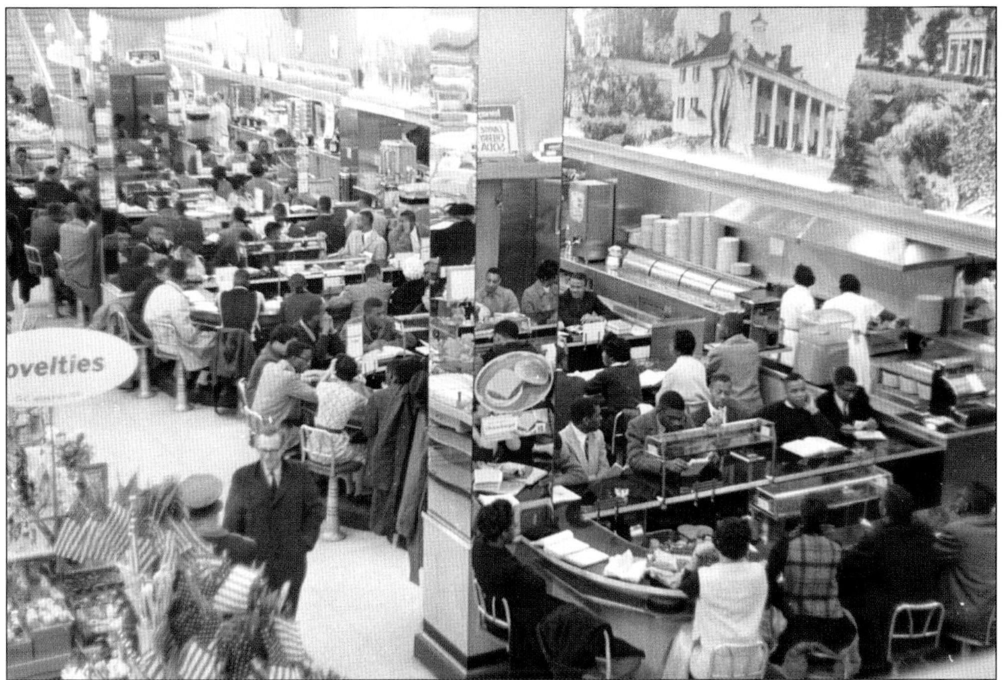

From this balcony view, there are police standing back from the counters. The police allowed some young white men to come in and taunt the seated demonstrators. The police waited for the sit-in demonstrators to react to the taunts so they could be arrested. (Malcolm O. Carpenter photograph, Prints & Photographs Division, Library of Congress.)

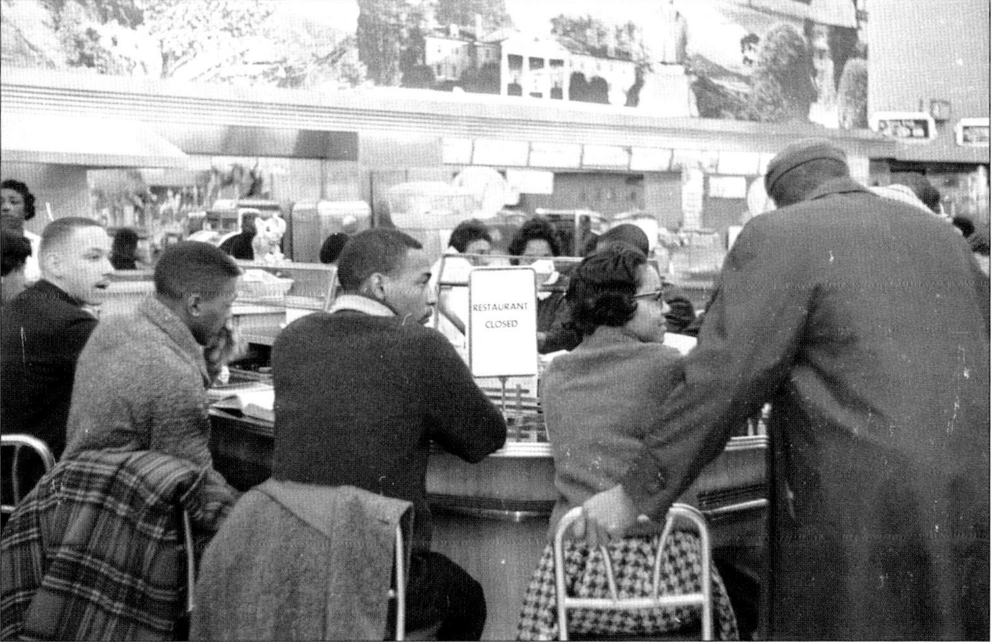

The demonstrators were well-trained in passive resistance and did not react to taunts. However, many of them were arrested for trespassing. (Malcolm O. Carpenter photograph, Prints & Photographs Division, Library of Congress.)

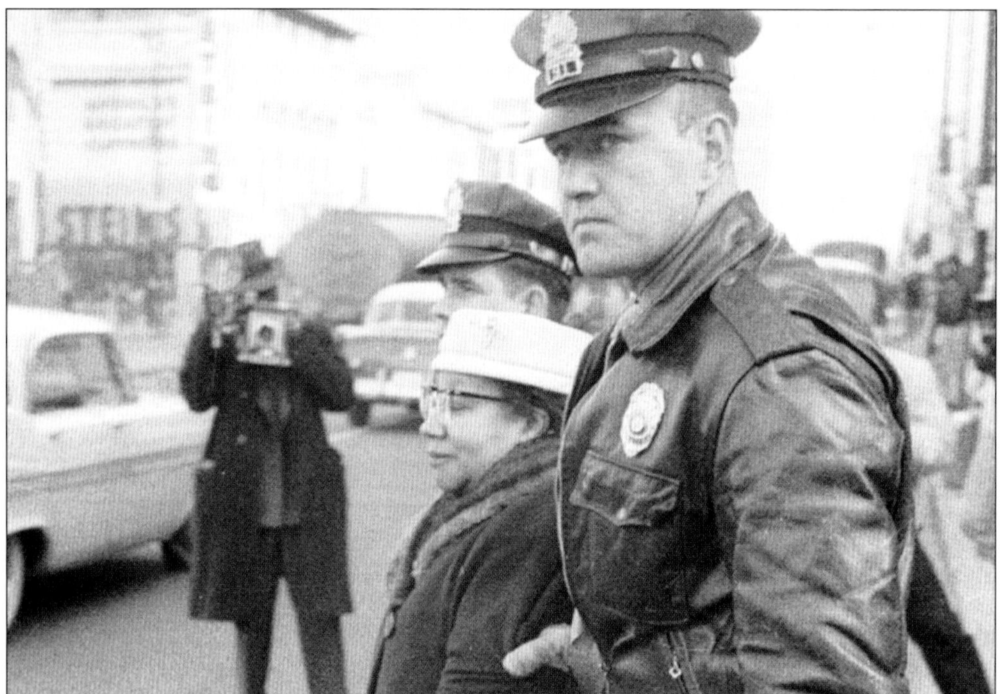

In 1960, police told Ruth Tinsley she could not stand still in a picketing area in front of a department store, but she refused to move and was arrested. (Malcolm O. Carpenter photograph, Prints & Photographs Division, Library of Congress.)

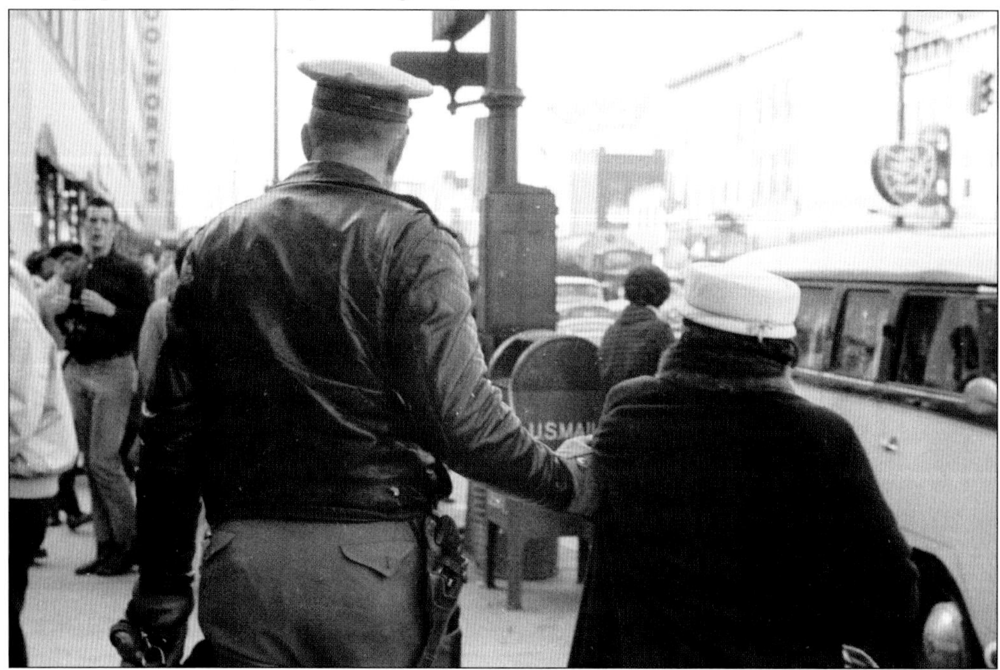

The police officer gripped Tinsley's arm and began to lead her toward the corner to cross Broad Street to the police station. (Malcolm O. Carpenter photograph, Prints & Photographs Division, Library of Congress.)

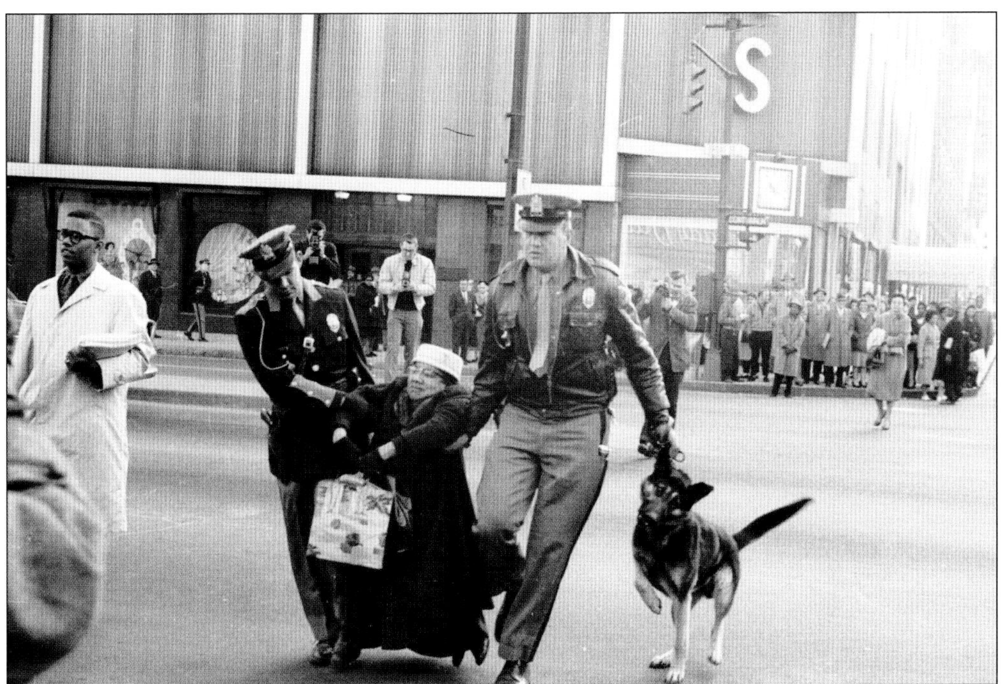

Joined by the second officer, they began to cross the street as the light changed. Halfway across the street, Tinsley suddenly sat down. The two officers were surprised and looked at her and then at each other. They then lifted her and, in a series of lifts and pauses, carried her across the street. (Malcolm O. Carpenter photograph, Prints & Photographs Division, Library of Congress.)

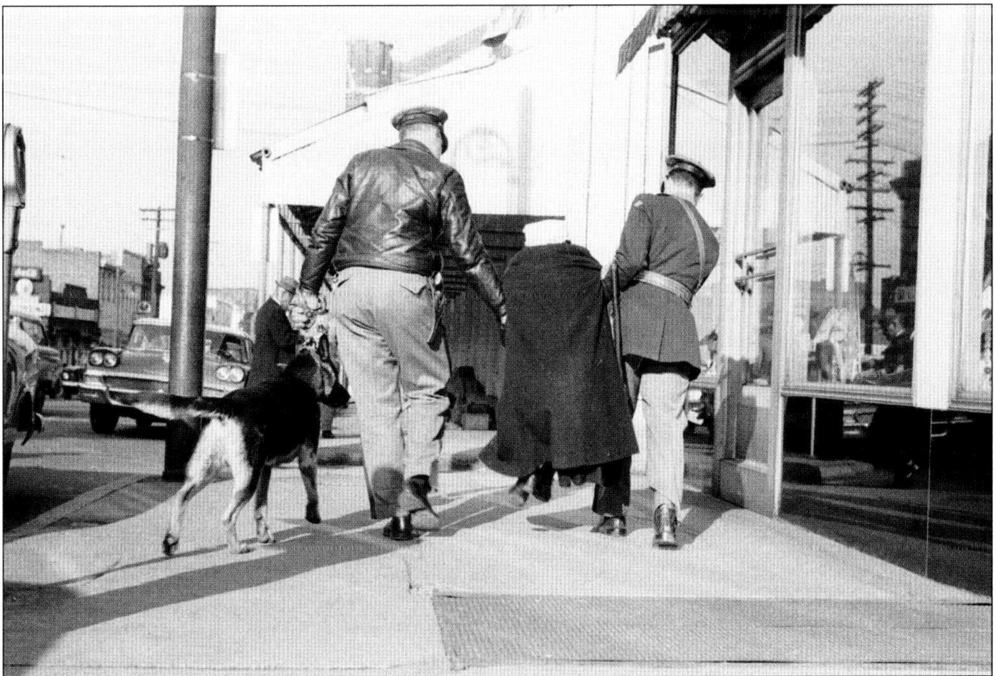

The officers continued carrying Tinsley down the street with a series of lifts to the police station. (Malcolm O. Carpenter photograph, Prints & Photographs Division, Library of Congress.)

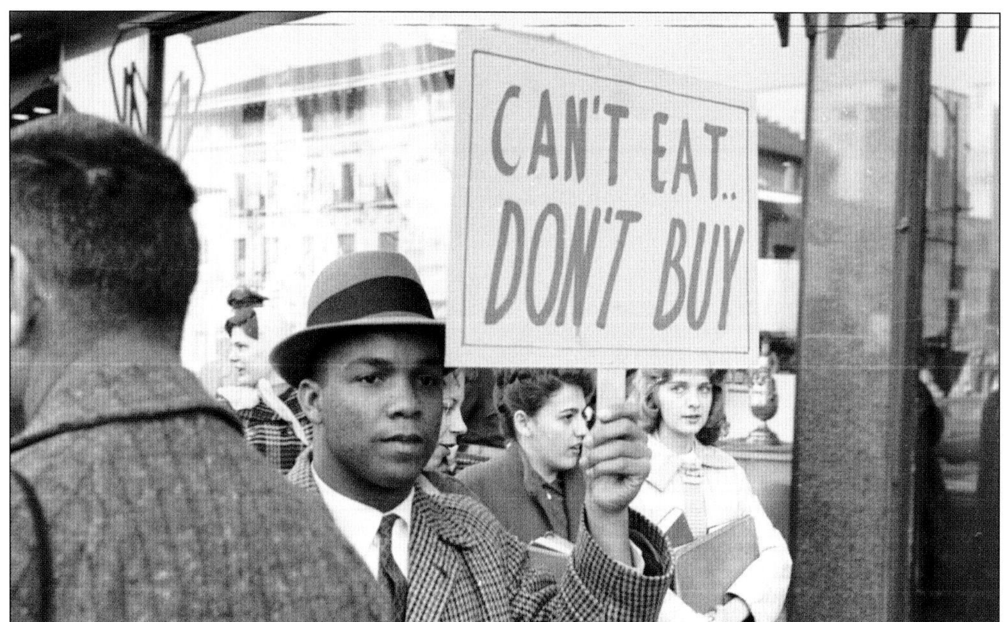

An unidentified young man pickets outside Richmond department stores where African Americans could purchase food for takeout only. (Malcolm O. Carpenter photograph, Prints & Photographs Division, Library of Congress.)

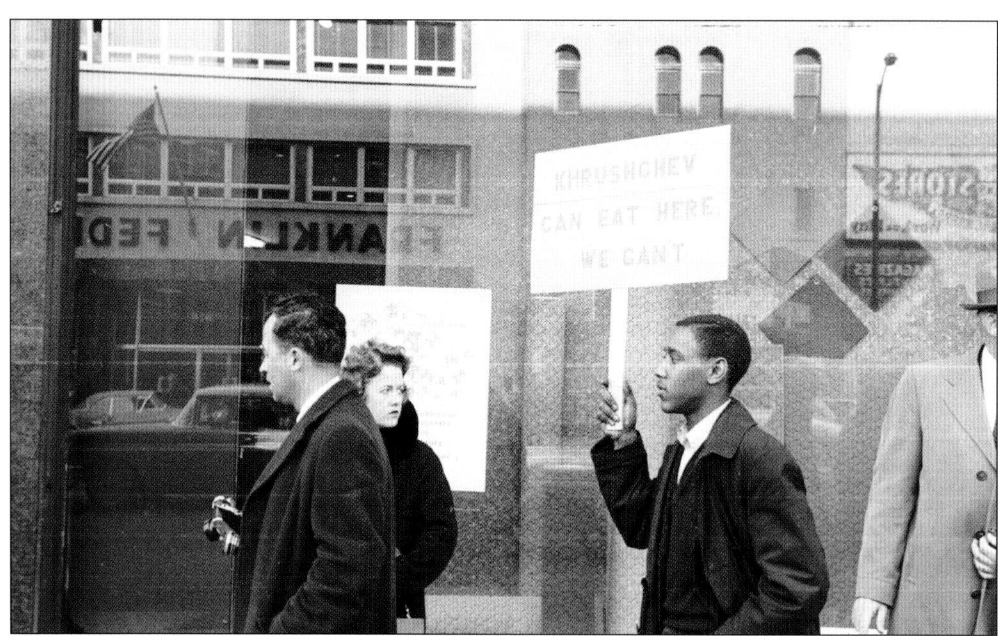

An unknown picketer carries a "Khrushchev Can Eat Here, We Can't" sign outside a department store on Broad Street. (Malcolm O. Carpenter photograph, Prints & Photographs Division, Library of Congress.)

The unidentified picketer was arrested as onlookers from the bus watched. (Malcolm O. Carpenter photograph, Prints & Photographs Division, Library of Congress.)

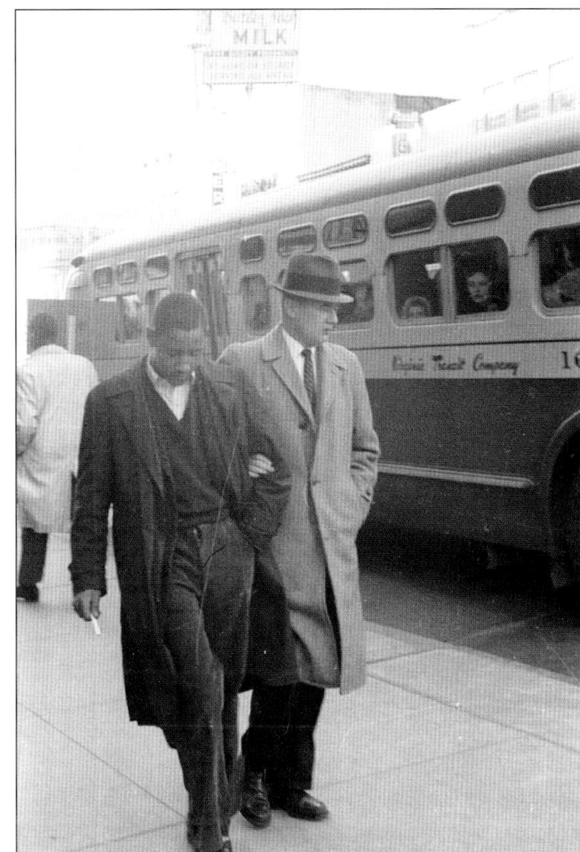

While being walked to the police station, the unidentified picketer was photographed by the media. (Malcolm O. Carpenter photograph, Prints & Photographs Division, Library of Congress.)

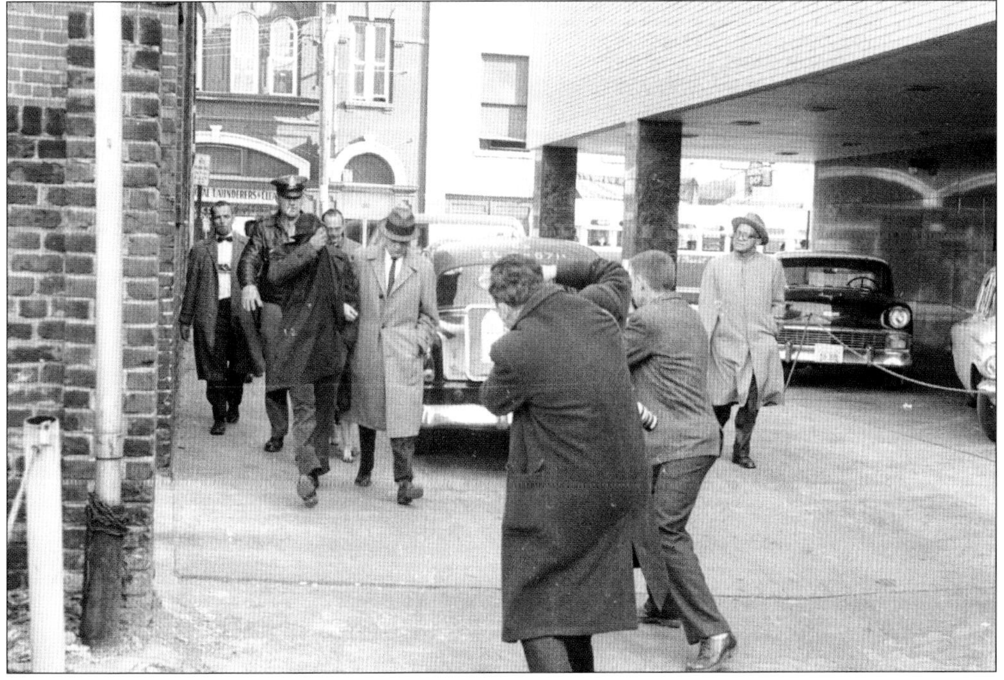

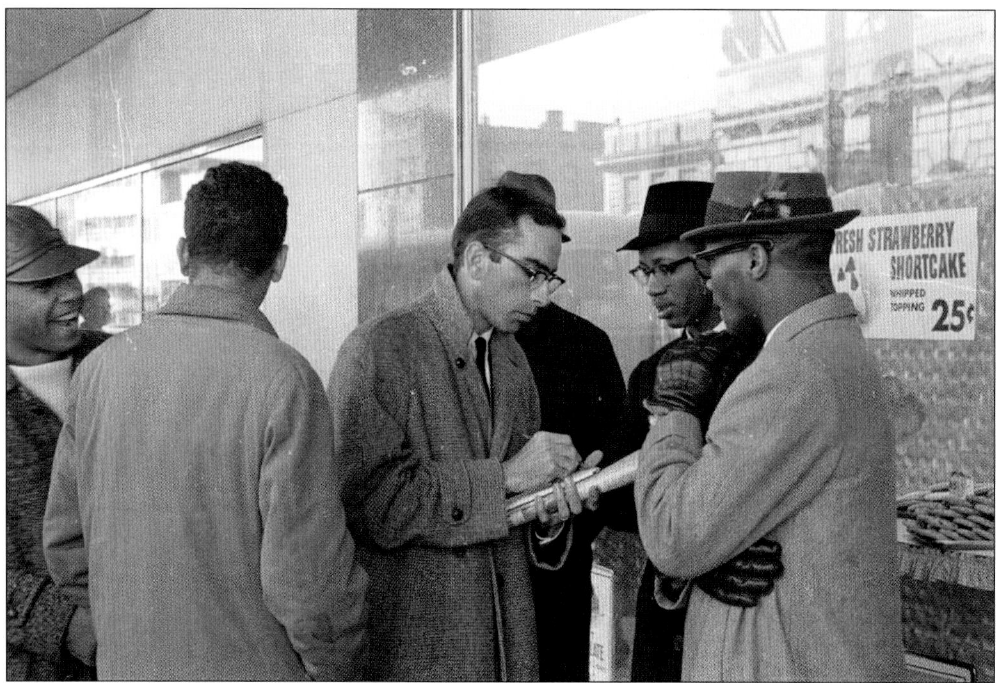

Reporters from the *Richmond Times-Dispatch* talk to African American organizers to solicit details and motives for the demonstrations. (Malcolm O. Carpenter photograph, Prints & Photographs Division, Library of Congress.)

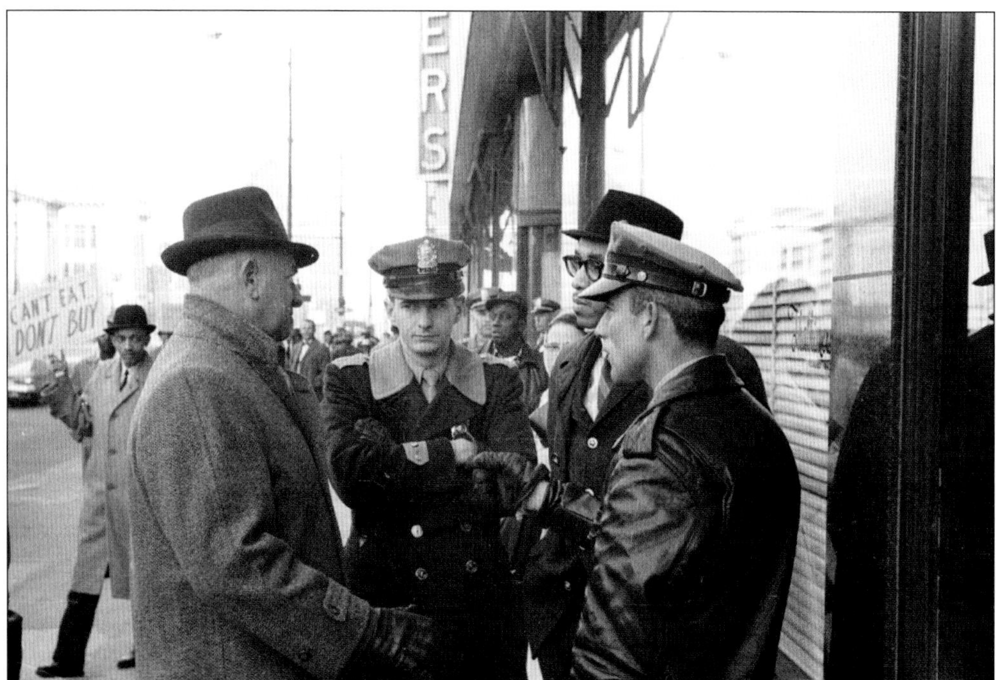

Police and detectives talk to one of the demonstration organizers with the hopes of a peaceful conclusion. (Malcolm O. Carpenter photograph, Prints & Photographs Division, Library of Congress.)

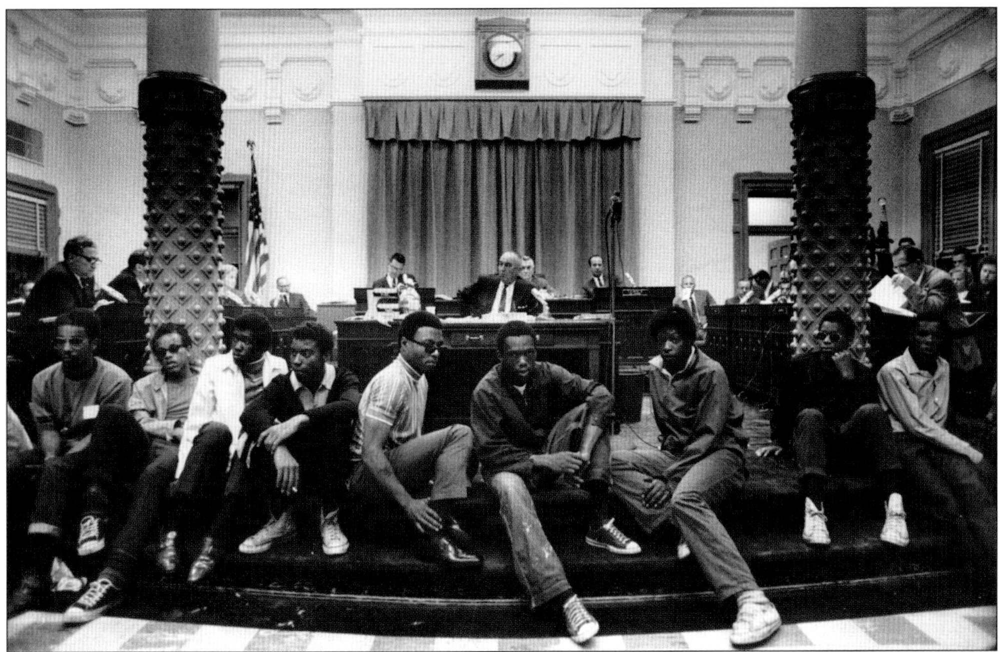

A group of young African American men sits on the steps of the dais leading to the desks of Richmond City Council members with the council members in the background in 1965. (Courtesy of the *Richmond Times-Dispatch* Collection, the Valentine.)

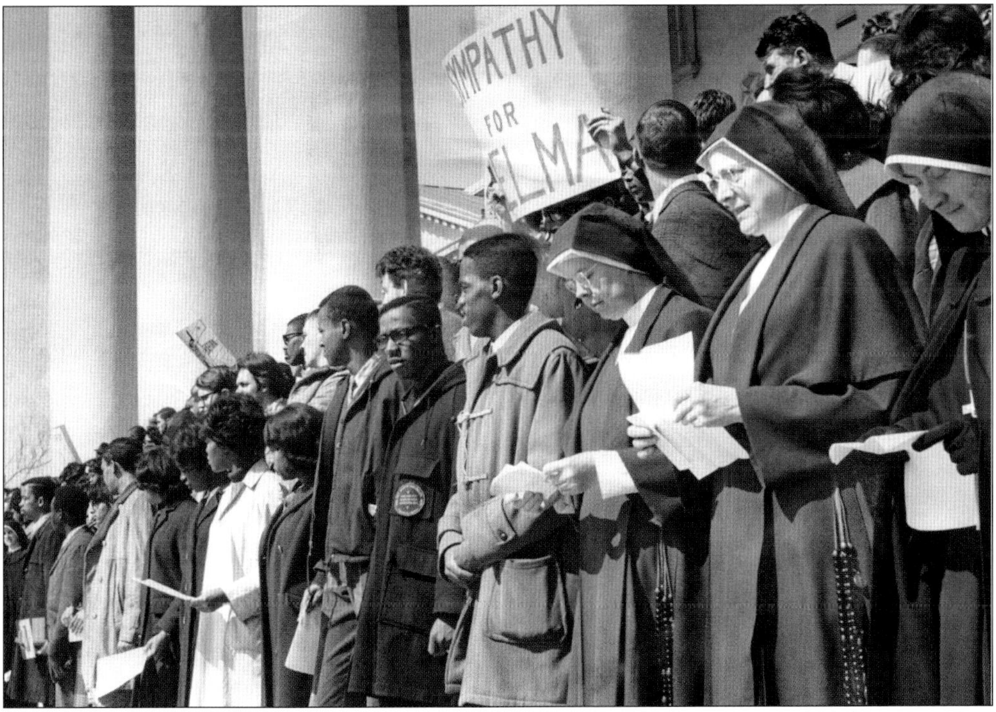

Over 700 people staged marches in four Virginia cities on March 16, 1965, in a demonstration for equality in voter registration. The Richmond rally ended on the steps of the state capitol. (Courtesy of the *Richmond Times-Dispatch*.)

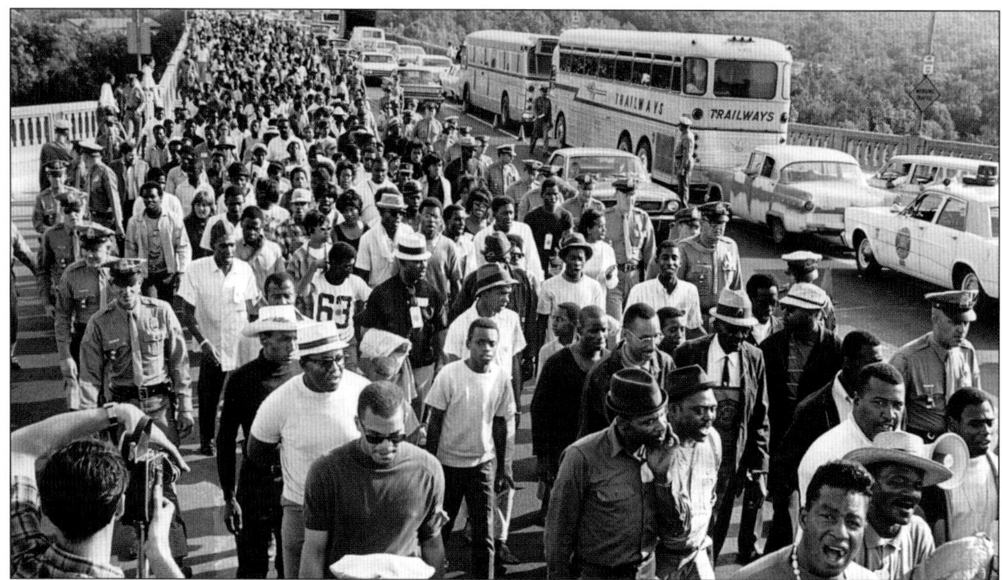

People march across the Robert E. Lee Bridge headed for Norfolk for the Poor People's Campaign on May 18, 1968. The purpose of the campaign was to gain economic justice for the nation's poor. The march was organized by Martin Luther King Jr. and the Southern Christian Leadership Conference (SCLC) but was carried out by Ralph Abernathy after King's assassination on April 4, 1968. (Courtesy of the *Richmond Times-Dispatch*.)

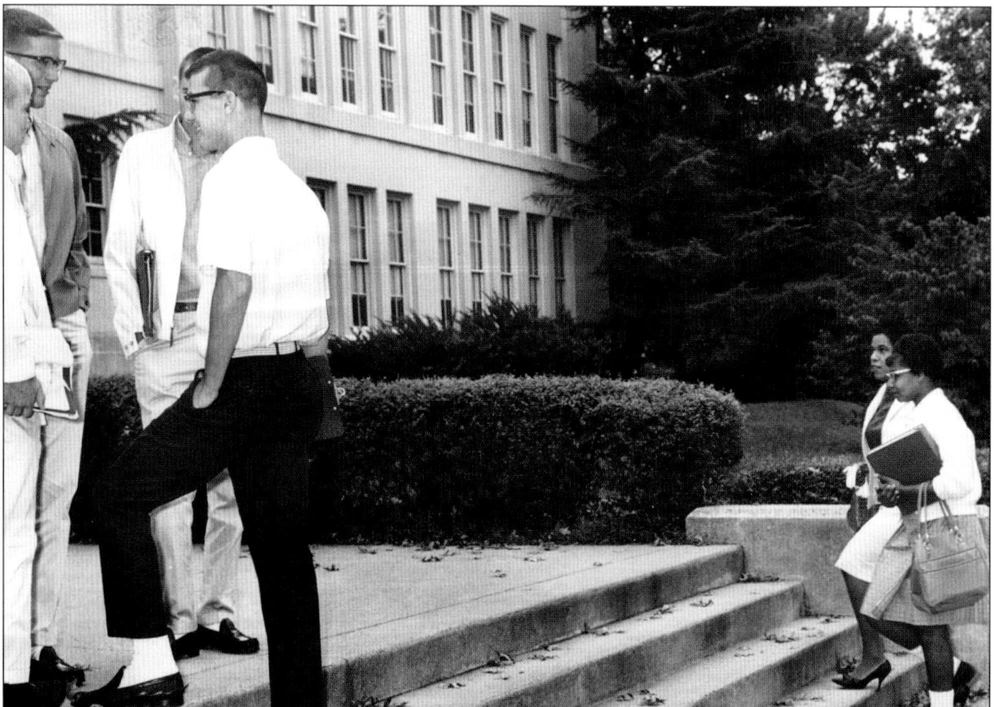

On September 6, 1962, Daisy Jane Cooper (right) and her mother, Elizabeth, walked into Thomas Jefferson School on the first day of integration, after a three-year desegregation court battle. Cooper was the only African American student. (Courtesy of the *Richmond Times-Dispatch*.)

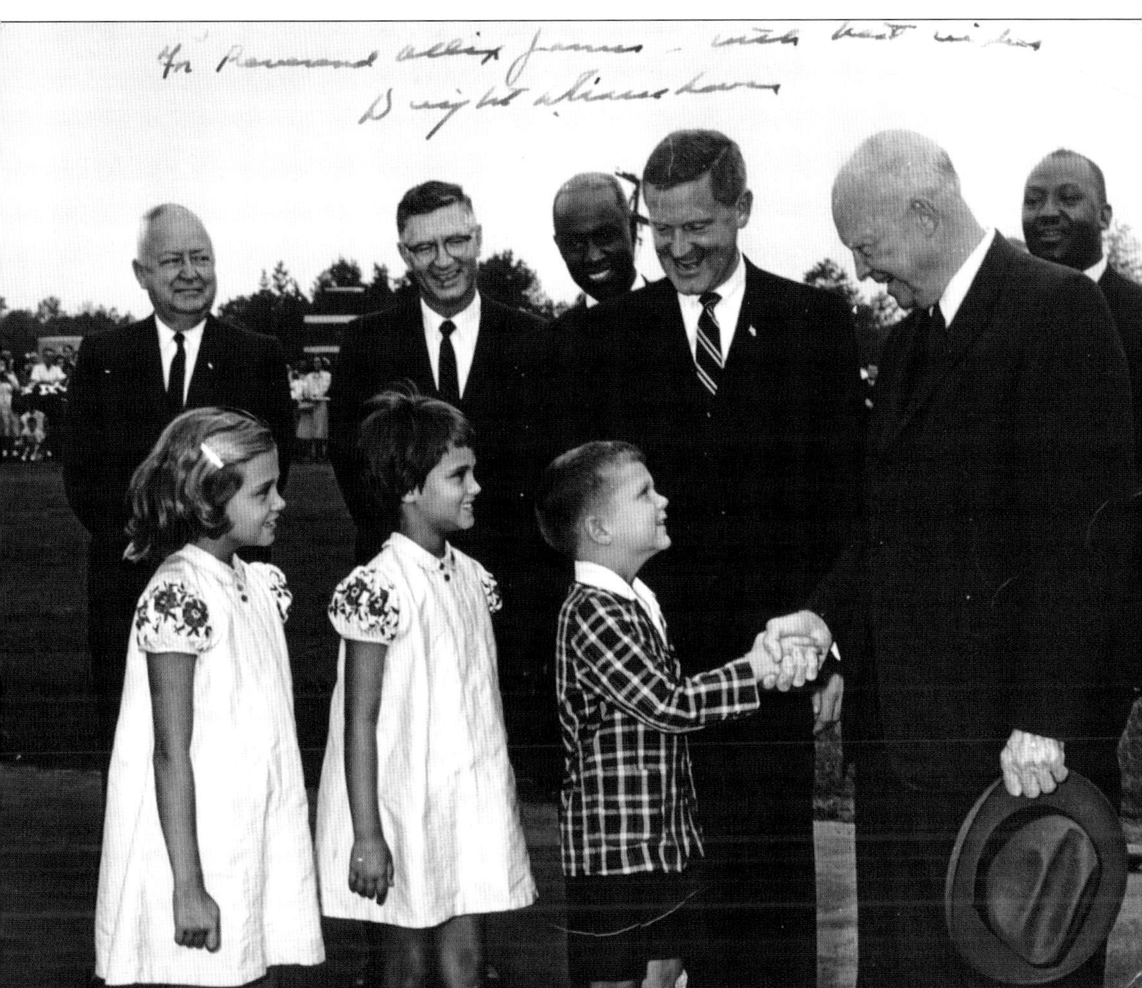

The 61st governor of Virginia, A. Linwood Holton Jr., was endorsed by the Richmond Crusade for Voters and was a champion for racial equality. Holton is pictured here (third from the right) with his children and former president Dwight Eisenhower (second from the right) on September 14, 1965. (Courtesy of the Odell Hobbs Collection, L. Douglas Wilder Library, Virginia Union University.)

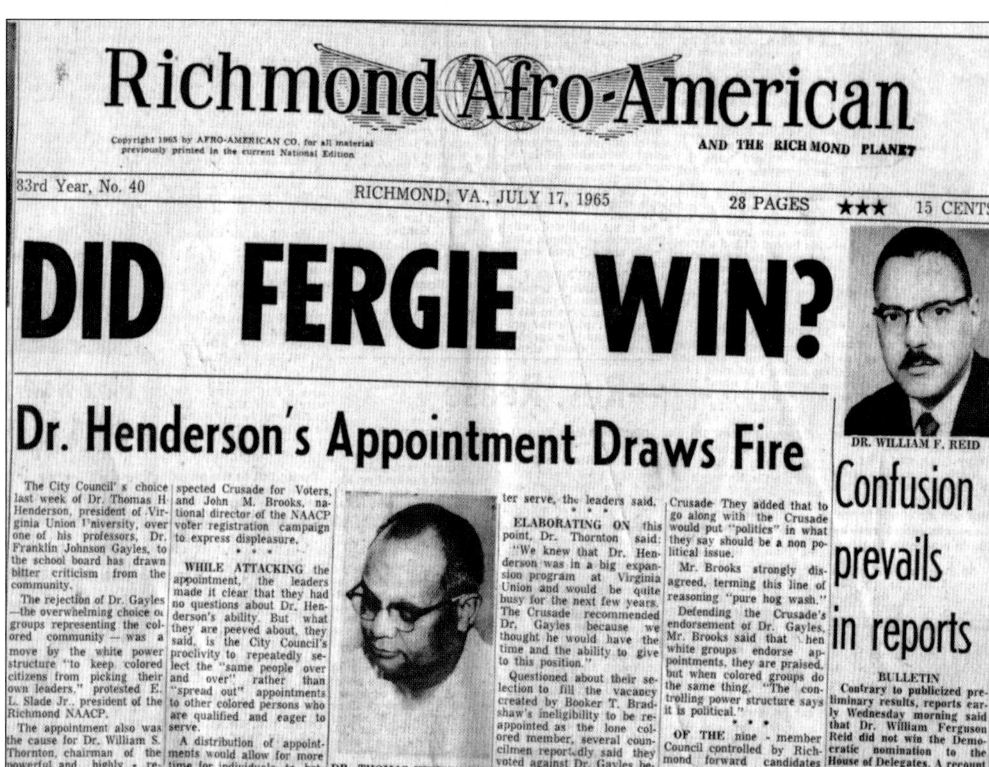

Richmond Afro-American

Copyright 1965 by AFRO-AMERICAN CO. for all material previously printed in the current National Edition

AND THE RICHMOND PLANET

83rd Year, No. 40 RICHMOND, VA., JULY 17, 1965 28 PAGES ★★★ 15 CENTS

DID FERGIE WIN?

Dr. Henderson's Appointment Draws Fire

The City Council's choice last week of Dr. Thomas H. Henderson, president of Virginia Union University, over one of his professors, Dr. Franklin Johnson Gayles, to the school board has drawn bitter criticism from the community.

The rejection of Dr. Gayles—the overwhelming choice of groups representing the colored community—was a move by the white power structure "to keep colored citizens from picking their own leaders," protested E. L. Slade Jr., president of the Richmond NAACP.

The appointment also was the cause for Dr. William S. Thornton, chairman of the powerful and highly respected Crusade for Voters, and John M. Brooks, national director of the NAACP voter registration campaign to express displeasure.

• • •

WHILE ATTACKING the appointment, the leaders made it clear that they had no questions about Dr. Henderson's ability. But what they are peeved about, they said, is the City Council's proclivity to repeatedly select the "same people over and over" rather than "spread out" appointments to other colored persons who are qualified and eager to serve.

A distribution of appointments would allow for more time for individuals to better serve, the leaders said.

DR. THOMAS HENDERSON

• • •

ELABORATING ON this point, Dr. Thornton said: "We knew that Dr. Henderson was in a big expansion program at Virginia Union and would be quite busy for the next few years. The Crusade recommended Dr. Gayles because we thought he would have the time and the ability to give to this position."

Questioned about their selection to fill the vacancy created by Booker T. Bradshaw's ineligibility to be reappointed as the lone colored member, several councilmen reportedly said they voted against Dr. Gayles because he was the pick of the Crusade. They added that to go along with the Crusade would put "politics" in what they say should be a non political issue.

Mr. Brooks strongly disagreed, terming this line of reasoning "pure hog wash."

Defending the Crusade's endorsement of Dr. Gayles, Mr. Brooks said that when white groups endorse appointments, they are praised, but when colored groups do the same thing, "The controlling power structure says it is political."

• • •

OF THE nine-member Council controlled by Richmond forward candidates

(Continued on Page 16)

DR. WILLIAM F. REID

Confusion prevails in reports

BULLETIN

Contrary to publicized preliminary results, reports early Wednesday morning said that Dr. William Ferguson Reid did not win the Democratic nomination to the House of Delegates. A recount shows otherwise, the reports

This July 17, 1965, headline from the *Richmond Afro-American* discusses the failed election of Dr. William Ferguson Reid to the General Assembly. (Courtesy of Afro-American Newspapers.)

Byrd Political Machine Crumbles—Fergie Wins!

RICHMOND

Black voters across the Commonwealth exercised their political muscles in Tuesday's Democratic primary balloting to help crumble the dominance of the old Sen. Harry F. Byrd political machine which oppressed minority citizens during its 40 long years of controlling the statehouse.

The biggest blow dealth to the Byrd machine was in the three-man gubernatorial race where Lt. Gov. Fred Pollard — the machine's candidate — came in last.

Moderate William C. Battle for the governor's mansion while liberal State Sen. Henry Howell of Norfolk, who got heavy black support, was a close runner-up.

Battle and Howell will meet in a runoff primary —the first in the state's history — on Aug. 19.

• • •

The Byrd machine also caught it on the chin in the race for lieutenant governor where State Sen. J. Sargeant Reynolds won the Democratic nomination by humiliating another machine man, State Sen. W. ... almost solid support from blacks despite the candidacy of a black hopeful in the four-man race, had polled 62.1 per cent of the votes cast at AFRO deadline to Thompson's 23.1 per cent.

Moses A. Riddick of Nansemond County, the lone black candidate in the primary, had won only 6.4 per cent of the vote and was in last place.

The only Byrd machine man to survive the primary was Guy Farley who ran close behind moderate Andrew Miller in the race for attorney general. They too will clash in the August runoff.

Miller, like Howell and Reynolds, won support from the Virginia Crusade for Voters — the state's most powerful black political organization.

Reactions in the black community to the fall of the Byrd machine was one of quiet satisfaction.

• • •

Typical of the mood in the black community was the reaction of Dr. William S. Thornton, Crusade chairman.

He was happy to observe that "Pollard is out of it completely" — but he spent no time commenting further on this obvious victory for his organization.

His emphasis was on the need for black people getting out to vote in the runoff.

"What this means is that more black voters will have to come out in August," said Dr. Thornton. "Every person who is qualified to vote should live up to his responsibility."

Henry L. Marsh III, the Richmond's lone black city councilman, saw things about the same way.

He said black people didn't turn out as well as they should have, adding that the job ahead is for black people to "form a coalition with low-income and average whites" to elect Henry Howell so that the government can be returned to the people."

This July 26, 1969, headline from the *Richmond Afro-American* proclaims the Byrd Machine's demise, as a result of Dr. William Ferguson Reid's election to the General Assembly in 1968. (Courtesy of Afro-American Newspapers.)

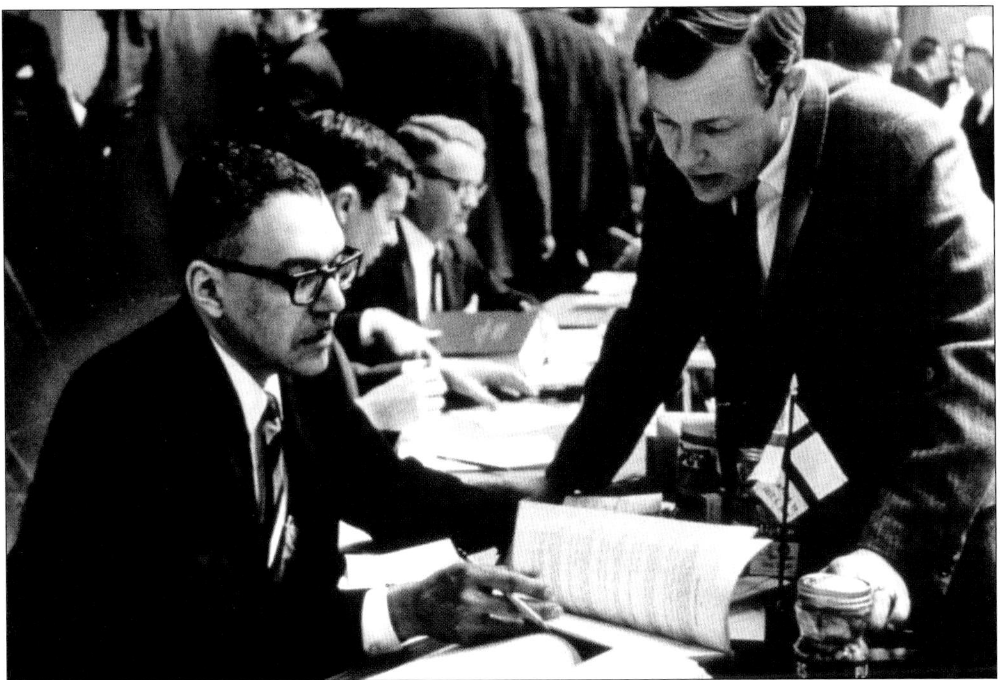

Delegate Dr. William Ferguson Reid reviews a document with an unidentified man in the Virginia General Assembly. Dr. Reid served six years in the Virginia House of Delegates. (Courtesy of Special Collections and Archives, James Branch Cabell Library, VCU Libraries.)

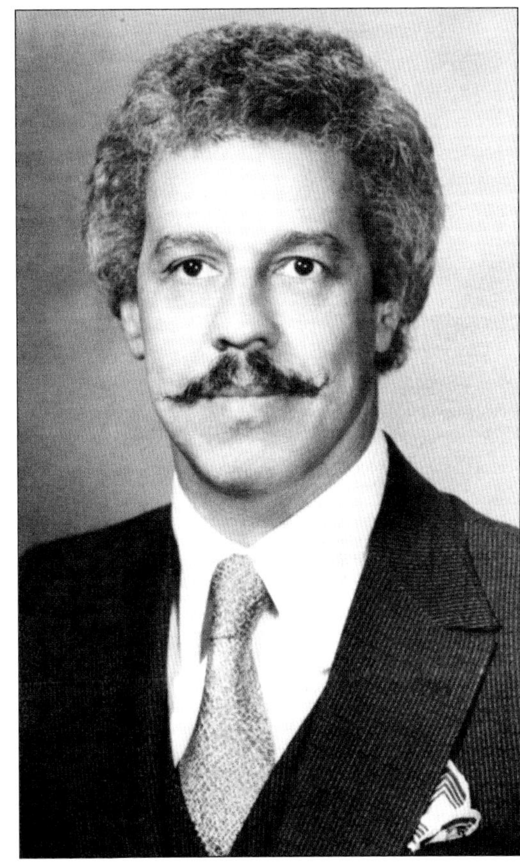

Sen. L. Douglas Wilder successfully ran for a Senate of Virginia seat in 1969. He was the first African American to hold such a position since Reconstruction. (Courtesy of the L. Douglas Wilder Library, Virginia Union University.)

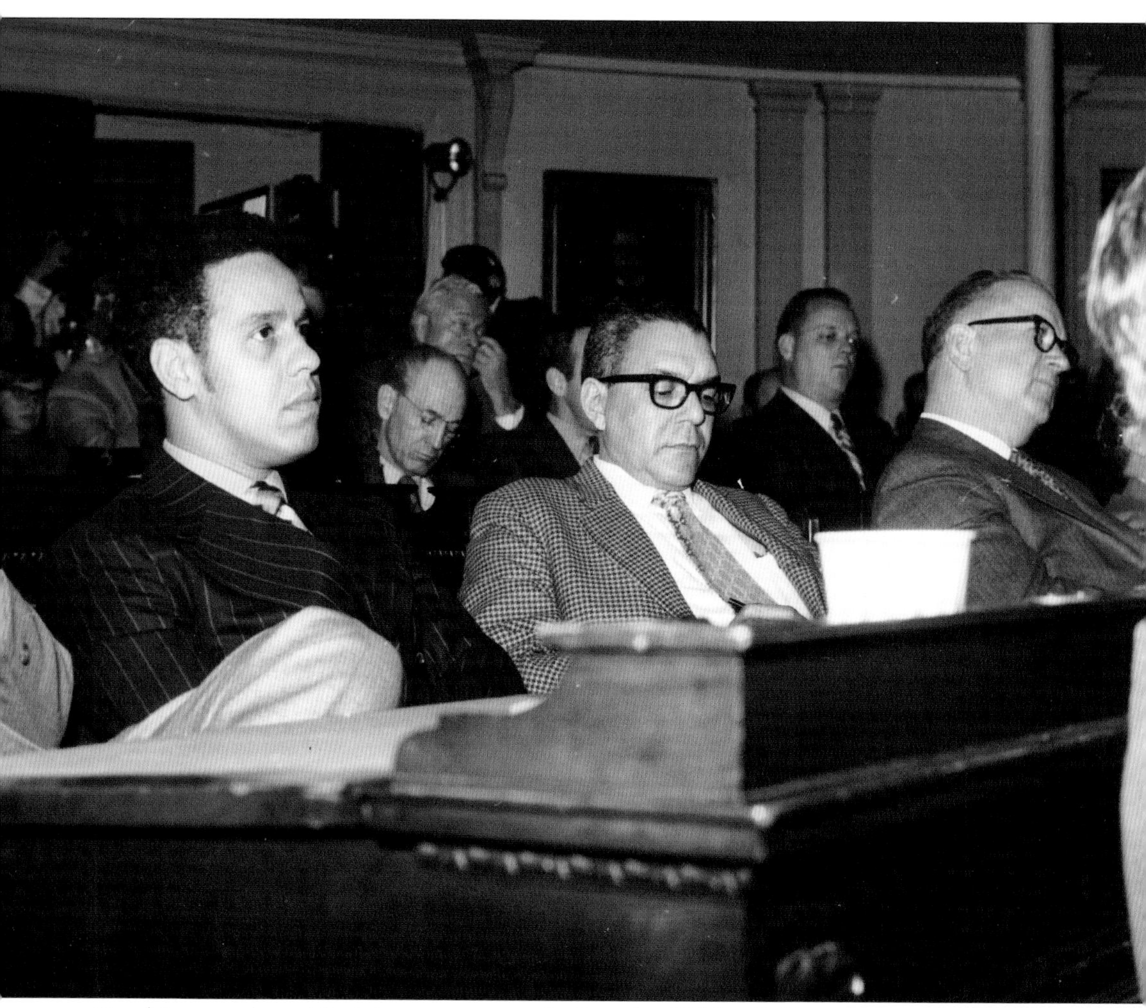

Two historymakers, Virginia state senator L. Douglas Wilder (left) and Virginia delegate Dr. William Ferguson Reid (center), sit together in the general assembly. The man at right is unidentified. (Courtesy of the Scott Henderson Collection, L. Douglas Wilder Library, Virginia Union University.)

Three

SEASON OF CHANGE

The Richmond Crusade for Voters gained significant political influence in the 1970s through elections, endorsements, and lawsuits. The city of Richmond saw voter registration quadruple among African Americans as a result of the Richmond Crusade for Voters' efforts. The organization credits its strong, well-developed precinct system, which included precinct captains, block meetings, and block leaders in predominately African American neighborhoods for the rise in voter participation. The community would eagerly await the Richmond Crusade for Voters' publication of the candidate endorsements list, which was often released the weekend before an election. As a result of the organization's success, some whites developed strategies to dilute the African American vote, specifically having sections of Chesterfield County annexed, adding over 40,000 white voters to the city. Consequently, lawsuits were filed and elections for Richmond City Council were not held from 1972 to 1976. The US Department of Justice concluded the annexation did weaken the African American vote, and the district system was created and implemented. This system led to Richmond's first African American majority city council in 1977, including Willie J. Dell, Walter T. Kenney, Claudette Black McDaniel, H.W. "Chuck" Richardson, and Richmond's first African American mayor, Henry L. Marsh III.

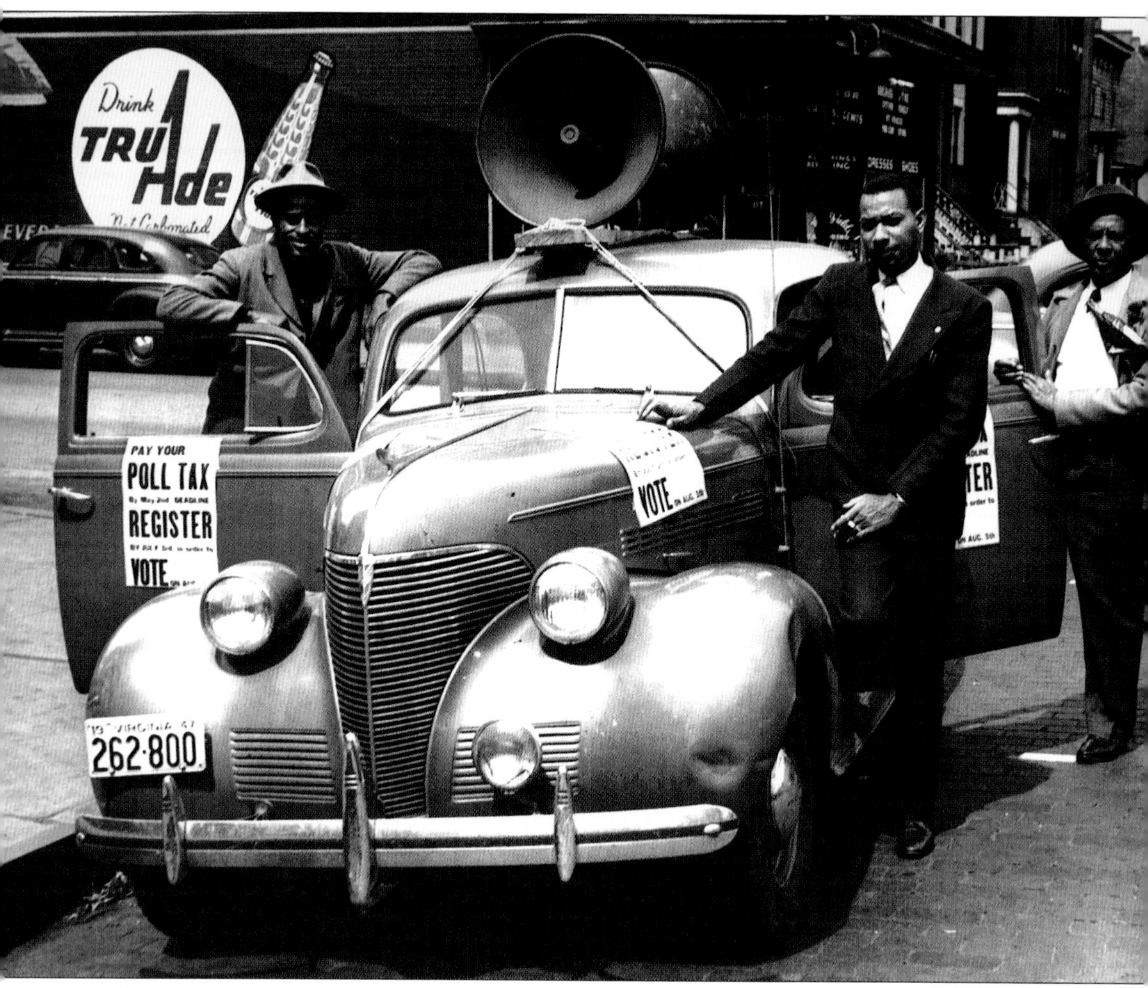

Calvin Hopkins (left), Lester Banks (center), and A. Washington "Puss" Owens of Richmond are active in a 1947 "Getting out the Vote" campaign. There were three standing committees of the Richmond Crusade for Voters: voter registration, get-out-the-vote, and research. The voter registration committee was responsible for registering as many voters as possible. There were goals and quotas set for this committee each year by the executive committee. The get-out-the-vote committee's responsibility was voter turnout. This committee would partner with churches and community organizations to provide rides to the polls. The research committee vetted candidates for public office. It was considered one of the most powerful committees, both inside and outside of the organization, because of its endorsement responsibilities. Each precinct had a captain, and the captain's duty was to hold meetings in the precinct area with the block leaders. The block leaders had officers and workers, who met directly with the community to disseminate information and to gather information about their community, such as the number of voters who needed rides to the polls and potential voters who needed assistance paying their poll tax. The precinct captains would relay that information directly to the executive committee, who would then devise plans based on that information. This organizational structure was deemed very successful and was emulated across the country. (Courtesy of the Scott Henderson Collection, L. Douglas Wilder Library, Virginia Union University.)

This November 21, 1964, headline from the *Richmond Afro-American* emphasizes and praises the voter strength of African Americans. This election was particularly important because of its connection to the enforcement of the Civil Rights Act of 1964. (Courtesy of Afro-American Newspapers.)

Leaders say heavy vote a 'milestone'

WASHINGTON

Civil rights leaders congratulated the colored voter last week for the unprecedented show of political strength at the polls.

Almost unanimously they view the lopsided vote for Johnson as a vote of confidence by the American people to continue a firm policy in eliminating racial discrimination.

WHITNEY M. YOUNG JR., executive director of the National Urban League, said that the election of President Johnson was a milestone for colored citizens.

"This milestone of achievement is growing evidence of the desire by colored citizens to share in the responsibilities as well as the privileges of citizenship. It evidences a more sophisticated knowledge of what the vote can achieve to bring relief from the poverty and despair which afflict so many," he continued.

He said the vote reflects the support of the overwhelming majority of Americans not only for Civil Rights Bill but for their backing of social security, medicare, and the war against poverty.

CONGRESSMAN ADAM CLAYTON POWELL (D.-N.Y.) said the "colored politicians had achieved a new dimension of power and respect as a result of the colored vote's heavily felt impact."

"As colored citizens become increasingly successful in American politics their intelligent use of the power of political offices to secure more patronage more jobs and a larger share of the political spoils — just as every minority group in this country has done to obviate the need for much of the civil rights activity per se."

ROY WILKINS executive director of the NAACP said the heavy colored vote showed an "awareness of the impact upon the nation and upon their lives of such vital issues as peace prosperity, and the anti-poverty war.

"They voted to support and accelerate the present national trend toward equal rights for all Americans and especially in anticipation that the Johnson Administration will enforce the Civil Rights Act of 1964 as vigorously as it worked for its enactment."

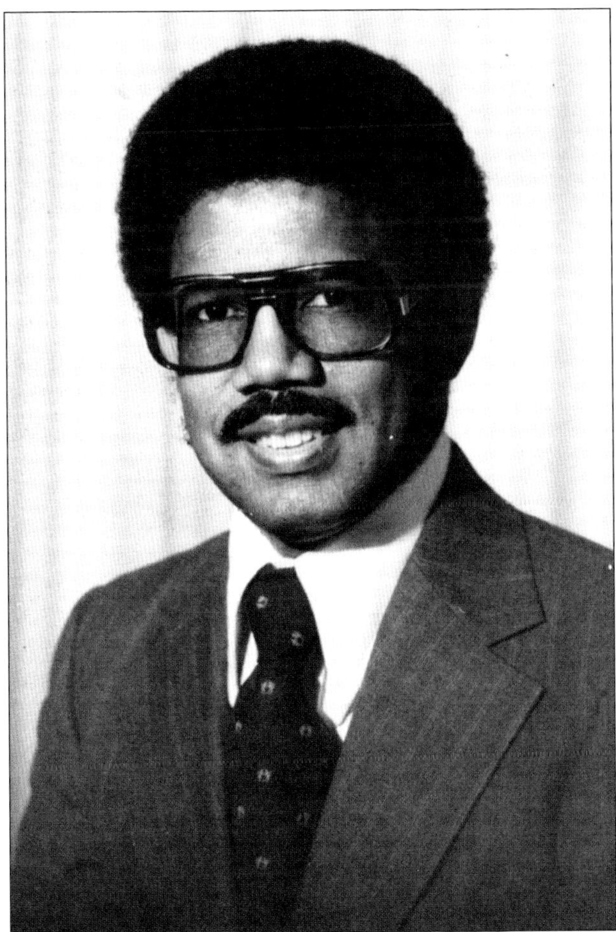

Civil rights attorney Henry L. Marsh III was elected to the Richmond City Council in 1966. He was selected to be the vice mayor in 1970 and became the first African American to serve as Richmond's mayor, from 1977 until 1982. The Richmond Crusade for Voters played a vital role in the election of the first majority African American city council, which selected Marsh as mayor. Marsh was elected to the Senate of Virginia in 1991, and he represented the Sixteenth District until 2014. (Courtesy of the L. Douglas Wilder Library, Virginia Union University.)

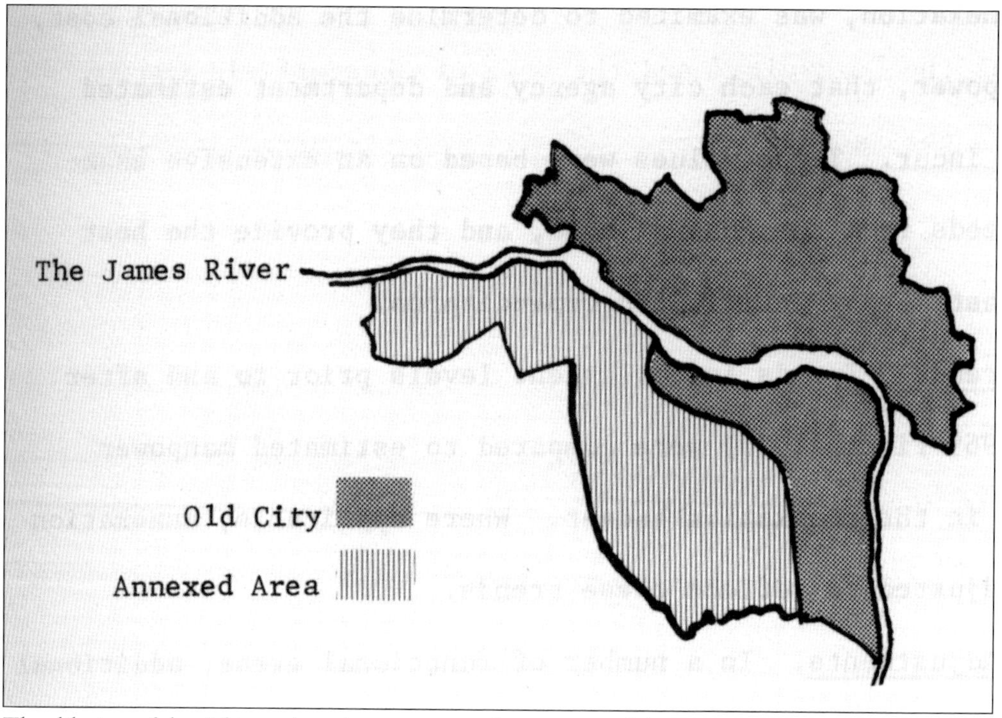

The James River

Old City

Annexed Area

The dilution of the African American vote was the purpose of the controversial 1970 Chesterfield County annexation. Pictured, the dark area was the existing city limits, and the striped section was the annexed area, which added over 40,000 white voters to the city of Richmond. (Courtesy of Special Collections and Archives, James Branch Cabell Library, VCU Libraries.)

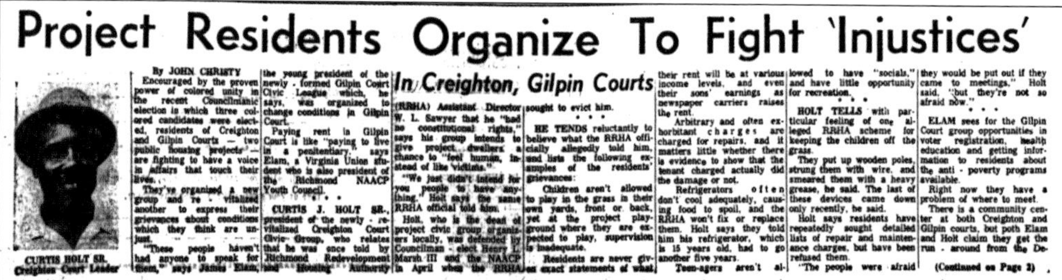

Project Residents Organize To Fight 'Injustices'

In Creighton, Gilpin Courts

CURTIS HOLT SR.
Creighton Court Leader

By JOHN CHRISTY

Encouraged by the proven power of colored unity in the recent Councilmanic election in which three colored candidates were elected, residents of Creighton and Gilpin Courts — two public housing projects — are fighting to have a voice in affairs that touch their lives.

They've organized a new group and re-vitalized another to express their grievances about conditions which they think are unjust.

"These people haven't had anyone to speak for them," says James Elam, the young president of the newly-formed Gilpin Court Civic League which, he says, was organized to change conditions in Gilpin Court.

Paying rent in Gilpin Court is like "paying to live in a penitentiary," says Elam, a Virginia Union student who is also president of the Richmond NAACP Youth Council.

* * *

CURTIS J. HOLT SR., president of the newly-revitalized Creighton Court Civic Group, who relates that he was once told by Richmond Redevelopment and Housing Authority (RRHA) Assistant Director W. L. Sawyer that he "had no constitutional rights," says his group intends to give project dwellers a chance to "feel human, instead of like victims."

"We just didn't intend for you people to have anything," Holt says the same RRHA official told him.

Holt, who is the dean of project civic group organizers locally, was defended by Councilman-elect Henry L. Marsh III and the NAACP in April when the RRHA sought to evict him.

* * *

HE TENDS reluctantly to believe what the RRHA officially allegedly told him, and lists the following examples of the residents' grievances:

Children aren't allowed to play in the grass in their own yards, front or back, yet at the project playground where they are expected to play, supervision is inadequate.

Residents are never given exact statements of what their rent will be at various income levels, and even their sons' earnings as newspaper carriers raises the rent.

Arbitrary and often exhorbitant charges are charged for repairs, and it matters little whether there is evidence to show that the tenant charged actually did the damage or not.

Refrigerators often don't cool adequately, causing food to spoil, and the RRHA won't fix or replace them. Holt says they told him his refrigerator, which is 15 years old, had to go another five years.

Teen-agers aren't allowed to have "socials," and have little opportunity for recreation.

* * *

HOLT TELLS with particular feeling of one alleged RRHA scheme for keeping the children off the grass.

They put up wooden poles, strung them with wire, and smeared them with a heavy grease, he said. The last of these devices came down only recently, he said.

Holt says residents have repeatedly sought detailed lists of repair and maintenance charges, but have been refused them.

"The people were afraid they would be put out if they came to meetings," Holt said, "but they're not so afraid now."

* * *

ELAM sees for the Gilpin Court group opportunities in voter registration, health education and getting information to residents about the anti-poverty programs available.

Right now they have a problem of where to meet.

There is a community center at both Creighton and Gilpin courts, but both Elam and Holt claim they get the run-around from the De-

(Continued on Page 2)

Curtis J. Holt Sr. (1920–1986) was a Richmond Crusade for Voters member, civil rights activist, and a resident of Creighton Court, a public housing community controlled by the Richmond Redevelopment and Housing Authority. Holt became a leader in the community by fighting inequalities and organizing the tenants to form the Creighton Court Civic Group. Structured tenant organizations were prohibited at the time by the Richmond Redevelopment and Housing Authority as a technique to suppress complaints about unsafe living conditions. Holt's activism continued when he successfully challenged the 1970 Chesterfield County annexation through the courts under the 1965 Voting Rights Act. (Courtesy of Afro-American Newspapers.)

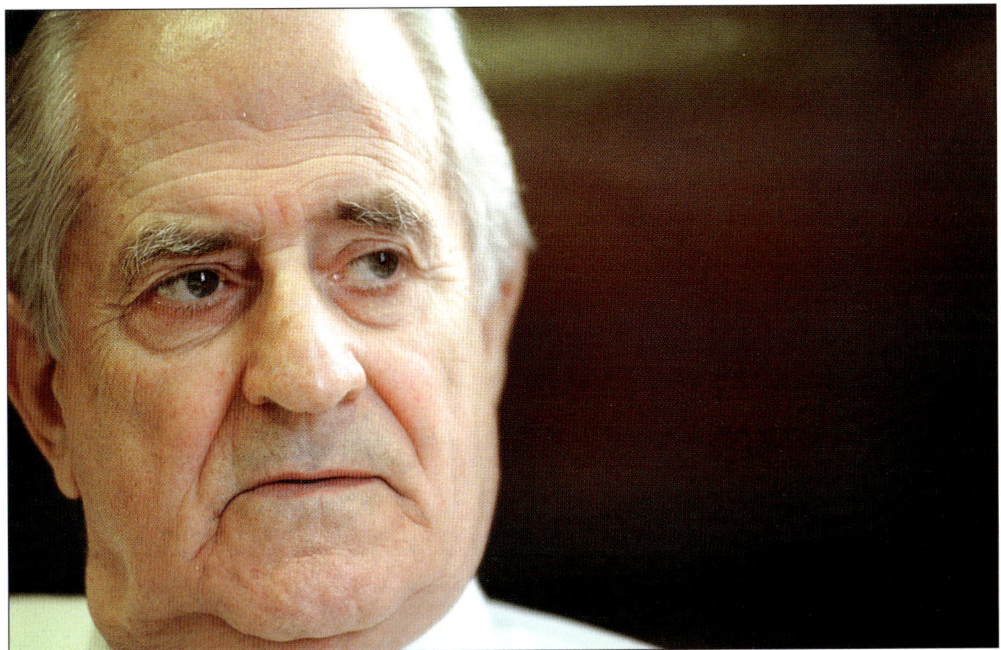

Federal judge Robert R. Merhige Jr. (1919–2005) was known for his controversial school integration rulings in the 1970s. Judge Merhige ruled that students in Henrico and Chesterfield Counties would have to be bused to Richmond to increase the percentage of non–African American students in Richmond Public Schools. (Courtesy of the *Richmond Times-Dispatch.*)

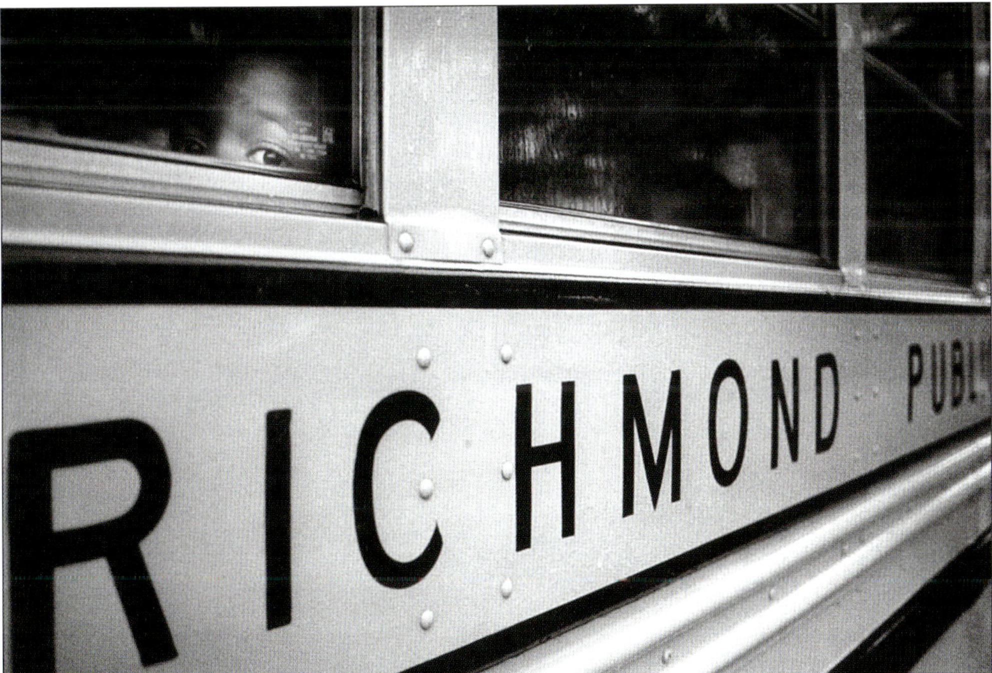

An African American student peers out of a Richmond Public School bus on the first day of busing, August 31, 1970. The Supreme Court invalidated most busing across city-county boundaries in the mid-1970s. (Courtesy of the *Richmond Times-Dispatch.*)

Crusade Wins Delay In Redistricting Fight

RICHMOND

The U.S. Attorney General has agreed to delay a quick decision on Virginia's legislative redistricting plan to allow the Virginia and Richmond Crusades for Voters to complete filing evidence in objection to the plan for the House of Delegates.

Leaders of the statewide and city Crusades expressed their pleasure at the decision by Atty. Gen. John N. Mitchell and predicted "that when all the evidence is in the attorney general will agree with us that the House of Delegates reapportionment plan violates the Voting Rights Act of 1965 and the 14th and 15th Amendments to the Constitution by having multi-member districts in areas of large concentrations of black citizens."

That assessment for the AFRO came from Dr. William S. Thornton, chairman of the Virginia Crusade and M. Philmore Howlette, chairman of the Richmond Crusade.

• • •

Mitchell called Gov. Linwood Holton Saturday to tell him that no decision would be forthcoming from the Justice Department on Virginia's redistricting plans in time for the reconvening of the General Assembly this past week because of the Crusades' objections.

Earlier, the governor had expressed optimism that the attorney general would issue a decision. This feeling was supported by a conversation which Virginia Attorney General Andrew P. Miller had with a Justice Department official last Friday. The official told Miller that the department had been sent to Mitchell for a final decision.

• • •

As a result, Dr. Thornton and Howlette sent a telegram to Mitchell last week. The message said, in part:

"We certainly would not oppose a decision by you to object to these changes at an early date to give the legislature ample time to devise a new plan. But we submit that if you were to decide now to register no objection, that decision would be premature and would defeat the law's purpose of giving 60 days to allow full inquiry and argument by opposing parties.

The 1965 Voting Rights Act provides that any changes in voting laws in states covered by the act must be approved by federal officials.

The Crusade is opposing the House of Delegates redistricting plan prim[illegible] because of it's tr[illegible] Richmond. The plan calls for all five city d[illegible] be elected at-large by the entire population of the city, which is predominantly white. However, any division of the city into single-member district would assure at least two districts in which black voters constitute a majority.

• • •

"We are presently compiling additional evidence to present to you in support of our position. We have a right to be heard and early approval of this plan would deprive us of that right," the telegram from Thornton and Howlette said.

"We understand Virginia's reasons for urging a speedy decision and we will, therefore, try to present our material as soon as practicable, but the state's desire for convenience is no justification for shortcutting the vital guarantees of the Voting Rights Act," the telegram added.

• • •

In the end, Mitchell agreed with the Crusades' arguments.

Virginia's Atty. Gen. Miller, however, saw an additional reason for which the federal officials might have decided to delay any ruling. The U.S. Supreme Court heard arguments in November on a case from Indiana which centered on the same question: at-large versus single-member districts.

A ruling in this case is expected soon and would appear to be applicable to the Crusades' objections to Virginia's plans.

This April 10, 1970, article from the *Richmond Afro-American* discusses the Richmond Crusade for Voters' redistricting victory. (Courtesy of Afro-American Newspapers.)

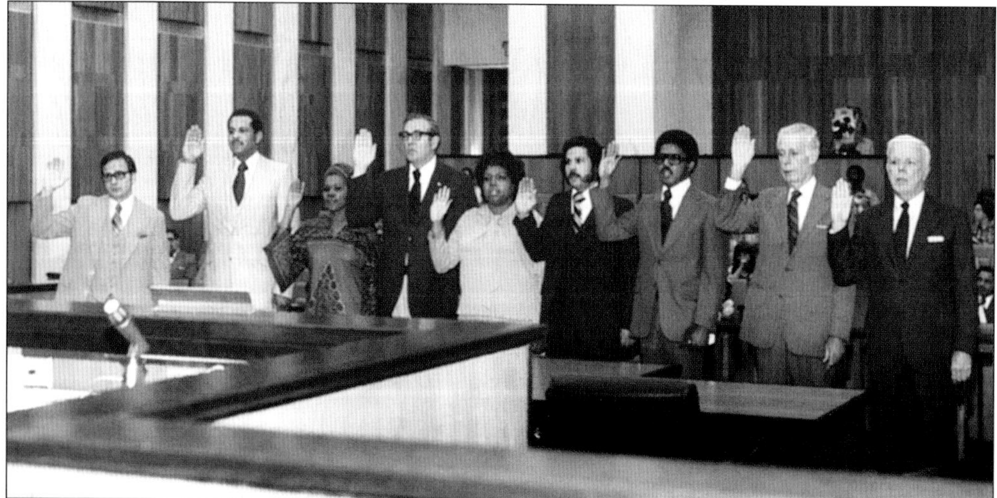

Richmond City Council elections were not held from 1972 until 1976 as a result of the annexation legal battle, and as a result, the ward system was created and implemented. This system led to Richmond's first African American–majority city council in 1977. Among those pictured are Walter T. Kenney (second from the left), Willie J. Dell (third from the left), Claudette Black McDaniel (fifth from the left), H.W. "Chuck" Richardson (sixth from the left), and Henry L. Marsh III (seventh from the left). (Courtesy of Richmond City Clerk's Office.)

John Houze moved to Richmond in 1955 and has been a member of the Richmond Crusade for Voters for over 40 years. Houze served as the treasurer for 22 years. (Courtesy of John Houze.)

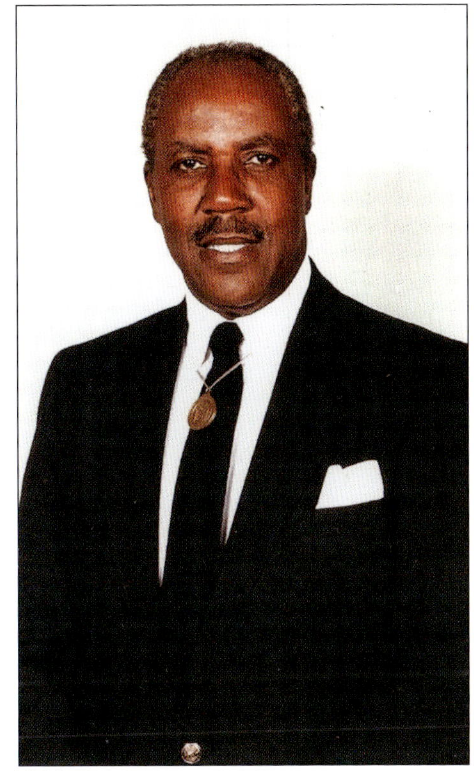

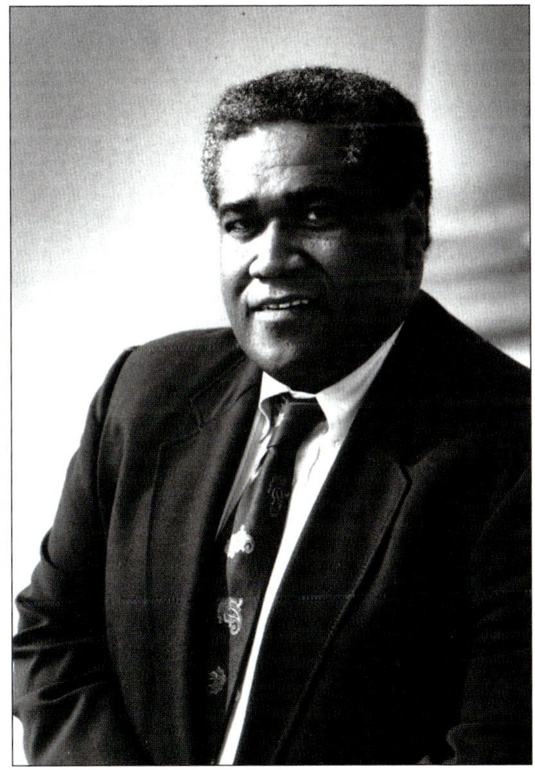

Native Richmonder and optometrist Benjamin J. Lambert III (1937–2014) served in the Virginia General Assembly from 1978 to 2006. In 1980, Lambert was the first African American man to represent Virginia on the Democratic National Committee. (Courtesy of University Relations Collection, L. Douglas Wilder Library, Virginia Union University.)

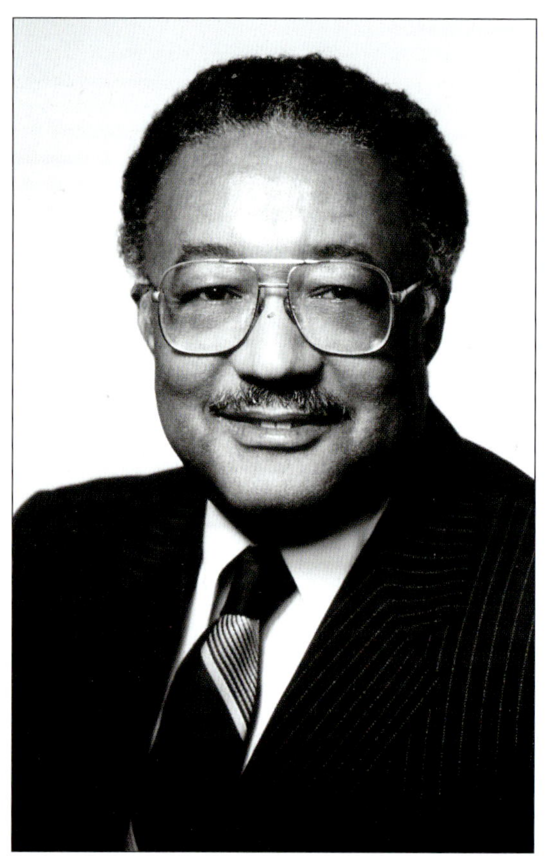

Native Richmonder, local businessman, and politician Clarence Lee Townes Jr. attended the 1964 Republican Convention as the first African American member of a Virginia delegation. Townes later chaired Richmond Renaissance, a nonprofit, biracial corporation formed to foster economic development in downtown Richmond. (Courtesy of Special Collections and Archives, James Branch Cabell Library, VCU Libraries.)

Despite protests from the African American community, the ground breaking for the Richmond Coliseum located 601 East Leigh Street took place in 1969 and opened August 21, 1971. The implementation of this project allowed for more destruction of the Jackson Ward community. (Courtesy of Special Collections and Archives, James Branch Cabell Library, VCU Libraries.)

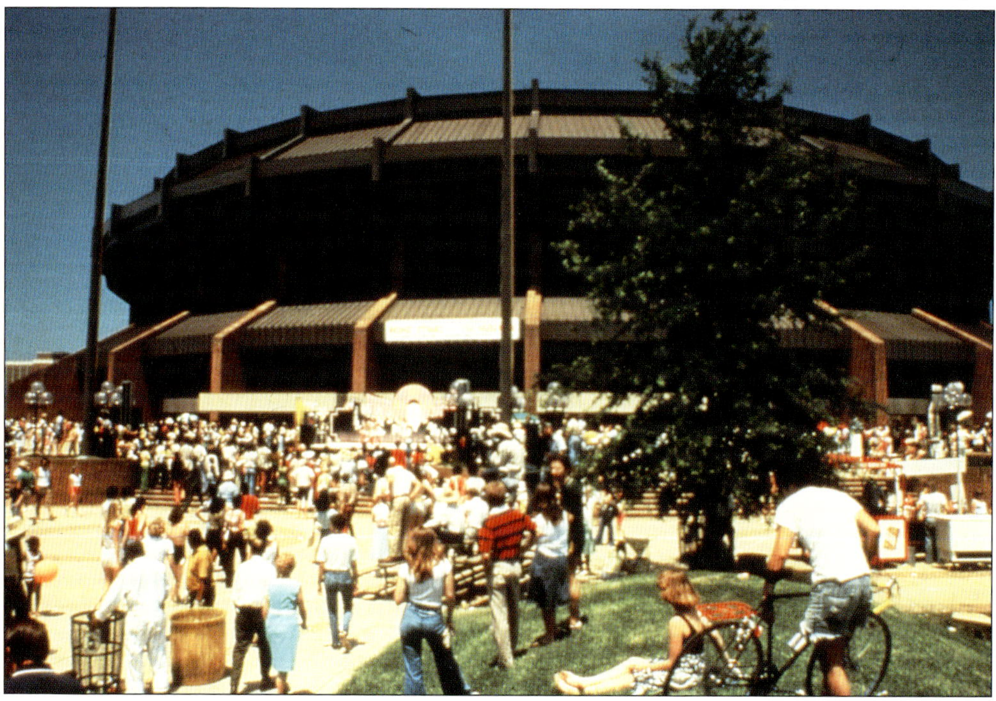

Four

History Is Made

In 1989, history was made in the state of Virginia and the United States with the election of L. Douglas Wilder, the first elected African American governor and a member of the Richmond Crusade for Voters. Before the historic election, both the Richmond City Council and the Richmond Crusade for Voters were struggling to come up with solutions to affect change for African Americans in the city. The Richmond City Council, which had been divided along racial lines, removed progressive Henry L. Marsh III as mayor and appointed conservative Dr. Roy A. West, who was supported by the white city council members and local business leaders in 1982. These two leaders, both African American, had ideological differences, which caused political infighting. One divisive topic was the revitalization of downtown Richmond. The Richmond Crusade for Voters, believed that, as a result of the infighting, issues that directly affected African Americans in the city were left off the table. During this time, the Richmond Crusade for Votes conducted its own self-examination, asking its members to study the organization's ability to relate to African American communities as a result of the special senatorial election held in 1982. The organization wanted to particularly focus on involving more youth and analyzing the value of their endorsement.

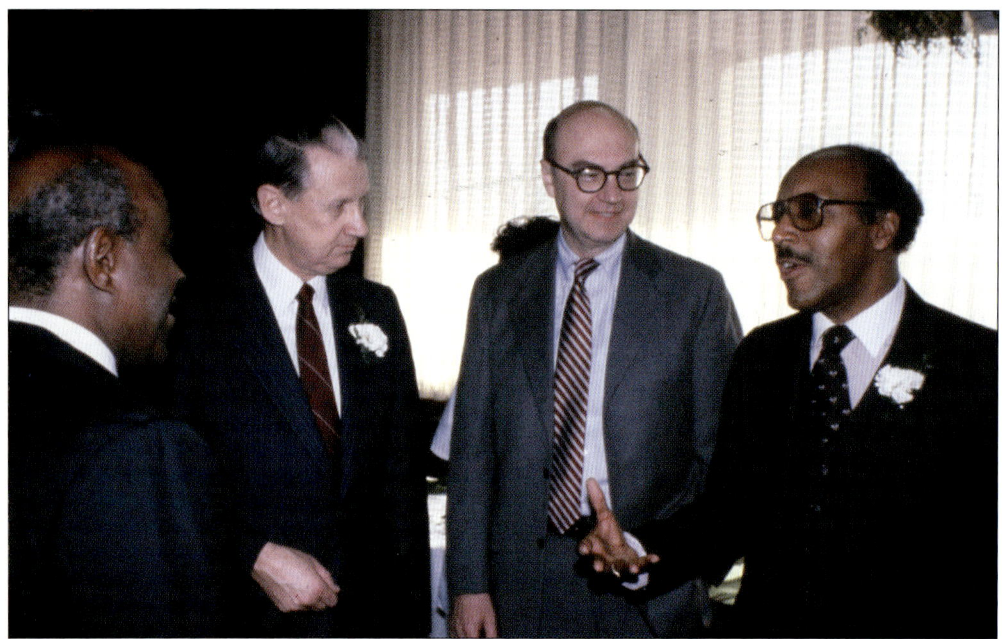

Richmond native Dr. Roy A. West (right) was mayor of Richmond from 1982 to 1988. Dr. West unseated his political rival Henry L. Marsh III. While serving as mayor, Dr. West served as the principal of multiple Richmond middle and high schools. (Courtesy of Special Collections and Archives, James Branch Cabell Library, VCU Libraries.)

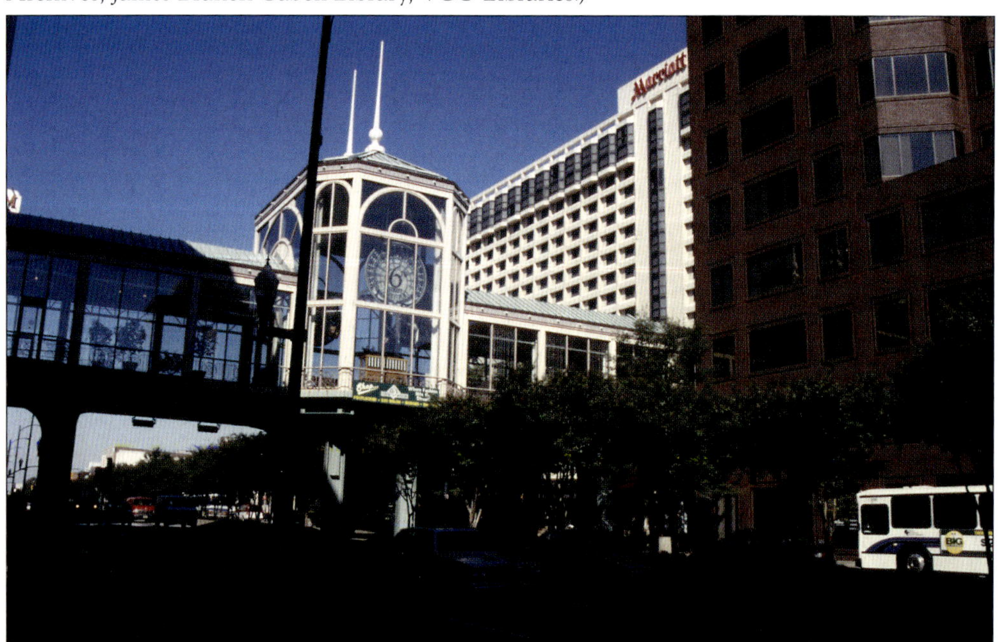

The Sixth Street Marketplace, a major project of the Richmond Renaissance to revitalize downtown, opened in 1985. The retail hub included restaurants and a bridge across Broad Street. Broad Street was seen as a symbol of racial division in the city of Richmond, separating predominantly African American Jackson Ward from the white retail and commercial district. (Courtesy of Special Collections and Archives, James Branch Cabell Library, VCU Libraries.)

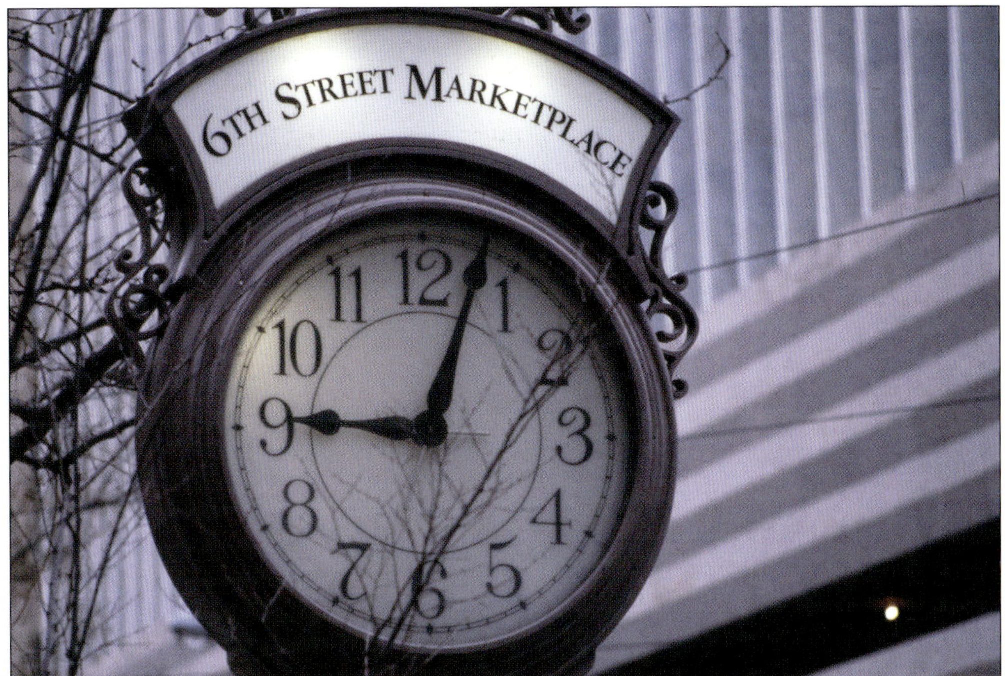

The Sixth Street Marketplace clock was seen as an icon of high hopes in the renewal of Richmond's downtown area. The closure of the two largest department stores, Miller & Rhoads and Thalhimers, contributed to the demise of Sixth Street Marketplace. The marketplace closed in 2003 after 18 years. (Courtesy of Special Collections and Archives, James Branch Cabell Library, VCU Libraries.)

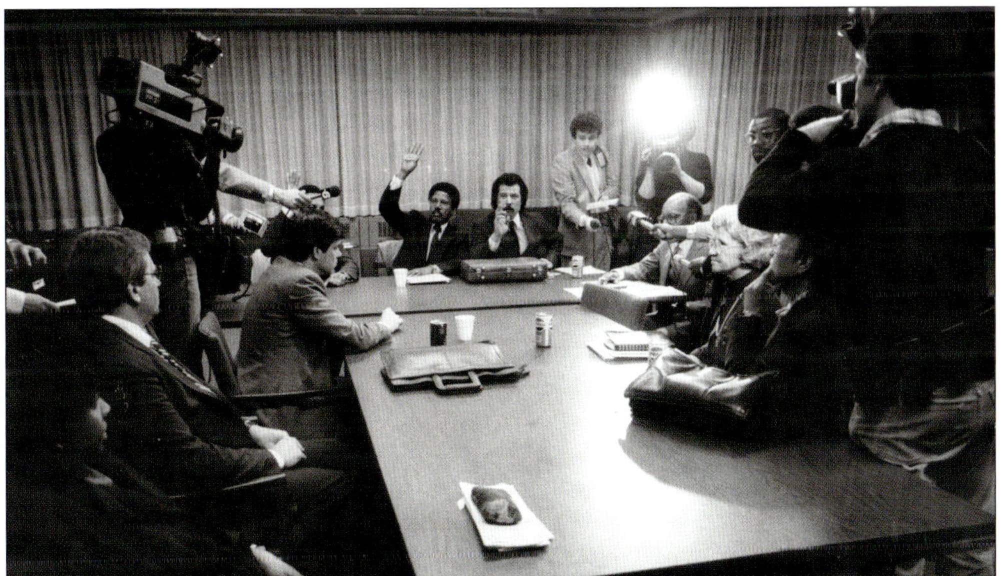
Richmond City Council members Henry L. Marsh III (left) and H.W. "Chuck" Richardson (right) sit next to one another at a table and raise their hands as reporters film the voting of William H. Hefty's resignation as Richmond city attorney on March 6, 1985. Hefty served as Richmond city attorney for four years. His ousting was not a surprise because city council appointed him during Marsh's mayoral term. (Courtesy of the *Richmond Times-Dispatch* Collection, the Valentine.)

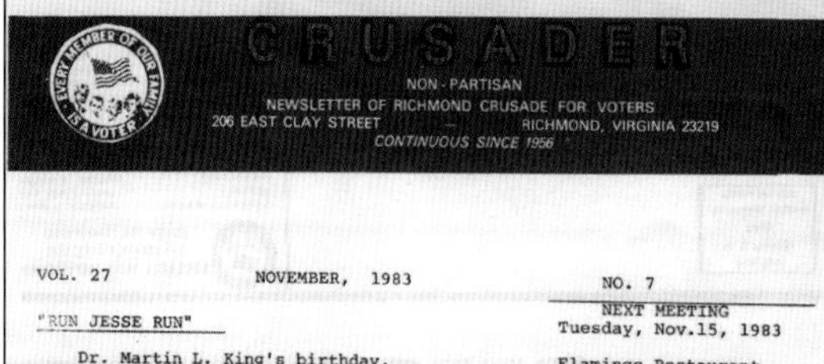

CRUSADER

NON-PARTISAN

NEWSLETTER OF RICHMOND CRUSADE FOR VOTERS

206 EAST CLAY STREET — RICHMOND, VIRGINIA 23219

CONTINUOUS SINCE 1956

EVERY MEMBER OF OUR FAMILY IS A VOTER

VOL. 27 NOVEMBER, 1983 NO. 7

"RUN JESSE RUN"

Dr. Martin L. King's birthday, 1981. Washington, D.C., snowy, impacted ice covered ground. Hundreds of thousands of sisters and brothers, members of all races, huddled together for warmth.

A man exhalts, "HE LIVES, HE LIVES, HE LIVES." The clouds part, the sun bursts forth and shines the first celestrial warmth of the day. Yet a chill passes through me, signifying not cold but a warmth for humanity that Dr. King had in his dream, which is still alive.

This man who spoke is the Rev.Jesse Jackson, a charismatic man. A man who is the needle guiding the threads of the rightness of Black political involvement in the truest sense of full participation. Not only for Blacks, but for women and other minority groups in America.

My wish is that you do not join the voices saying, "America is not ready for a Black to be president, much less run for the nomination," "A Black can't win" and other such statements.

Let's say, RUN JESSE, SPEAK FOR US, ARTICULATE OUR NEEDS, JESSE.

America needs Jesse Jackson. It is past time for Blacks to exercise our full Constitutional powers. Wake up Richmond. When America sends Blacks to kill their likenesses in Africa and in Granada shouldn't we have a voice in foreign policy decisions?

It's all connected and Jesse Jackson can and will show you the whole picture. FIGHT JESSE FIGHT AND WIN.

Jean Roland-Pender

NEXT MEETING
Tuesday, Nov.15, 1983

Flamingo Restaurant
2909 North Ave.
8:00p.m.

CONGRATULATIONS

Congratulations to all of the Richmond delegation who were reelected to the Virginia Assembly. Even though all of you were unopposed, persons voting for tou gave you a vote of confidence. This means that we will expect you to support the bills which benefit your constituency.

IGA COMMUNITY FOOD STORE

IGA Community food store is a predominately Black owned full service grocery located about 2500 Mechanicsville Tpk.

The Crusade has adopted the patronage support of this store.

Each time Crusaders shop at IGA, sign the Crusade roster posted in the store. Ask for it.

ROBERT MORTON BELL- HONOR

The United Food and Commercial Workers International Union, Local 157, will honor Mr. Bell, Sr., at a retirement dinner, Sat. Nov. 19, 1983, 6:00 p.m. at the Holiday Inn-Midtown, 3600 W. Broad Street.

continued on back

The November 1983 edition of the *Crusader*, the Richmond Crusade for Voters newsletter, provided an editorial about Rev. Jesse Jackson's run for president, honors, get-well wishes, and announcements. (Courtesy of Special Collections and Archives, James Branch Cabell Library, VCU Libraries.)

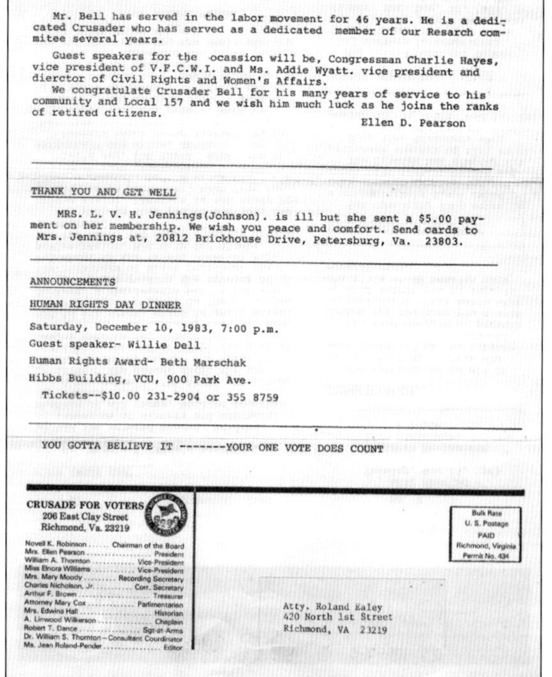

MORTON cont'd

Mr. Bell has served in the labor movement for 46 years. He is a dedicated Crusader who has served as a dedicated member of our Resarch commitee several years.

Guest speakers for the ocassion will be, Congressman Charlie Hayes, vice president of V.F.C.W.I. and Ms. Addie Wyatt. vice president and dierctor of Civil Rights and Women's Affairs.

We congratulate Crusader Bell for his many years of service to his community and Local 157 and we wish him much luck as he joins the ranks of retired citizens.

Ellen D. Pearson

THANK YOU AND GET WELL

MRS. L. V. H. Jennings(Johnson). is ill but she sent a $5.00 payment on her membership. We wish you peace and comfort. Send cards to Mrs. Jennings at, 20812 Brickhouse Drive, Petersburg, Va. 23803.

ANNOUNCEMENTS

HUMAN RIGHTS DAY DINNER

Saturday, December 10, 1983, 7:00 p.m.

Guest speaker- Willie Dell

Human Rights Award- Beth Marschak

Hibbs Building, VCU, 900 Park Ave.

Tickets--$10.00 231-2904 or 355 8759

YOU GOTTA BELIEVE IT -------YOUR ONE VOTE DOES COUNT

CRUSADE FOR VOTERS
206 East Clay Street
Richmond, Va. 23219

Novell K. Robinson ...... Chairman of the Board
Mrs. Ellen Pearson ...... President
William A. Thornton ...... Vice-President
Miss Elnora Williams ...... Vice-President
Mrs. Mary Moody ...... Recording Secretary
Charles Nicholson, Jr. ...... Corr. Secretary
Arthur F. Brown ...... Treasurer
Attorney Mary Cox ...... Parlimentarian
Mrs. Edwina Hall ...... Historian
A. Linwood Wilkerson ...... Chaplain
Robert T. Dance ...... Sgt-at-Arms
Dr. William S. Thornton—Consultant Coordinator
Ms. Jean Roland-Pender ...... Editor

Bulk Rate
U. S. Postage
PAID
Richmond, Virginia
Permit No. 434

Atty. Roland Ealey
420 North 1st Street
Richmond, VA 23219

The *Crusader*, the Richmond Crusade for Voters newsletter, was sent monthly to members. Items in the newsletter included community partnerships, support for African American–owned businesses, and fundraising events. (Courtesy of Special Collections and Archives, James Branch Cabell Library, VCU Libraries.)

This February 11, 1984, headline from the *Richmond Afro-American* shows the endorsement of the Richmond Crusade for Voters for Rev. Jesse Jackson for president of the United States. Reverend Jackson became only the second African American to launch a nationwide campaign for US president; Shirley Chisholm was the first. (Courtesy of Afro-American Newspapers.)

Crusade endorses Jesse Jackson

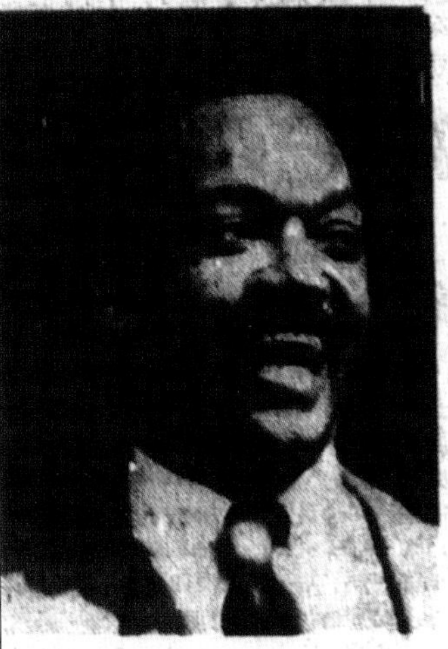

Rev. Jesse Jackson

The Richmond Crusade for Voters has endorsed the Rev. Jesse Jackson for President, but has stopped short of pledging to raise funds for his campaign.

Crusade President Ellen Pearson said the black political action group will be working for Jackson's candidacy in the two areas where the Crusade is usually active—voter registration and education.

Despite the Crusade's support, Jackson's bid for the Democratic nomination is likely to gain little support in Virginia since this state does not hold a primary election. Even some prominent black Democrats are not supporting Jackson's bid. Richmond City Councilman Henry L. Marsh III, for example is backing the candidacy of former Vice President Walter Mondale.

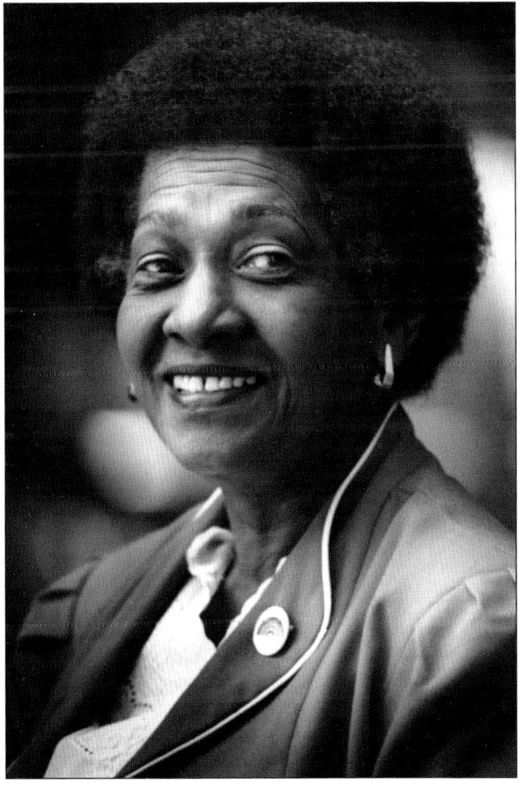

Ellen D. Pearson, born in Orangeburg, South Carolina, served as the ninth president of the Richmond Crusade for Voters from 1981 to 1984. While president, Pearson's goal was to increase African American turnout and the number of African American elected officials. (Courtesy of Special Collections and Archives, James Branch Cabell Library, VCU Libraries.)

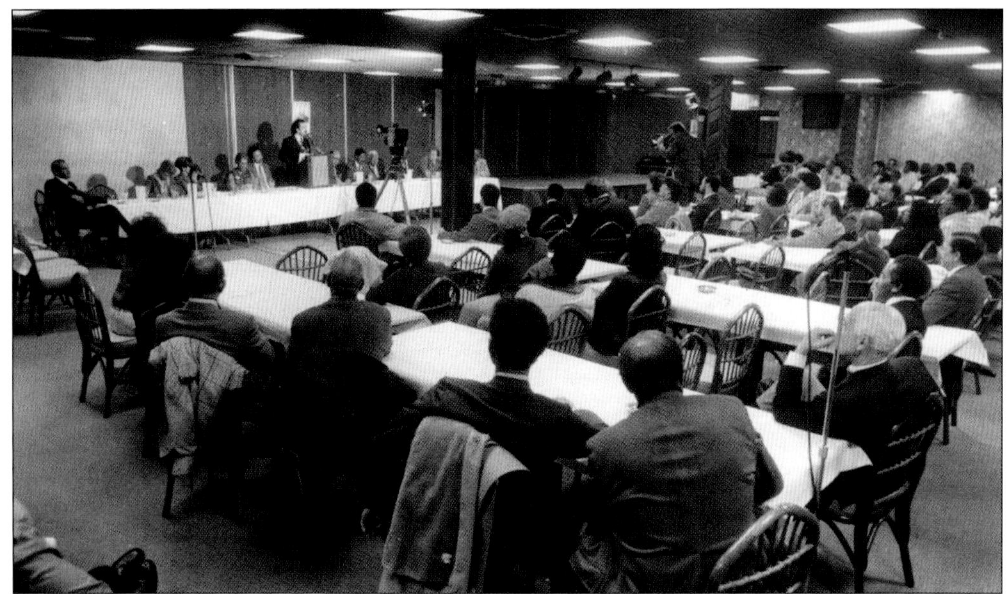

A panel of candidates for Richmond City Council and city councilman H.W. "Chuck" Richardson (at lectern) are shown during the March 18, 1986, meeting of the Richmond Crusade for Voters at the Military Retirees' Club on Chamberlayne Avenue. Local, state, and national candidates for office would visit the Richmond Crusade for Voters to seek the organization's endorsement. (Courtesy of the *Richmond Times-Dispatch* Collection, the Valentine.)

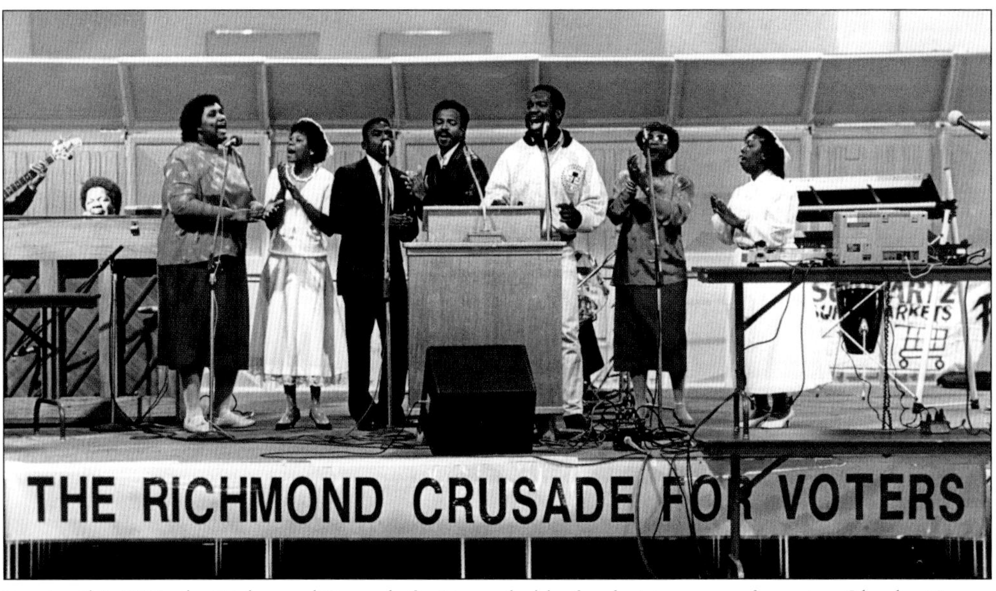

On April 9, 1988, the Richmond Crusade for Voters held a fundraising event featuring Charles Turner and the Agape Singers. (Courtesy of the *Richmond Times-Dispatch* Collection, the Valentine.)

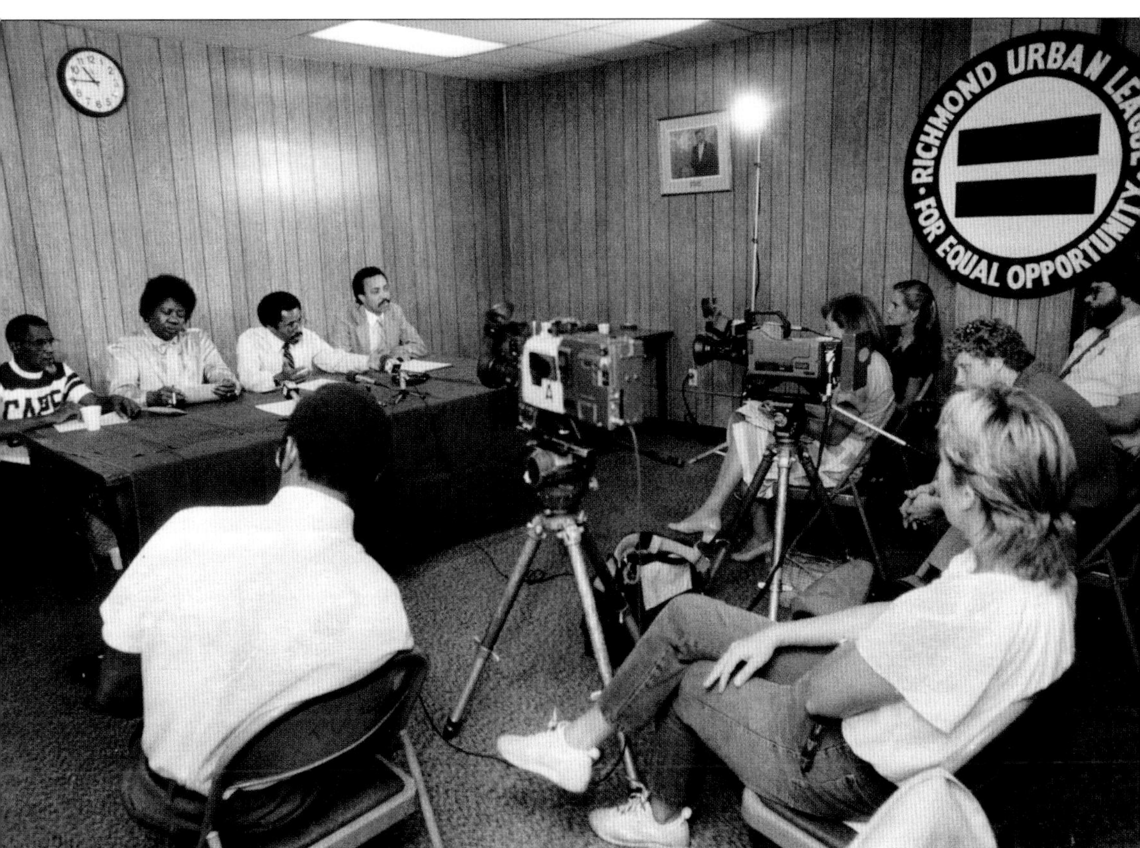

The Urban League and the Richmond Crusade for Voters convened a press conference on September 6, 1985, to encourage voter registration and education. Seated at the table are, from left to right, Eugene Banks; Alma M. Barlow, president of the Richmond Tenants Organization; Rev. Tyler C. Millner, president of the Richmond Branch of the NAACP; and J. Earl Ricks, a youth counselor with the Virginia Department of Corrections. (Courtesy of the *Richmond Times-Dispatch* Collection, the Valentine.)

CRUSADE FOR VOTERS
GET-OUT-THE-VOTE HEADQUARTERS
522 Brook Avenue
Phone; 648-2102

Dear Crusader:

The Crusade For Voters and the Research Committee of the Crusade urge you to support and vote for President JIMMY CARTER and Vice President WALTER MONDALE and JOHN MAPP, the third district congressional candidate on November 4, 1980.

President Carter has kept us at peace. He has created thousands of new jobs, including youth employment programs. He has led the fight against inflation, strengthened the social security system, and supported the food stamp program. President Carter's national urban policy has helped cities like Richmond revive their downtowns and improve housing and neighborhoods. And, the President has nominated more black judges to the federal judiciary than all the other presidents in the history of this nation combined.

In contrast, Ronald Reagan who was endorsed by the Ku Klux Klan, has called the poor "a faceless mass waiting for handouts." He would eliminate the Department of Education and Health and Human Services. Reagan has called urban aid programs "one of the biggest phonies that we have in the system."

JOHN MAPP, an able democrat, has endorsed the Democratic Party platform and the principles of equal opportunity. On the other hand, his republican opponent, Tom Bliley supported the 1970 annexation of Chesterfield county and is opposed to the social programs which were established to ensure equal opportunity to all.

On the Constitutional Amendments Vote NO on Question #2 and YES on 1, 3, and 4. We did not include those amendments in this mailing because it would make for too much bulk.

We are proud to be able to say, *"Neither money nor self-interest groups can influence the recommendation of the CRUSADE FOR VOTERS."*

Your vote counts. In this important election, VOTE!

Crusadingly yours,

M. Philmore Howlette, *Chairman of the Board*
John Howlette, *Chairman Research*
Norvell K. Robinson, *President*
Ellen D. Pearson, *Vice-President*
William S. Thornton, *Consultant*

By Authority of Arthur Brown, Treasurer

A Richmond Crusade for Voters endorsement document from 1980 is pictured. The report discusses a constitutional amendment and the reasons for the group's endorsements of Jimmy Carter, Walter Mondale, and John Mapp. (Courtesy of Special Collections and Archives, James Branch Cabell Library, VCU Libraries.)

CRUSADE FOR VOTERS

SAMPLE BALLOT

GENERAL ELECTION

Tuesday, November 4, 1980

PRESIDENT AND VICE PRESIDENT
(Vote for not more than one)

☒ DEMOCRATIC PARTY
Election for
JIMMY CARTER, President
WALTER F. MONDALE, Vice President
CHRISTOPHER W. HUTTON
WILLIAM P. ROBINSON, SR.
WILLIAM N. PAXTON, JR.
MUSCOE GARNETT
WALTER D. SOUTHALL
ROBERT B. LAMBETH, JR.
ROBERT W. FARMER
DONALD N. HENRY
ANNABEL C. JENNINGS
ELIZABETH B. BASKERVILLE
C. FLIPPO HICKS
JAMES M. HEILMAN

CRUSADE FOR VOTERS

SAMPLE BALLOT

GENERAL ELECTION

Tuesday, November 4, 1980

Member
House of Representatives
Third District
(Vote for not more than one)

☒ JOHN A. MAPP
☐ THOMAS J. "TOM" BLILEY, JR.
☐ JAMES B. TURNEY
☐ HOWARD H. CARWILE

Only You Can Stop The Conservative Take-Over Of Our Community And The Nation! Help Protect Our Elderly And The Education Of Our Children.

Cast Your Vote On November 4th For JIMMY CARTER For President And JOHN MAPP For Congress!

Polls Will Be Open From 6:00 a.m. to 7:00 p.m.

For additional information call 648-2102

By Authority of Arthur Brown, Treasurer

This is a sample ballot for the Tuesday, November 4, 1980, election endorsing the Democratic ticket. (Courtesy of Special Collections and Archives, James Branch Cabell Library, VCU Libraries.)

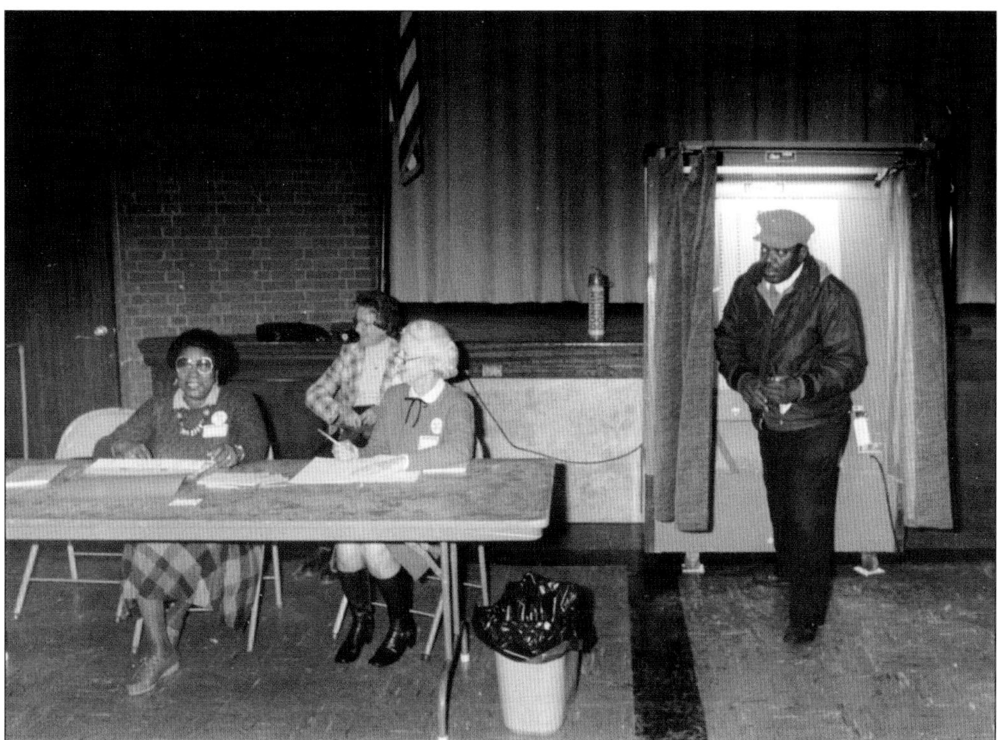

Aaron Battle Jr. (right) walks out of a voting booth at Northminster Baptist Church, located at Westwood and Moss Side Avenues on Richmond's north side, on December 16, 1985. From left to right, Addie L. Mosby, Ann Nell Johnson, and Margaret C. Hiner run the voting process. (Courtesy of the *Richmond Times-Dispatch* Collection, the Valentine.)

CRUSADE'S CONCERNS FOR 1986

1. *Does the Crusade for Voters still maintain the ability to relate to the Black Community?*

2. *What is the value of the Crusade's endorsement and what impact does it have on the Black Community in the late 80's, i.e., Senate Race Special Election?*

3. *The Research Committee needs to take a look at its method of endorsement.*

4. *The time has come for Crusade to explain to the Black Community why the organization endorses a candidate and be ready to substantiate choice.*

5. *Crusade must provide a firm stand for only one candidate for each office available. To split support among one or more candidates for the same office will only tend to split the vote.*

6. *Crusade has to do a better job of "reading" the Black Community, i.e., Senate Race Special Election.*

7. *The role of the Crusade Consultants should be changed, i.e., supply information to the Research Committee about a candidate on how the Black Community is receiving a certain candidate - be realistic and factual.*

8. *Consultants attending Crusade's Research meeting should not be permitted to make campaign speeches or introduce fallacious and misleading statements, i.e. endorsing a certain candidate would split the Black Community. Then that same candidate received 80% of the Black vote.*

9. *A Get Out the Vote Committee is needed within the organization instead of one or two people trying to do the job.*

10. *What and who are Grass Roots Voters in the late 80's?*

11. *The 71st House Race is coming up in a Special Election January 7, 1986. What role will the Crusade for Voters organization play in this election?*

12. *The Special Election will take place January 7, 1986. Because the city of Richmond is Democratic, candidates proclaiming to be demonstrats and who are not willing to file and seek the Party's nomination, but choose to run as Independents, are "fighting an uphill battle."*

This 1985 Richmond Crusade for Voters document addresses concerns and questions for the upcoming year. Maintaining the ability to relate to the African American community and the value of the organization's endorsement are the top concerns. (Courtesy of Special Collections and Archives, James Branch Cabell Library, VCU Libraries.)

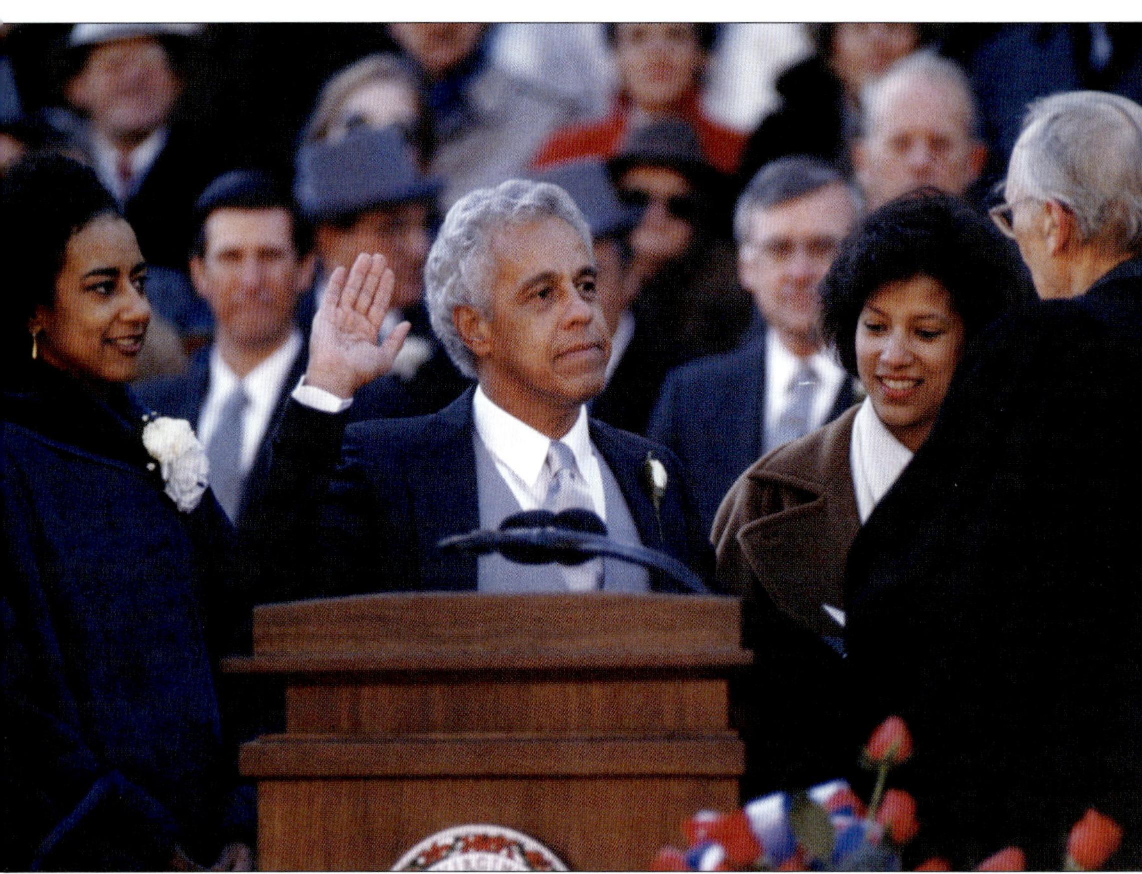

Native Richmonder Lawrence Douglas Wilder became the first elected African American governor in the United States in 1989. The grandson of a former slave, Wilder was born on January 17, 1931, and named after abolitionist Frederick Douglass and poet Paul Laurence Dunbar. The Korean War veteran and Bronze Star recipient was not allowed to enroll in a Virginia law school upon his return to the States because of segregation laws; therefore, he pursued a career as an attorney at Howard University in Washington, DC. He is shown here with his daughters Lynn Wilder (left) and Loren Wilder (right) taking the oath of office January 13, 1990, to become the 66th governor of Virginia. (Courtesy of the L. Douglas Wilder Library, Virginia Union University.)

Five

Trials and Triumphs

In the 1990s, the crime rate in the city of Richmond reached a new high, with 161 homicides in 1994. The city was in trouble. The Richmond Crusade for Voters experienced its own trials and triumphs during the 1990s with the accusation that members of the powerful and long-standing research committee delivered endorsements for money, and the once-thriving State Crusade for Voters became defunct. The organization acquired its first office space at Second and Jackson Streets in Jackson Ward and reached a milestone anniversary of 40 years. The Richmond Crusade for Voters made purposeful efforts during this time to reach out to the community and to work with other Richmond civic organizations to find new leadership for the city of Richmond. In 1994, the Richmond Crusade for Voters endorsed a progressive slate of candidates for city council, including John Conrad, Tim Kaine, Viola Osborne Baskerville, H.W. "Chuck" Richardson, L. Shirley Harvey, Adolphus C. "Carl" Prince, and Anthony D. Jones.

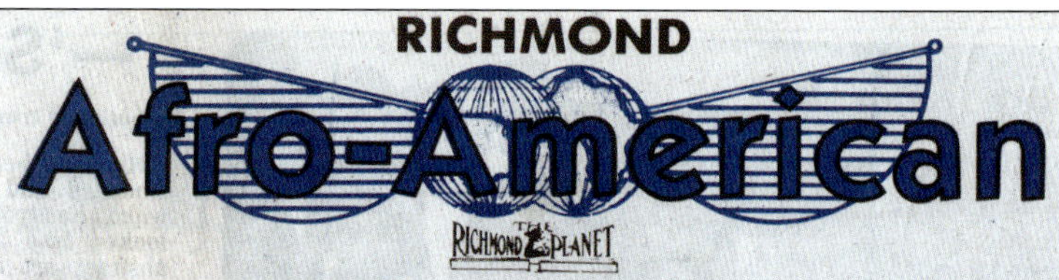

Volume 109 No. 7 | Copyright by the AFRO-AMERICAN Company | January 26, 1991

Crusade re-establishes vision

By Hazel Trice Edney
AFRO Staff Writer

Richmond Crusade for Voters newly-installed President Roxie Raines Kornegay says the 34-year-old organization will work to re-establish the vision and purpose of its founders.

"When we turn our attention to the founding fathers of the Richmond Crusade for Voters, we see men who took the time to initiate the fight for equality . . . Their major thrust was to approach the social, educational, political and economic problems of our community through the political door. Voter registration, voter education and get out the vote were the primary items of their agenda," she told the audience at the installation service on Jan. 15.

Like the Crusade of old, Ms. Kornegay said the new administration will seek to form a coalition with other like-minded organizations in order to carry out an effective agenda for African-American causes.

"The objective appears to have been, 'Take it to the Ballot Box. Do it at the polls.' Combining this effort with our brother and sister organizations, a difference was made and can continue to be made," she said.

The coalition of organizations is in the process of being formed and is expected to meet very shortly, sources say.

At least 200 people attended the installation ceremony at the Military Retirees Club. Outgoing president, Robert J. Grey Jr., who was awarded a

(Continued on Page A2)

This January 26, 1991, headline from the *Richmond Afro-American* emphasizes the Richmond Crusade for Voters' renewed commitment to African American issues, voter registration, and voter education. During the mid-1980s, the organization experienced a decrease in membership and influence on the African American community, citing the lack of grassroots efforts that once connected the organization and the community. (Courtesy of Afro-American Newspapers.)

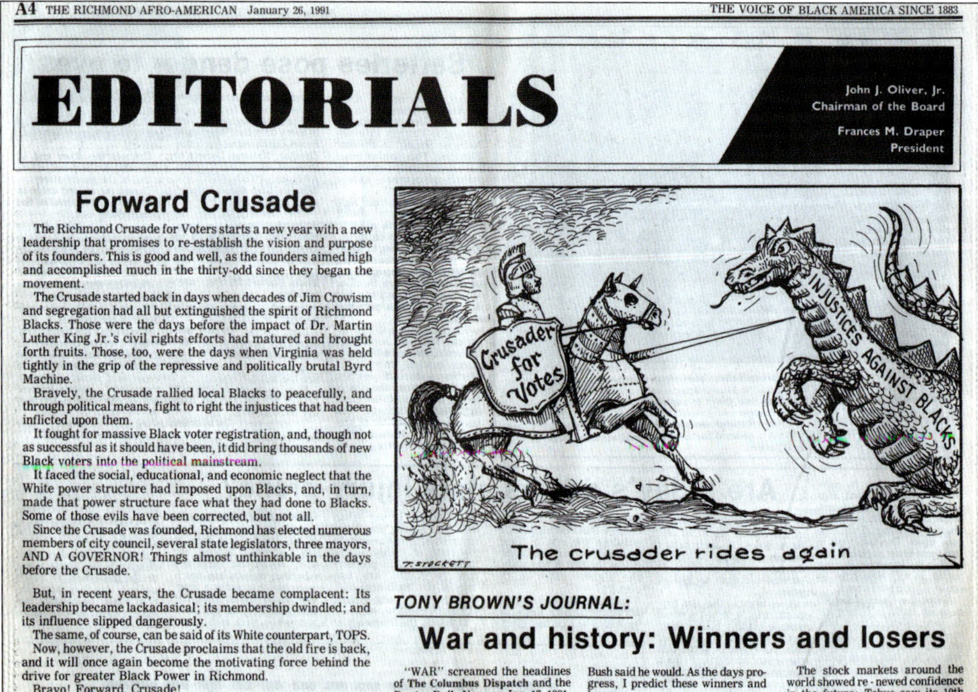

A4 THE RICHMOND AFRO-AMERICAN January 26, 1991 | THE VOICE OF BLACK AMERICA SINCE 1883

EDITORIALS

John J. Oliver, Jr.
Chairman of the Board
Frances M. Draper
President

Forward Crusade

The Richmond Crusade for Voters starts a new year with a new leadership that promises to re-establish the vision and purpose of its founders. This is good and well, as the founders aimed high and accomplished much in the thirty-odd since they began the movement.

The Crusade started back in days when decades of Jim Crowism and segregation had all but extinguished the spirit of Richmond Blacks. Those were the days before the impact of Dr. Martin Luther King Jr.'s civil rights efforts had matured and brought forth fruits. Those, too, were the days when Virginia was held tightly in the grip of the repressive and politically brutal Byrd Machine.

Bravely, the Crusade rallied local Blacks to peacefully, and through political means, fight to right the injustices that had been inflicted upon them.

It fought for massive Black voter registration, and, though not as successful as it should have been, it did bring thousands of new Black voters into the political mainstream.

It faced the social, educational, and economic neglect that the White power structure had imposed upon Blacks, and, in turn, made that power structure face what they had done to Blacks. Some of those evils have been corrected, but not all.

Since the Crusade was founded, Richmond has elected numerous members of city council, several state legislators, three mayors, AND A GOVERNOR! Things almost unthinkable in the days before the Crusade.

But, in recent years, the Crusade became complacent: Its leadership became lackadasical; its membership dwindled; and its influence slipped dangerously.

The same, of course, can be said of its White counterpart, TOPS.

Now, however, the Crusade proclaims that the old fire is back, and it will once again become the motivating force behind the drive for greater Black Power in Richmond.

Bravo! Forward, Crusade!

TONY BROWN'S JOURNAL:

War and history: Winners and losers

"WAR" screamed the headlines of The Columbus Dispatch and the Dayton Daily News on Jan. 17, 1991,

Bush said he would. As the days progress, I predict these winners and losers:

The stock markets around the world showed re-newed confidence in the future; Tokyo saw its 10th

This editorial cartoon from the *Richmond Afro-American* underscores the renewed spirit the Richmond Crusade for Voters generated in the 1990s. The column provides a brief history of the organization, its successes, and challenges. (Courtesy of Afro-American Newspapers.)

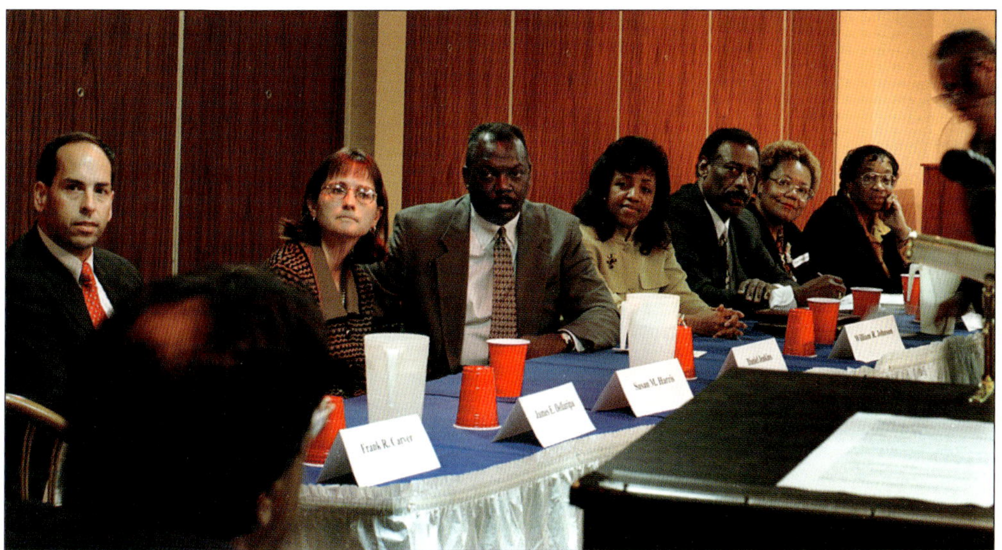

A Third District candidate's forum was held by the Richmond Crusade for Voters in December 1997 at the Military Retiree Club. Viola Baskerville was elected to the Virginia House of Delegates in November, which left her district seat vacant. From left to right are James Dellaripa II, Susan Harris, W. Randolph Johnson Jr., Kathy Thompson, Charles Walker, Viesta Washington, and Jean Williams. (Courtesy of the *Richmond Times-Dispatch*.)

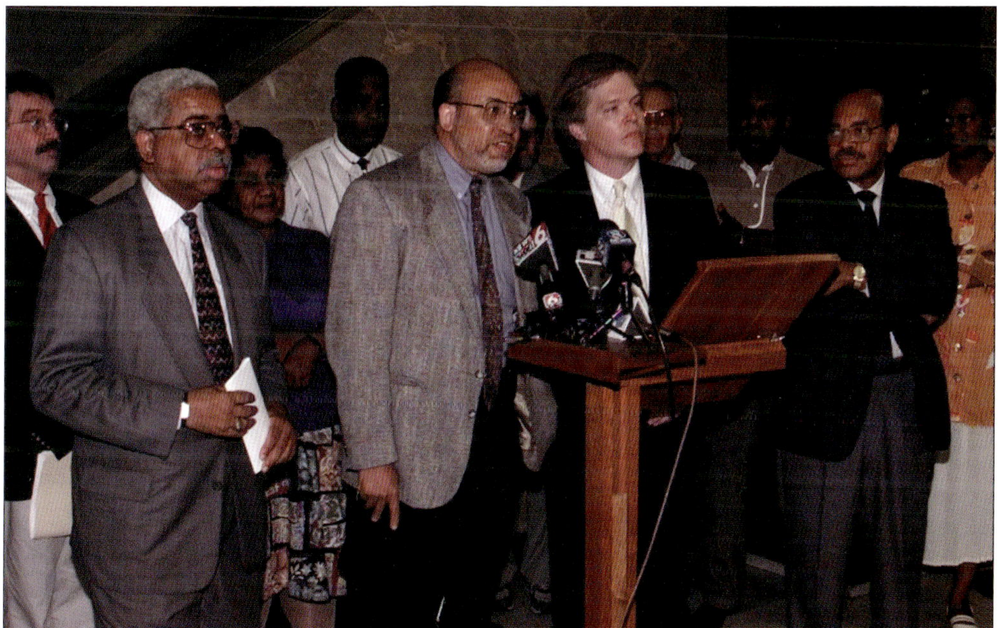

At a city hall press conference denouncing school violence on June 24,1998, are, from left to right, Charles Chambliss with the Richmond Crusade for Voters, Warren Kennedy with the Richmond chapter of the NAACP, Ernie Brown with the Coalition for a Safer Richmond, and Melvin Law, chairman of the Richmond School Board and a member of the Richmond Crusade for Voters. As rates of violence increased in the city of Richmond, the Richmond Crusade for Voters began to address these issues and hold public officials accountable by inviting them to meetings to discuss their plans to combat the violence. (Courtesy of the *Richmond Times-Dispatch*.)

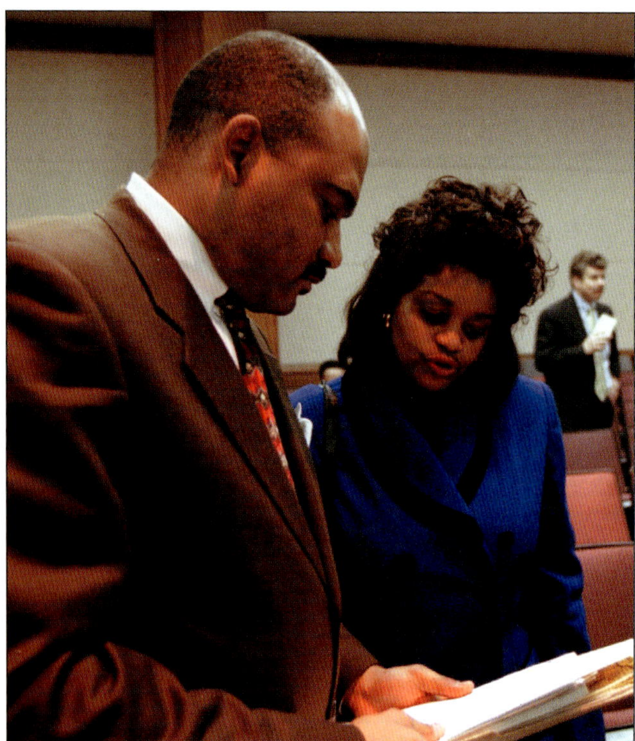

Richmond Crusade for Voters' member Rudy McCullum (left) and executive secretary for the Richmond chapter of the NAACP Linda Byrd-Harden review papers before the February 7, 1996 House Counties, Cities and Towns Committee. The committee was considering a bill to allow at-large mayoral elections in the city of Richmond. McCullum and Byrd-Harden were opposed to the bill. The city would eventually elect its mayor at-large beginning in 2005. (Courtesy of the *Richmond Times-Dispatch*.)

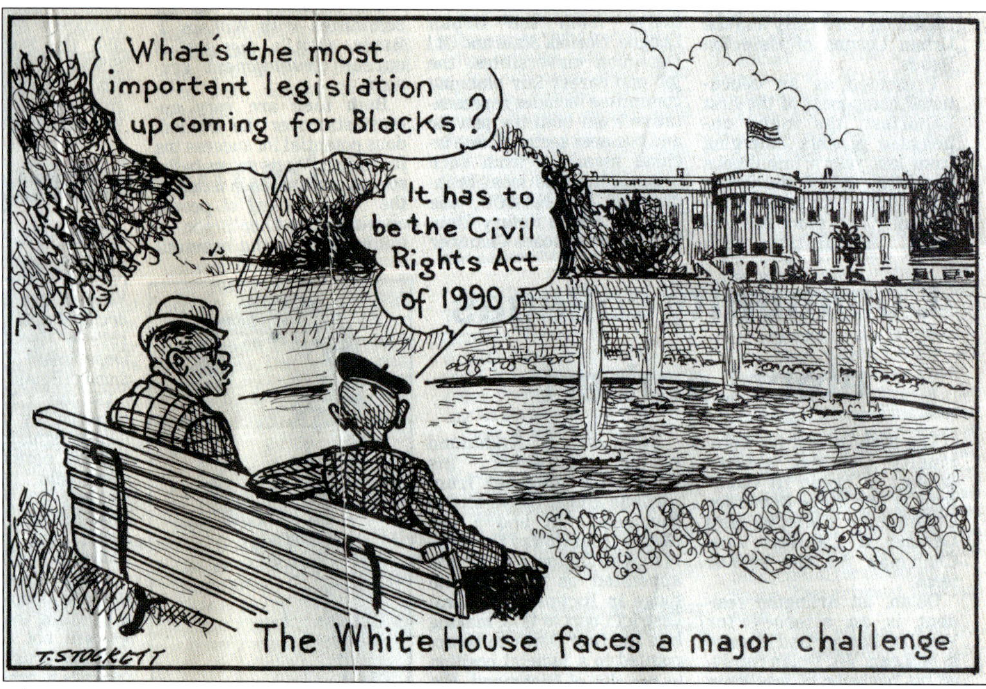

This August 4, 1990, editorial cartoon from the *Richmond Afro-American* highlights the importance of the Civil Rights Act of 1990. The act passed in 1991 in response to Supreme Court decisions that limited the rights of employees who had sued their employers for discrimination. (Courtesy of Afro-American Newspapers.)

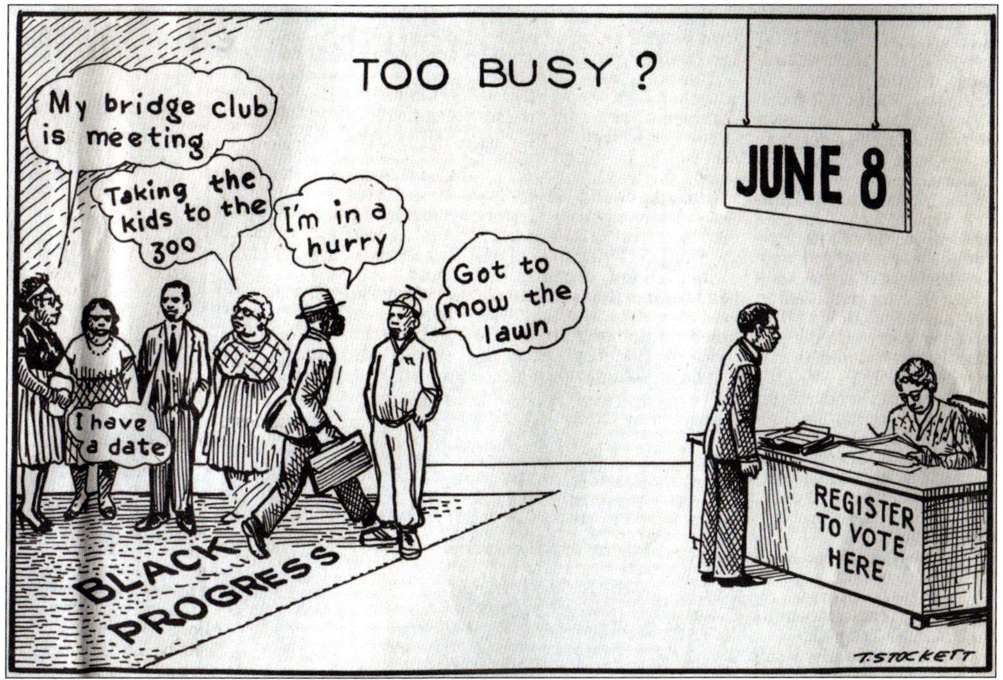

This June 8, 1991, editorial cartoon from the *Richmond Afro-American* connects the importance of voting with African American progress. It provides some common excuses and how those excuses will delay progression. (Courtesy of Afro-American Newspapers.)

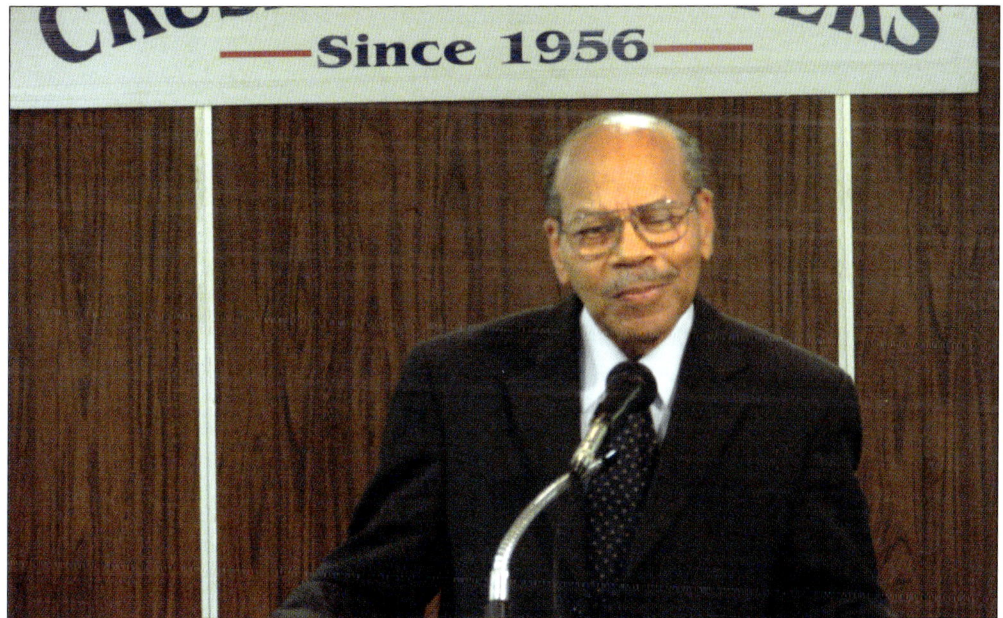

Melvin Law was the 18th and 21st president of the Richmond Crusade for Voters, serving from 1998 to 2000 and 2004 to 2006. While president, Law focused on electing the best people for the community regardless of race. During his tenure, Tim Kaine was endorsed as Richmond's mayor in 1998 and as Virginia governor in 2006. Law believes firmly that voting is a duty. (Courtesy of Ralph Cramer.)

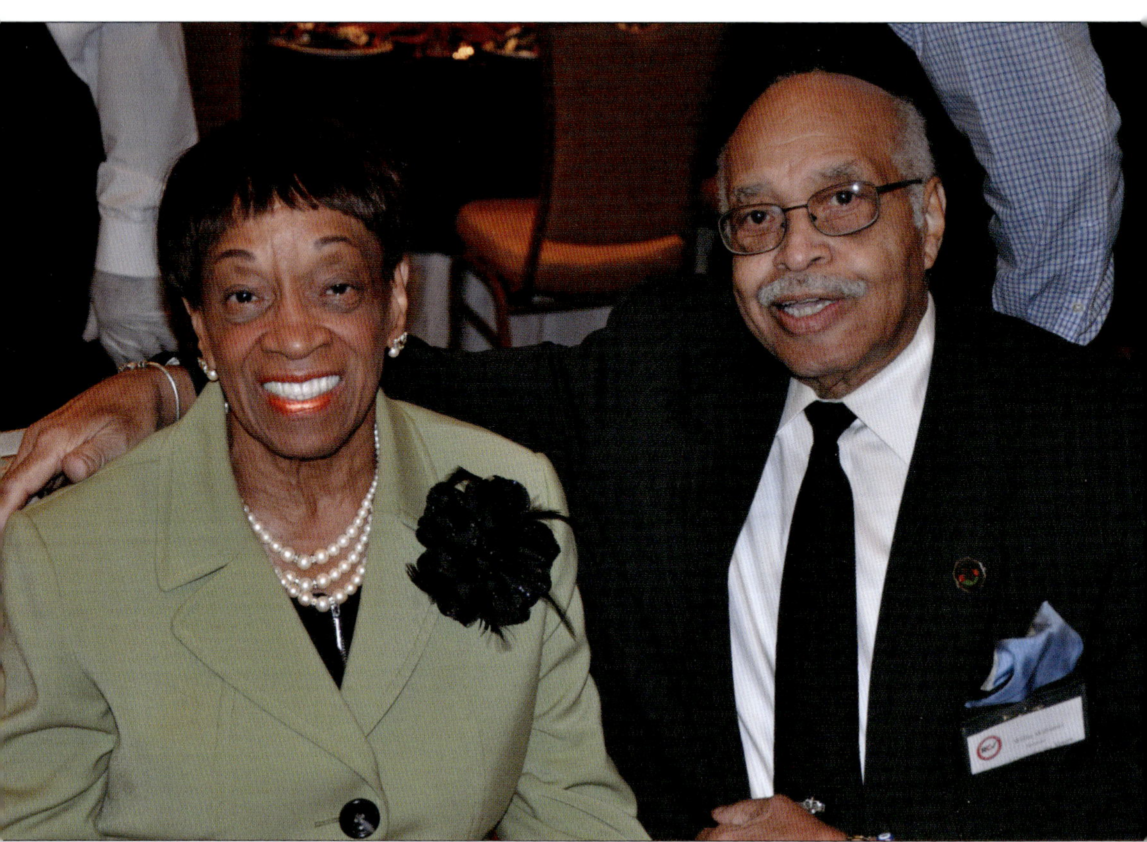

Richmond native and former naval officer Willie Williams III was the 15th president of the Richmond Crusade for Voters, serving from 1995 to 1997. Williams's goal as president was to put the organization back on course by increasing membership and reaching out to the community youth and college students. Churches and civic organizations were vital to his goal of registering and educating people. Williams is pictured with his wife, Jean Williams. (Courtesy of Pamela Eddie.)

Six

Hope for the Future

Over the last two decades, the Richmond Crusade for Voters has received praise for its commitment to the city of Richmond, most notably a commendation from the Virginia General Assembly in 2008 with House Joint Resolution No. 229. The organization endured presidential impeachments and a decrease in membership, productivity, and influence, and it elected its youngest president. The organization has vowed to return to the basics through grassroots efforts in all Richmond neighborhoods and to become more inclusive by inviting those from diverse backgrounds, races, and political affiliations to join and share their ideas for the advancement of the city, with a focus on the issues. The Richmond Crusade for Voters has held candidate forums; conducted voter registration drives at colleges, universities, community festivals, and churches; and hosted candidate meet-and-greet events as well as holiday celebrations. In November 2015, the organization held a celebration honoring Dr. William Ferguson Reid's 90 for 90 campaign, to register 90 new voters in each precinct in the commonwealth of Virginia with the goal of a quarter million new voters. Sixty years after its creation, the Richmond Crusade for Voters continues to fight for political empowerment through voter registration and voter education.

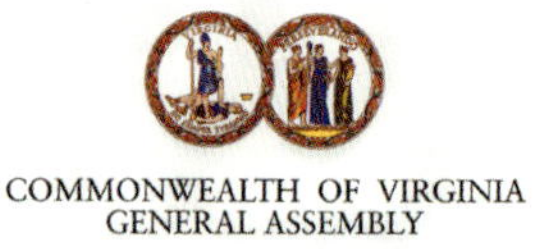

COMMONWEALTH OF VIRGINIA
GENERAL ASSEMBLY

HOUSE JOINT RESOLUTION NO. 229

Commending the Richmond Crusade for Voters.

Agreed to by the House of Delegates, January 18, 2008
Agreed to by the Senate, January 24, 2008

WHEREAS, the Richmond Crusade for Voters has served the Richmond Metropolitan Community and its citizens for over 50 years; and

WHEREAS, in 1956 the Richmond Crusade for Voters was established by three distinguished cofounders, Dr. William S. Thornton, Dr. William Ferguson Reid, and John M. Brooks, who were visionary and influential leaders in the Commonwealth; and

WHEREAS, the Richmond Crusade for Voters grew out of the Council to Save Public Schools, a Richmond organization formed to fight a January 1956 law that allowed cities in Virginia the option of closing rather than integrating public schools; and

WHEREAS, the 1988 November-December edition of *Richmond Surroundings* published the original goal of the Richmond Crusade for Voters as "increasing effective black participation in Richmond's political process"; and

WHEREAS, the Richmond Crusade for Voters' mission continues to be "to increase the voting strength of the population of the City of Richmond and to improve the moral, social, economic, educational and general welfare of our people"; and

WHEREAS, the Richmond Crusade for Voters strives to increase the voice and influence of all African Americans in the political process by encouraging voter registration among black citizens, endorsing excellent candidates, and increasing voter turnout citywide; and

WHEREAS, the Richmond Crusade for Voters was instrumental in electing the first black majority on the Richmond City Council, which picked Henry L. Marsh III as the city's first African-American mayor in 1977; and

WHEREAS, twelve years after the Richmond Crusade for Voters was formed, cofounder Dr. William Ferguson Reid became the first black member of the General Assembly of Virginia since Reconstruction, and he represented Richmond and Henrico County with distinction in the House of Delegates from 1968 to 1973; and

WHEREAS, over the years, the Richmond Crusade for Voters has touched the lives of many citizens in the City of Richmond by educating them on the importance of their privilege to vote and how their vote can make a difference, providing a forum for the candidates, and providing information on important public issues of concern to all of Virginia's citizens; now, therefore, be it

RESOLVED by the House of Delegates, the Senate concurring, That the General Assembly commend and congratulate the Richmond Crusade for Voters for its outstanding service to the Richmond Metropolitan Community for over 50 years; and, be it

RESOLVED FURTHER, That the Clerk of the House of Delegates prepare a copy of this resolution for presentation to the Richmond Crusade for Voters as an expression of the General Assembly's gratitude to the organization for its commitment to the voters of the Commonwealth.

House Patrons: Hall, Alexander, Amundson, Armstrong, BaCote, Barlow, Bouchard, Cox, Dance, Eisenberg, Howell, A.T., Hull, Jones, D.C., Lewis, Loupassi, Massie, McClellan, Melvin, Moran, Morrissey, Nichols, O'Bannon, Peace, Poisson, Shannon, Spruill, Toscano, Tyler, Valentine, Vanderhye, Ward, Ware, O. and Ware, R.L.

Senate Patrons: Marsh and McEachin

Clerk of the House of Delegates

In 2008, the Richmond Crusade for Voters received a commendation from the Virginia General Assembly for its 52 years of service to the city of Richmond. The tribute provides a brief history of the organization, its mission, and its successes. (Courtesy of Jennifer McClellan.)

Richmond native Antione M. Green was recruited to join the Richmond Crusade for Voters in 1998. He was elected first vice president in 2004 and president in 2007. At age 28, Green was the youngest president in the Richmond Crusade for Voters' history. In tandem with the organization's responsibilities, Green was also enrolled as a student at Virginia Commonwealth University. As president, Green was a staunch supporter for greater voter empowerment in the city of Richmond and had a mission to strengthen the Richmond Crusade for Voters' legacy by recruiting new and diverse members. Green ran for a seat on the Henrico County School Board in 2003 and in the Sixty-Ninth District in the Virginia House of Delegates in 2009. (Courtesy of Antione M. Green.)

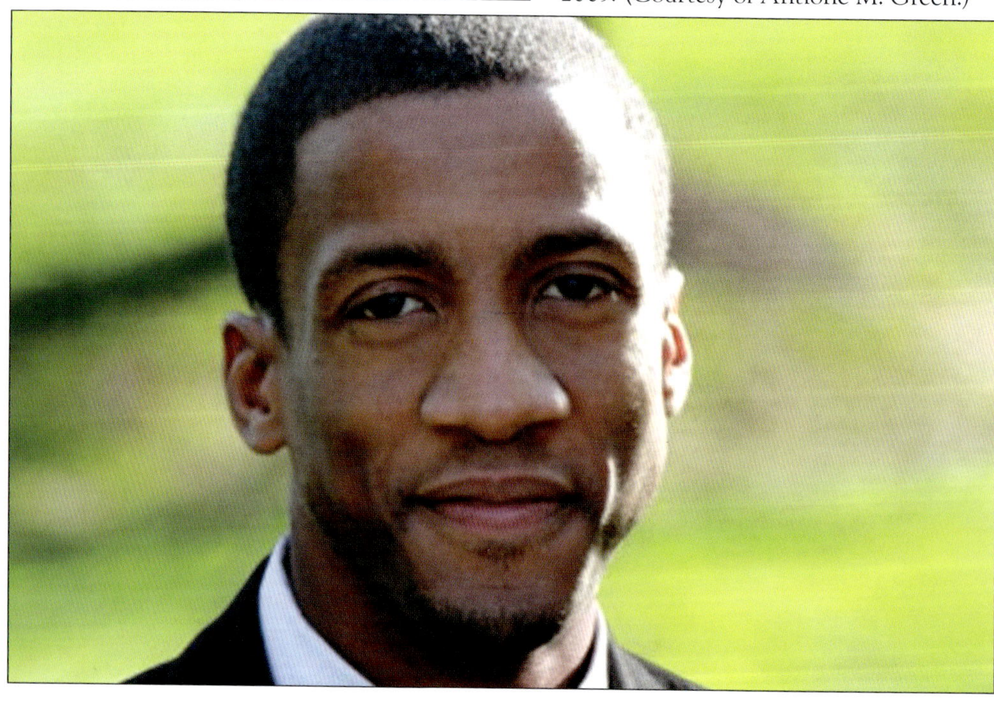

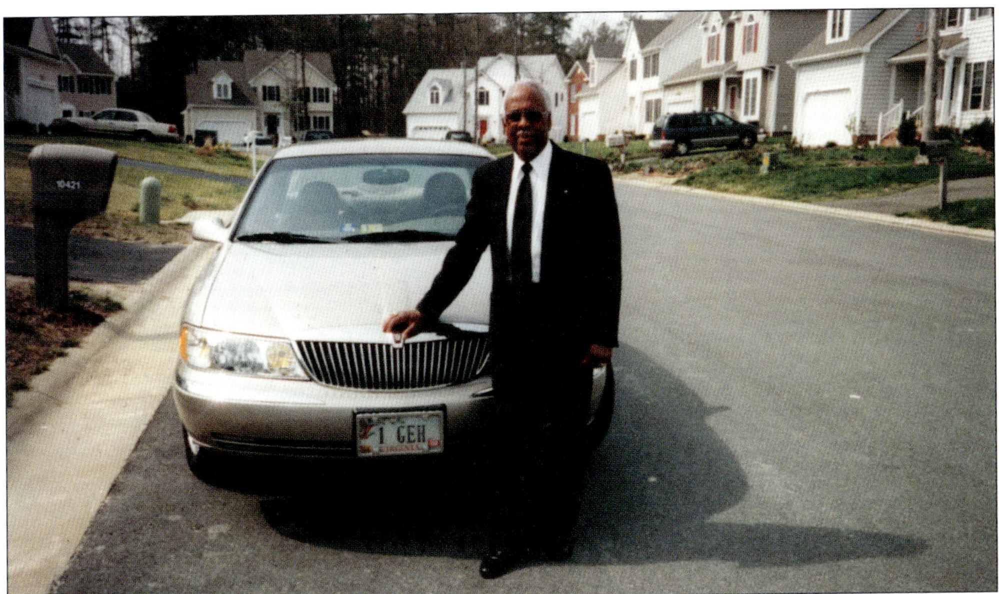

George Hicks has been a devoted member of the Richmond Crusade for Voters for over 15 years. Hicks was active on the get-out-the-vote committee by providing rides to the polls on election day and going door-to-door delivering voter education materials. He is a vocal community activist and volunteer. Hicks was a mail clerk at Reynolds Metals Company for 35 years. He believes that for the Richmond Crusade for Voters to thrive, it must make deliberate efforts to recruit and retain young people. (Courtesy of George Hicks.)

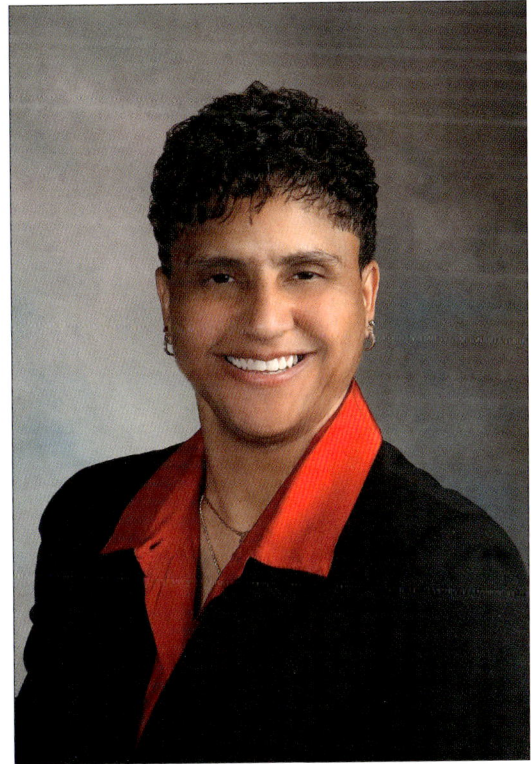

Antionette V. Irving has been a member of the Richmond Crusade for Voters for over two decades. Irving is a social activist, community leader, and doctoral student. She is a 1983 graduate of Armstrong-Kennedy High School and earned a bachelor of arts degree in criminal justice in 1987 from Shaw University and a master's degree in administration from Central Michigan University in 1993. She created the Antionette V. Irving Foundation, Inc. in 2004, with the goal to assist and empower youth to make positive changes and solid decisions. (Courtesy of Antionette V. Irving.)

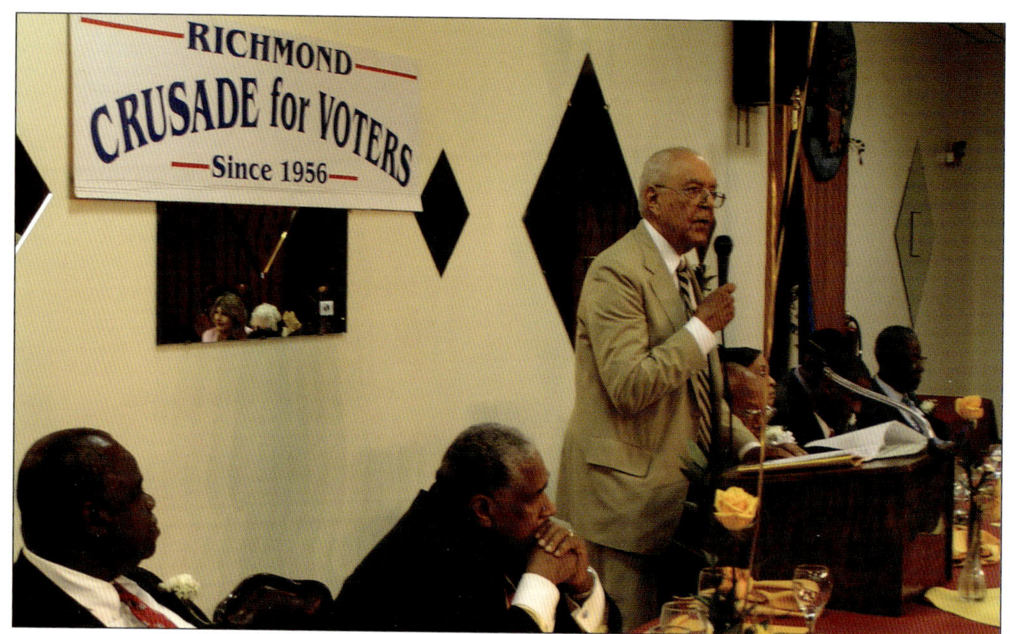

Dr. William Ferguson Reid, one of the cofounders of the Richmond Crusade for Voters, speaks to an audience at the organization's 50th anniversary dinner in 2006. The celebration was held at the Military Retirees Club, at 2220 Chamberlayne Avenue. The evening was filled with good food, fellowship, and speeches reminiscing about the past and providing hope for the future of the city of Richmond and the Richmond Crusade for Voters. (Courtesy of Ralph Cramer.)

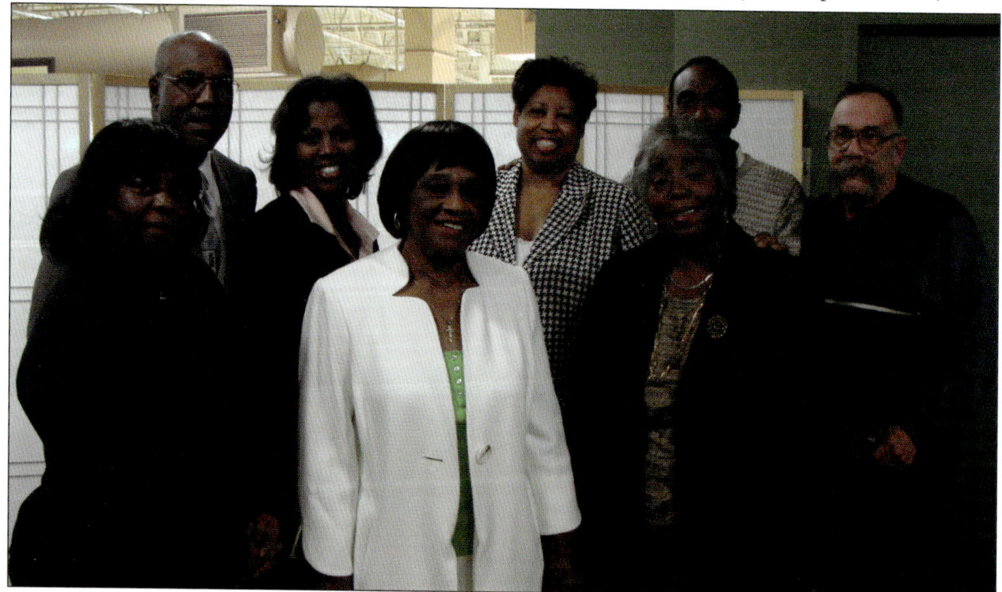

For the 55th anniversary banquet held at the Crowne Plaza Richmond Downtown, the fundraising committee raised over $7,000. A patron list raised the funds. The committee developed a list of people to call and meet with about contributing funds to the anniversary banquet. The patrons were residents of the city of Richmond and the surrounding areas. From left to right are (first row) Carrie Cox, Amelia Lightner, and Ophelia Daniels; (second row) John Houze, Dawn Page, Francine Young, Art Burton, and Ralph Cramer. (Courtesy of Ralph Cramer.)

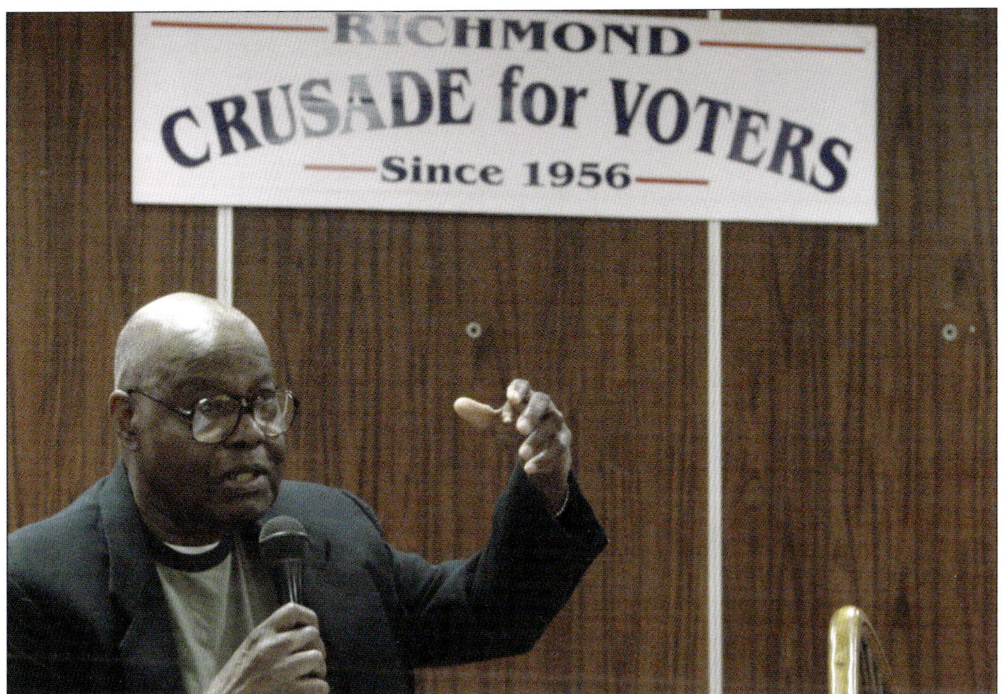

Richmond native William A. Thornton was born on December 29, 1924. He was a product of Richmond Public Schools, graduating from Armstrong High School in 1942, and Howard University, graduating in 1949. Thornton was a charter member of the Richmond Crusade for Voters, with over 50 years of service. He served on the executive committee, and as a mentor to new members and historian for many years. Thornton took great pride in his duty to collect, save, and protect the historical information on the Richmond Crusade for Voters. He is affectionately referred to as the walking encyclopedia. Thornton is pictured speaking at the Richmond Crusade for Voters' June 2006 meeting at the Military Retirees Club. (Courtesy of Ralph Cramer.)

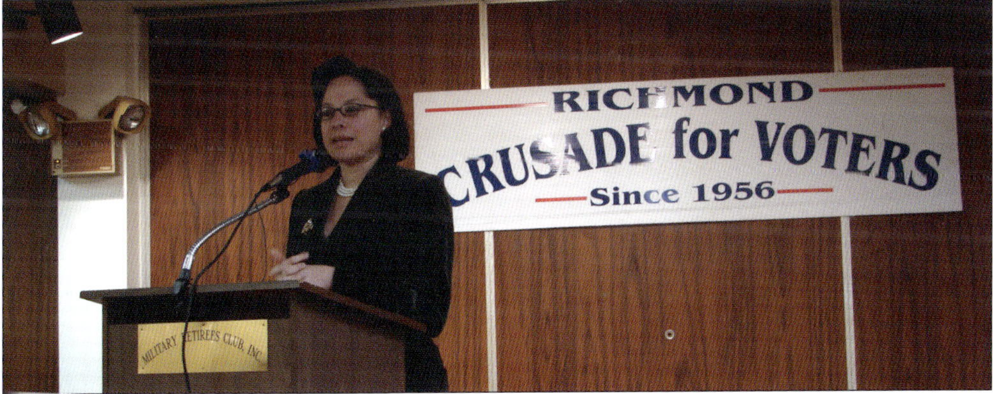

Petersburg native Delegate Jennifer McClellan has been a longtime supporter of the Richmond Crusade for Voters. Since 2006, she has been a member of the Virginia House of Delegates representing the Seventy-First District, which includes sections of the city of Richmond and Henrico County. Delegate McClellan received her bachelor of arts from the University of Richmond in 1994 and a juris doctor from the University of Virginia in 1997. Pictured, Delegate McClellan speaks to the Richmond Crusade for Voters at the holiday dinner held at the Military Retirees Club in December 2007. (Courtesy of Ralph Cramer.)

Richmond Crusade for Voters, Inc.
2012 Election Endorsements
Our Voice, Our Vote, Our Future

President	
Barack Obama	X

Vice President	
Joseph "Joe" Biden, Jr.	X

U S Senate	
Timothy Michael "Tim" Kaine	X

U S House of Rep.- 3rd District	
Robert C. "Bobby" Scott	X

U S House of Rep. - 7th District	
E. Wayne Powell	X

Richmond Mayor At-Large	
Dwight C. Jones	X

Richmond City Council	
District 1 – Bruce W. Tyler	X
District 2 – Charles R. Samuels	X
District 3 – Christopher A. Hilbert	X
District 4 – Johnny Walker	X
District 5 – E Martin Jewell	X
District 6 – Ellen F. Robertson	X
District 7 – Cynthia Newbille	X
District 8 – Dawn C. Page	X
District 9 – Douglas G. Conner	X

Richmond School Board	
District 1 – Glen H. Sturtevant Jr.	X
District 2 – Kimberly B. Gray	X
District 3 – Jeffery M. Bourne	X
District 4 – Vanessa W. Easter	X
District 5 – Mamie Taylor	X
District 6 – Shonda L. Harris-Muhammed	X
District 7 – Donald L. Coleman	X
District 8 – Derik Jones	X
District 9 – Tichi L Pinkey-Eppes	X

Need a ride to the polls? Call 804-484-4476

Richmond Crusade for Voters Inc. Founded 1956

Richmond Crusade for Voters, Inc.
P. O. Box 25302
Richmond, VA 23260
Sylvia C. Wood, President
www.rcfv.org

In 2008, the Richmond Crusade for Voters endorsed the first African American president, Barack Obama. This is the Richmond Crusade for Voters 2012 endorsement ballot. The Richmond Crusade for Voters endorsed Pres. Barack Obama for a second term, Tim Kaine for US Senate, Robert "Bobby" Scott for the Third District in the US House of Representatives, E. Wayne Powell for the Seventh District in the US House of Representatives, and Dwight C. Jones for mayor of the city of Richmond. (Courtesy of Sylvia C. Wood.)

Michael Brown is pictured at the lectern at the October 2010 endorsement meeting. Brown has been involved with the Richmond Crusade for Voters since childhood and officially joined the organization in the 1970s. As a grade school student, he participated in newspaper drives as class projects. The newspapers were sold for recycling, and the money was used to pay poll taxes for those who could not afford to pay the tax. At age 10, Brown delivered Richmond Crusade for Voters literature, such as the endorsement lists in the Northside of Richmond including Ginter Park and North Highland Park. (Courtesy of Ralph Cramer.)

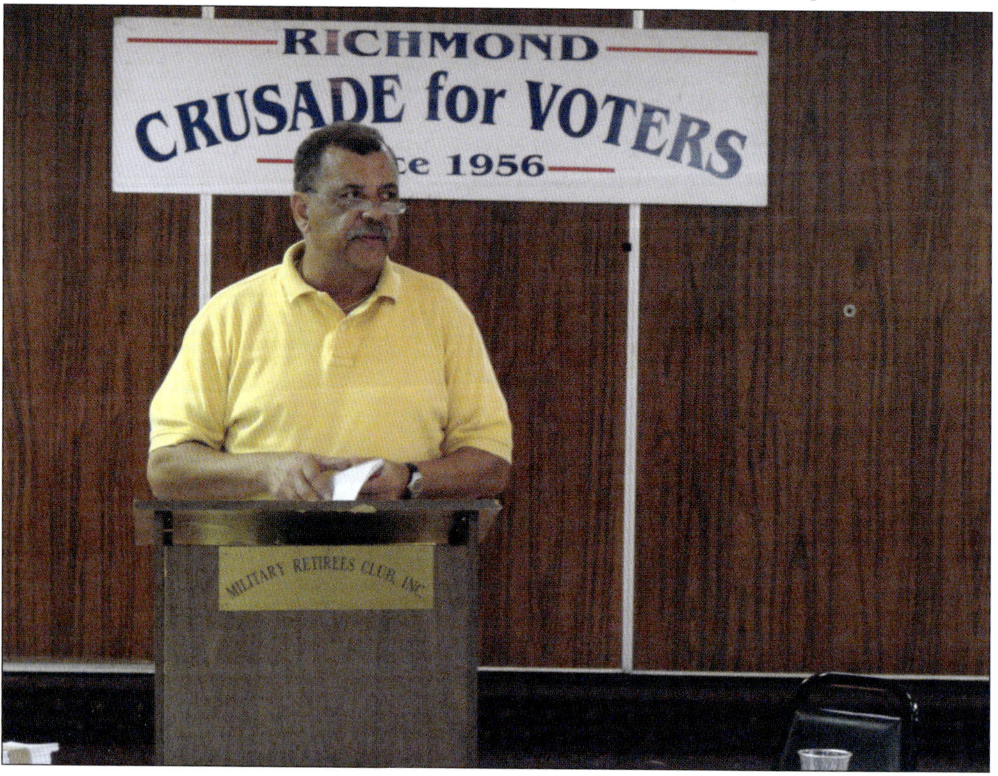

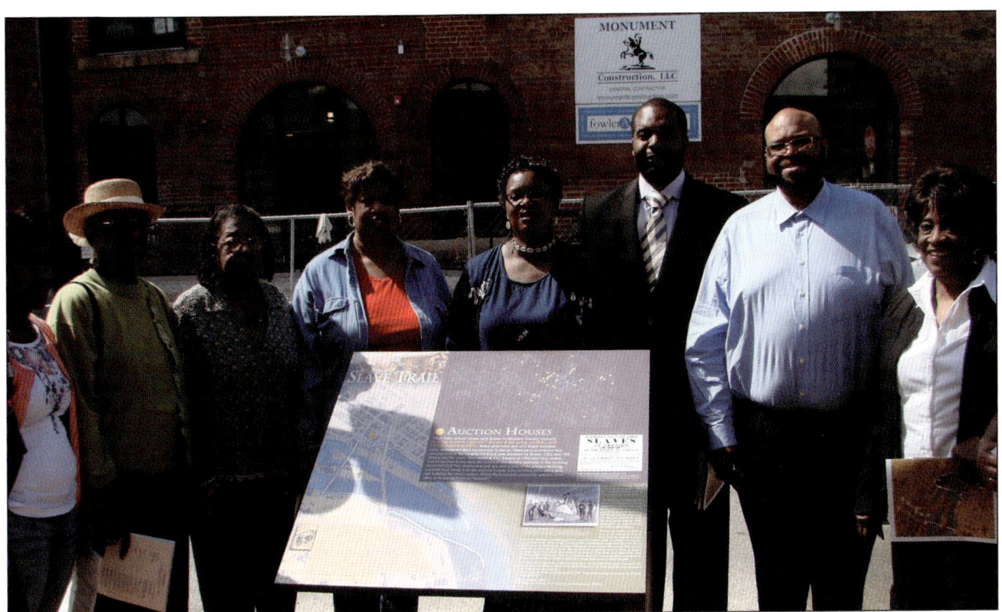

In March 2011, the Richmond Crusade for Voters commemorated the 12th marker along the Richmond Slave Trail, which is for the Slave Auction House. The Slave Trail is a walking trail that chronicles the history of the trade of enslaved Africans from Africa to Virginia until 1775. Richmond was the largest source of enslaved Africans on the East Coast of America from 1830 to 1860. The trail includes a path through the slave markets of Richmond, Lumpkin's Slave Jail, and the Negro Burial Ground. Delegate Delores L. McQuinn, representing the Seventieth District in the Virginia House of Delegates, was instrumental in the creation and commemoration of Richmond's slave trail. Pictured from left to right are unidentified, Ruth Thierry, Francine Young, Sylvia C. Wood, LaMar Dixon, Roderick Bullock, and Amelia Lightner. (Courtesy of Ralph Cramer.)

Civil rights activist and Culpeper native Sylvia C. Wood served as the 24th president of the Richmond Crusade for Voters. Woods was involved with the organization for over 20 years before becoming president. She is a graduate of Saint Paul's College in Lawrenceville, Virginia, and in 1998 was the first women president of the NAACP Richmond Branch. Remaining focused on the Richmond Crusade for Voters' mission to register and educate voters was Wood's top priority. (Courtesy of Sylvia C. Wood.)

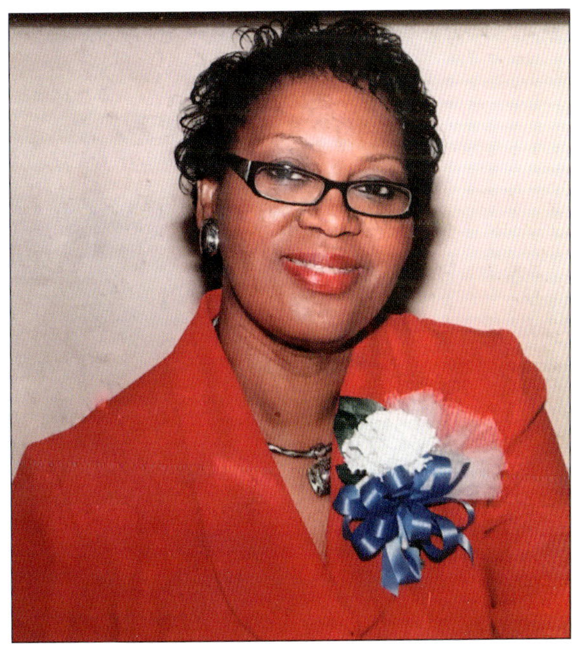

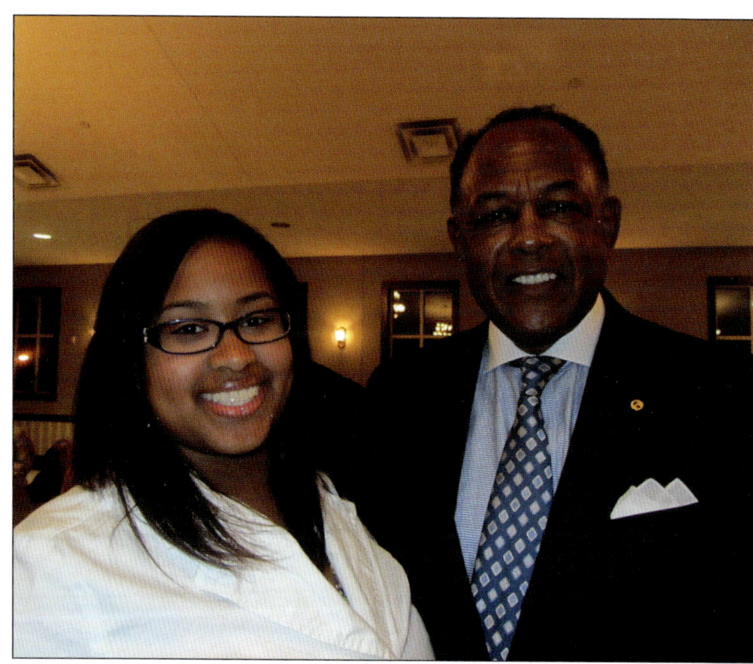

Shakira W. Johnson and Richmond mayor Dwight C. Jones attend a dinner sponsored by the Richmond Crusade for Voters at Six Street Baptist Church in 2012. The night was full of good food, fellowship, and celebration. Johnson was the soloist for the evening. (Courtesy of Margaret S. Johnson.)

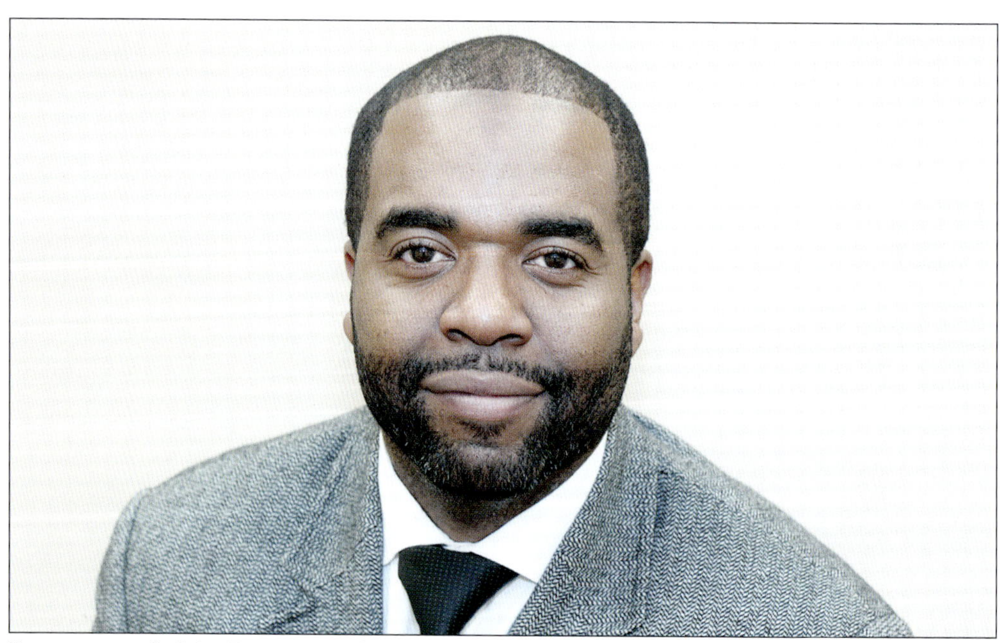

Entrepreneur LaMar Dixon served as the 25th president of the Richmond Crusade for Voters. He is a graduate of Virginia Union University and cofounded the Steel Jacket Club, a group that supports the school's athletics program. Dixon continues to be an advocate for community development and wealth building for African Americans in the city of Richmond. (Courtesy of LaMar Dixon.)

Amelia Lightner has been a member of the Richmond Crusade for Voters for 40 years and served as the second vice president from 2014 to 2016. Lightner is an advocate for the city of Richmond, particularly the Eighth District, where she resides. She is the president of the Brookbury Civil Association in the Upper Reservoir District in the city of Richmond. Lightner is on the board of directors of GroundWork RVA, which is an organization that encourages young conservationists from local high schools to create green infrastructure in Richmond's urban neighborhoods, such as community gardens. (Courtesy of Amelia Lightner.)

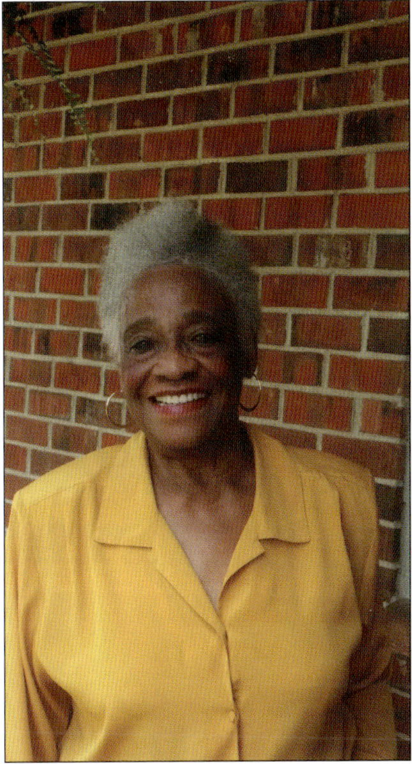

Richmond business owner Ralph Cramer has been a member of the Richmond Crusade for Voters for over 35 years. Cramer served as the organization's treasurer and recording secretary during multiple administrations. (Courtesy of Ralph Cramer.)

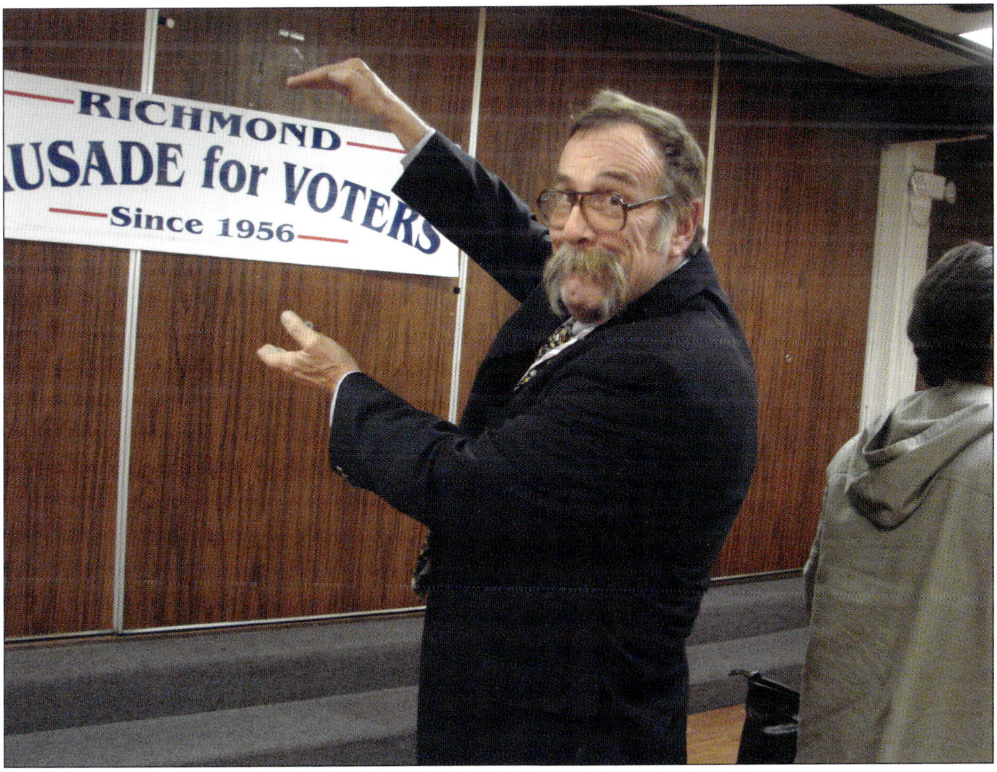

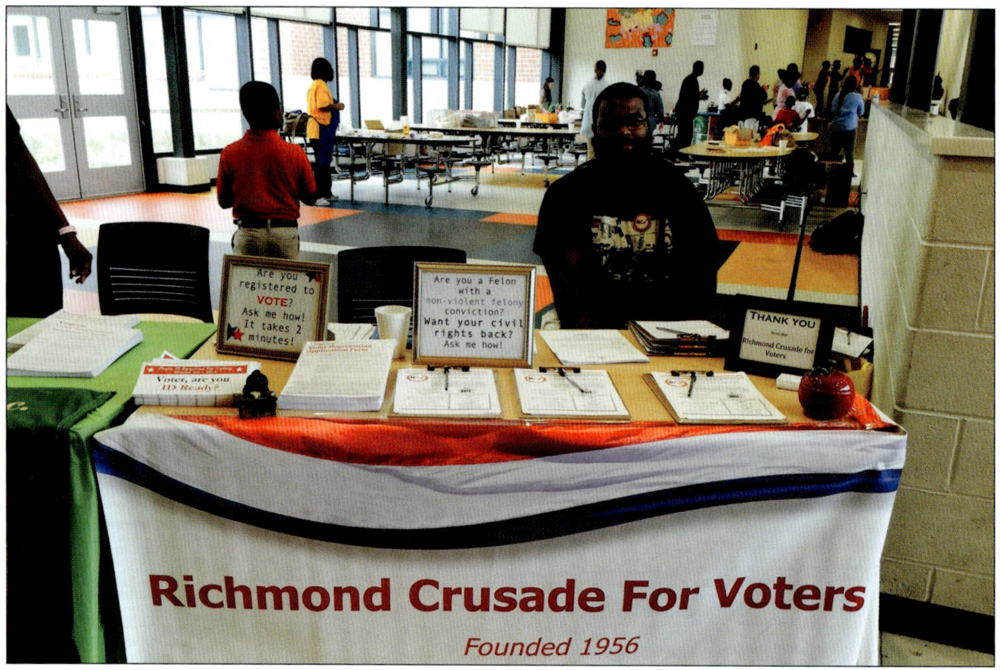

Native Richmonder and Virginia Union University student Steven Armstrong served as a summer and fall 2015 intern for the Richmond Crusade for Voters. During his tenure, he was very active with the voter registration committee. Pictured is Armstrong registering voters at a back-to-school event on August 8, 2015, at Martin Luther King Jr. Middle School in Richmond. (Courtesy of Kathy Wilson Jones.)

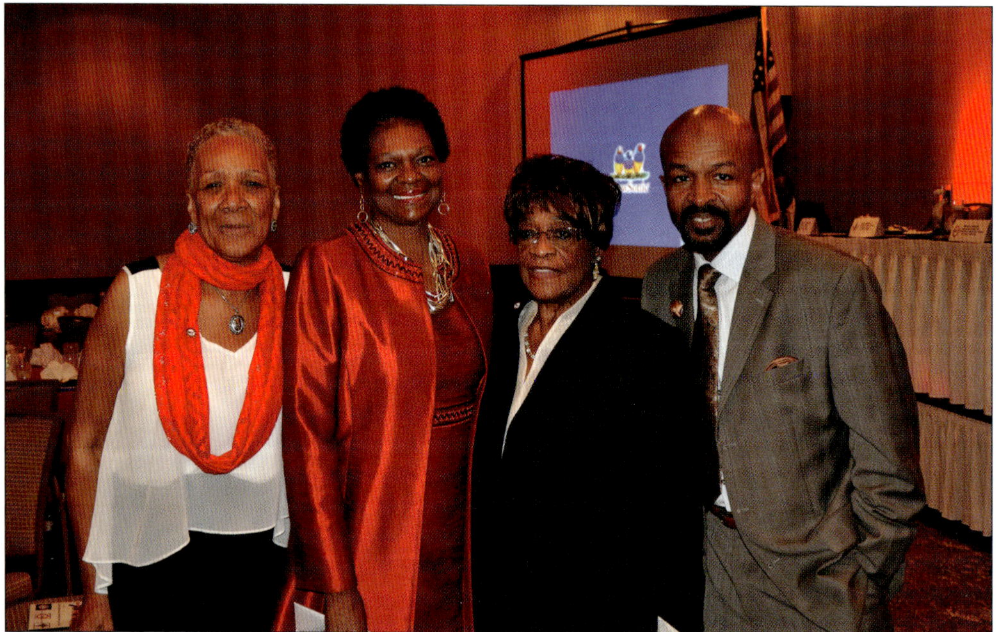

In attendance at the 90 for 90 event on November 1, 2016, from left to right, are Vivian Richardson, Richmond Crusade for Voters member; Delegate Delores L. McQuinn; Amelia Lightner, Richmond Crusade for Voters member; and Jonathan McQuinn. (Courtesy of Pamela Eddie.)

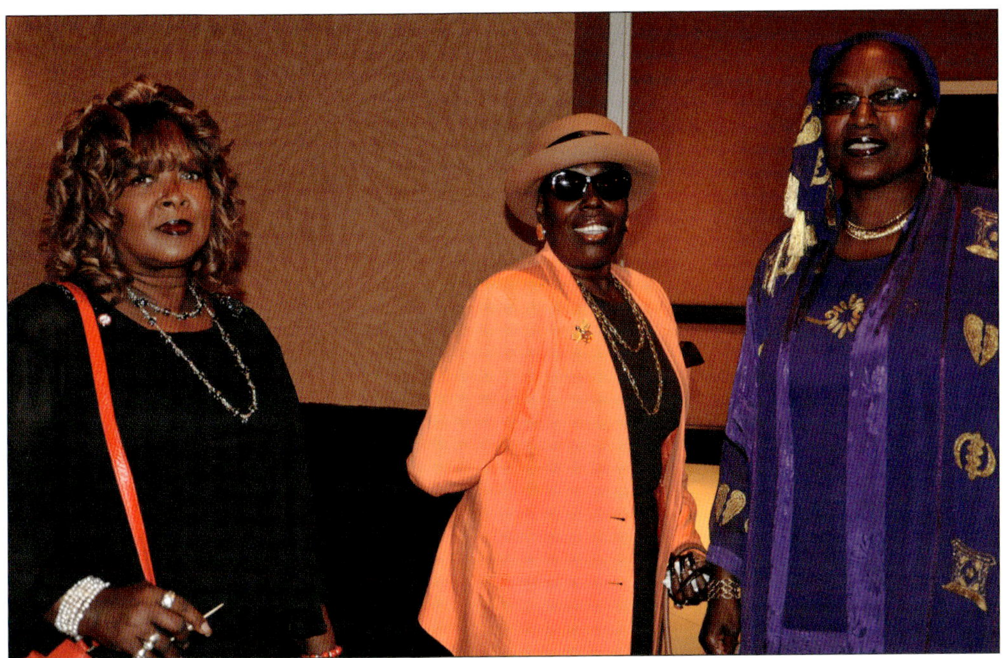

Pictured from left to right are Dorothy Ware, Richmond Crusade for Voters member; Vera Smith; and Lynetta Thompson, president of the NAACP Richmond Branch, at the 90 for 90 gala held at the Crowne Plaza Richmond Downtown. (Courtesy of Pamela Eddie.)

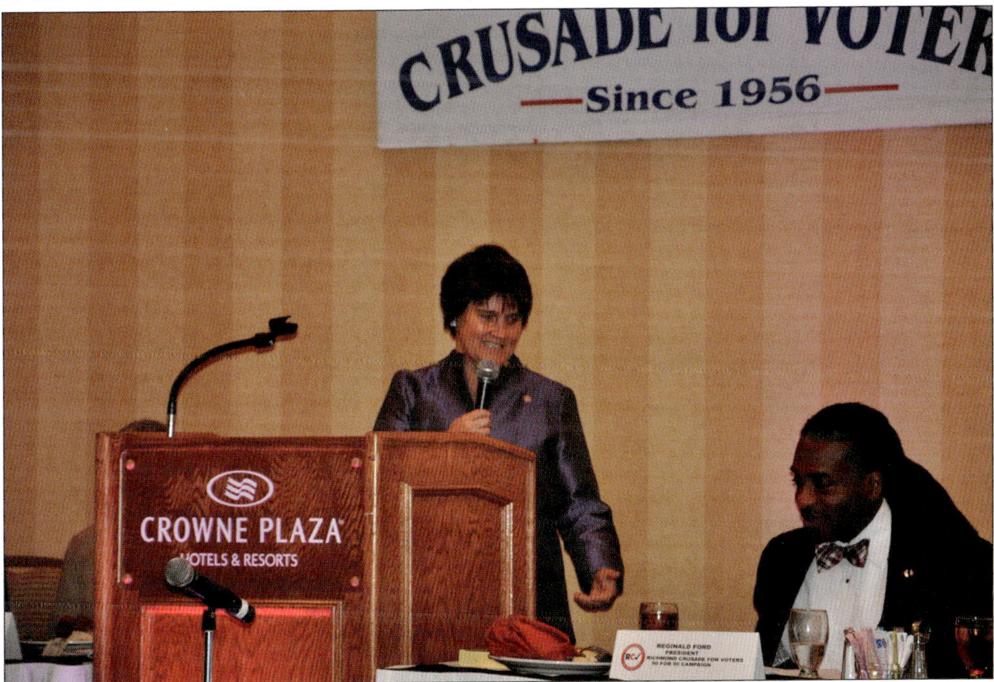

Pictured are Ann Holton, guest speaker at the 90 for 90 gala, and Reginald D. Ford, president of the Richmond Crusade for Voters. Holton served as secretary of education for the commonwealth of Virginia from 2014 to 2016. During her speech, Secretary Holton discussed the importance of equal education for all. (Courtesy of Pamela Eddie.)

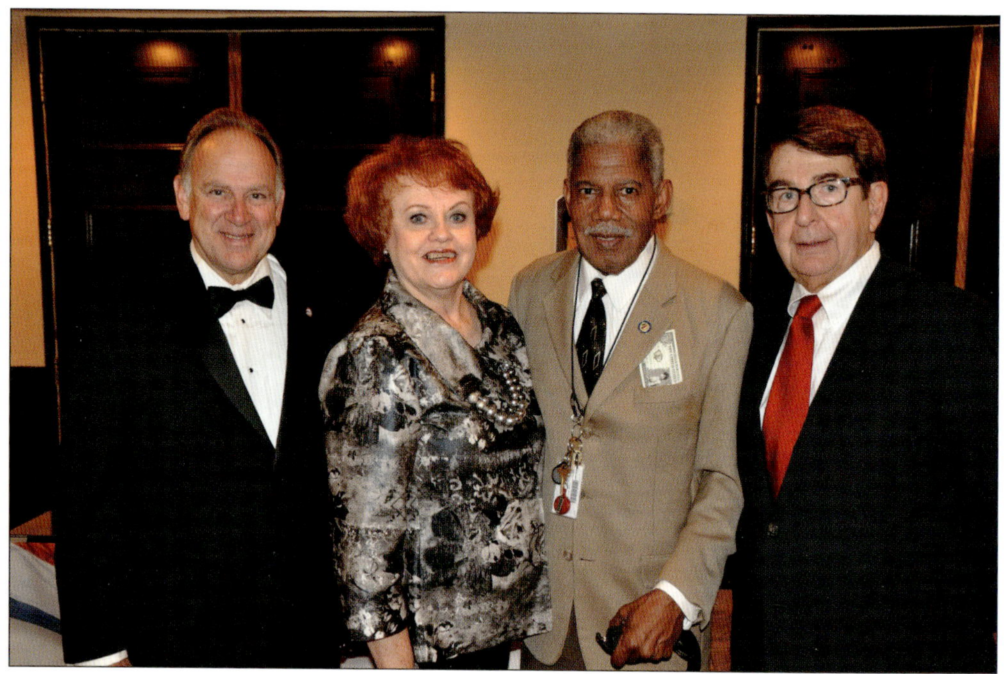

From left to right are David Bernard, Cheryl Ragsdale, Sen. Henry L. Marsh III, and Ben Ragsdale at the 90 for 90 gala. (Courtesy of Pamela Eddie.)

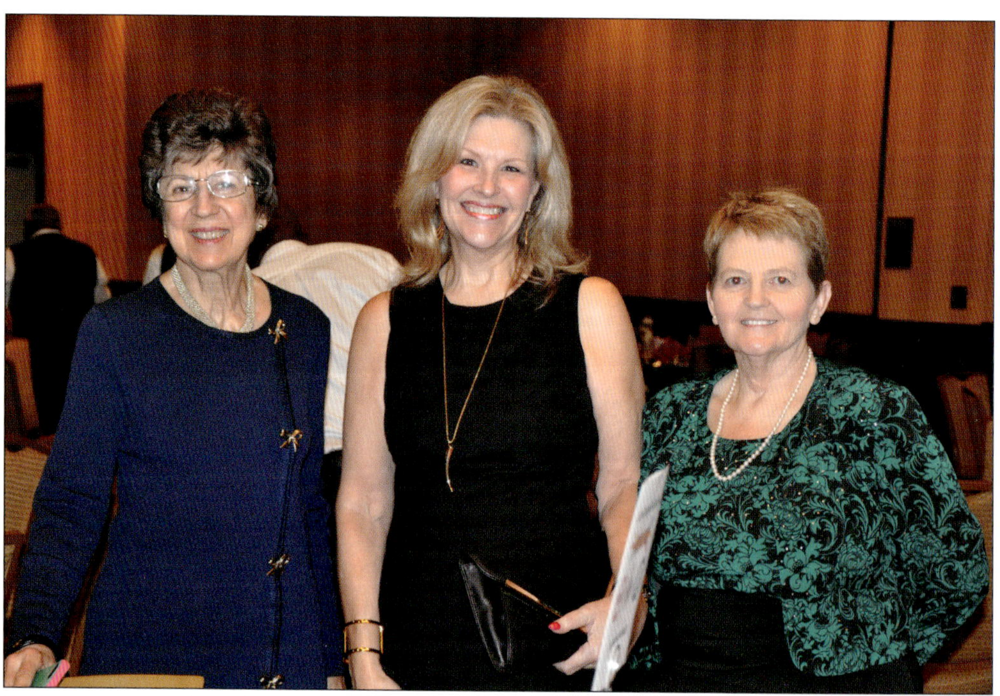

Pictured here are, from left to right, Melissa Marion, Kathy Carle, and Brenda Hill, the 90 for 90 campaign chair and community activist. (Courtesy of Pamela Eddie.)

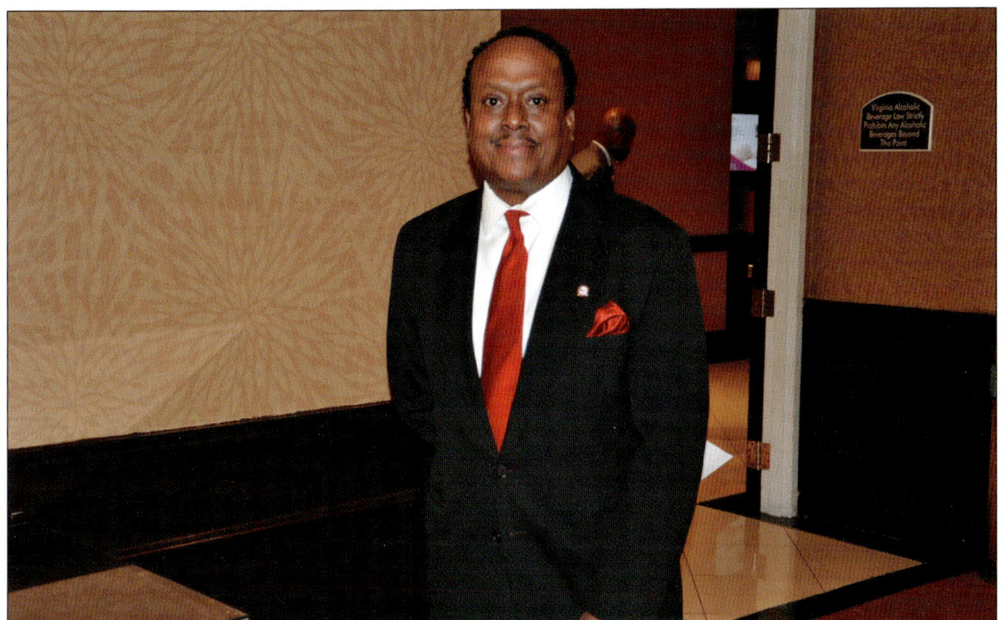

Keith Hicks has been a member of the Richmond Crusade for Voters since 2013. Hicks has served as the recording secretary, audit committee chair, and as research committee chair for a candidates' forum. He was appointed by Virginia governor Terry R. McAuliffe to the Virginia Manufactured Housing Board for a four-year term. (Courtesy of Pamela Eddie.)

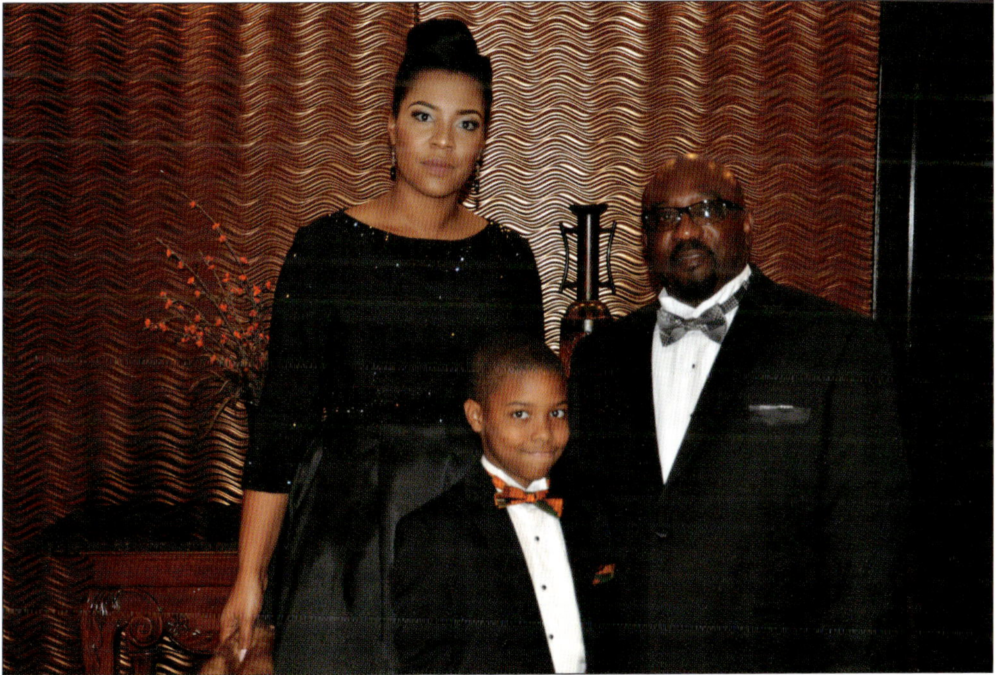

Francesca Leigh-Davis served on the voter registration committee for the Richmond Crusade for Voters for two years and was the chair of the committee the second year. During her tenure, she collected over 300 voter registration applications. The Davis family (pictured) includes, from left to right, Francesca Leigh-Davis, Carter Davis, and Calvin Davis. (Courtesy of Pamela Eddie.)

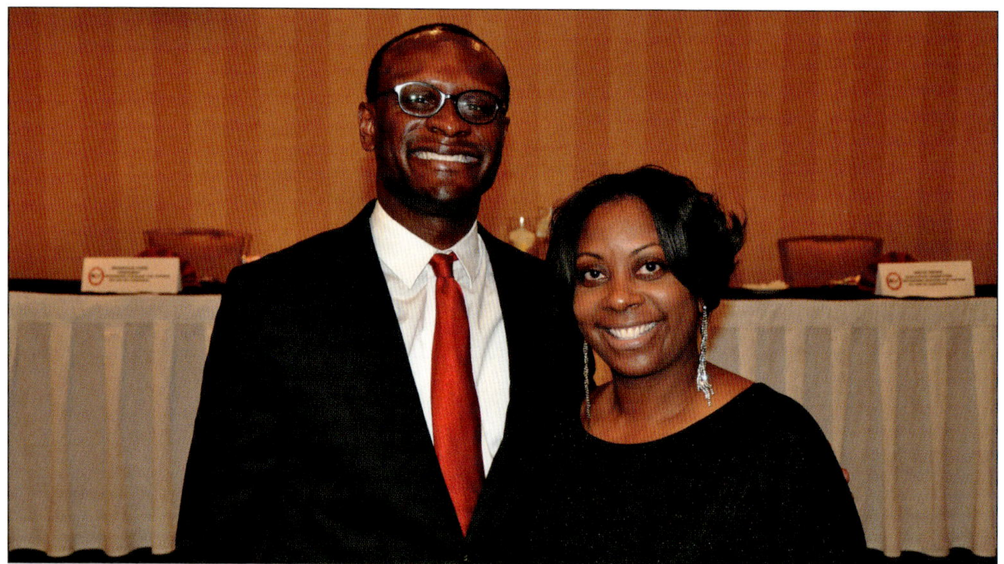

Garrett Sawyer (left) was appointed membership chair of the Richmond Crusade for Voters in January 2015 and previously served as treasurer. Lisa Hicks (right), a new member of the Richmond Crusade for Voters, has been an educator for over 25 years with Richmond Public Schools. (Courtesy of Pamela Eddie.)

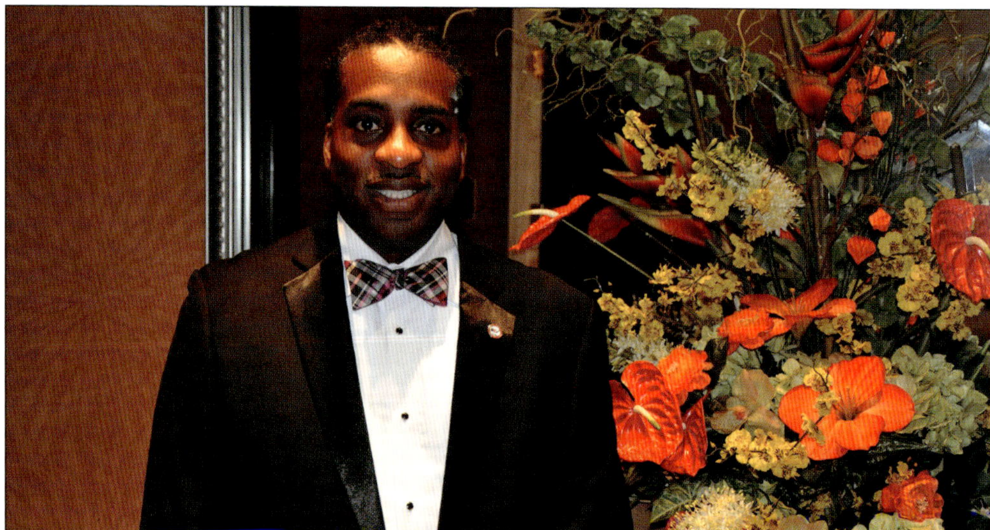

Texas native Reginald D. Ford was the 26th president of the Richmond Crusade for Voters. Ford joined the organization in 2013 to increase his awareness of Richmond's politics and Richmond's African American history. While president, he held candidate forums, meet-and-greet events, and educational seminars for local middle and high school students; provided dinner to a retirement community; and sponsored a trip to the Virginia General Assembly for a group of Richmond Public Schools high school students, where they were able to talk to Virginia senators Rosalyn Dance and Donald McEachin. Ford's primary focus for the Richmond Crusade for Voters was to be visible, vocal, and educating. During his tenure as president of the Richmond Crusade for Voters, he served as District 66 director of Toastmasters International, a communication and leadership organization, and completed a bachelor's degree in banking and leadership. (Courtesy of Pamela Eddie.)

Bibliography

Moeser, John, and Rutledge M. Dennis. *The Politics of Annexation: Oligarchic Power in a Southern City*. Cambridge, MA: Schenkman Publishing Company, 1982.

Randolph, Lewis, and Gale T. Tate. *Rights for a Season: The Politics of Race, Class, and Gender in Richmond, Virginia*. Knoxville: University of Tennessee Press, 2003.

Silver, Christopher. *Twentieth-Century Richmond*. Knoxville: University of Tennessee Press, 1984.

Silver, Christopher, and John V. Moeser. *The Separate City: Black Communities in the Urban South 1940–1968*. Lexington: University Press of Kentucky, 1995.